EBURY

UNSTO

Manthan Shah is a young author, ...dent and
Schwarzman Scholar.

He is a two-time Under-18 SGFI .....an Table Tennis National
Champion, and he won medals for India at the Pacific School Games
2015 in Adelaide, Australia. He hosts *Planet Impact*, the podcast that
shares the stories of young changemakers with its 10,000 listeners.

He is set to pursue a master's degree in global affairs at Tsinghua
University, Beijing. He was a Dean's List student and Global Citizenship
awardee at the SP Jain School of Global Management, Sydney. He
has a diploma in creative writing from Symbiosis College of Distance
Learning, Pune.

He had the privilege of meeting HH Pope Francis in a private
sitting at Vatican City in 2019 and meeting HH the Dalai Lama at
Dharamshala in 2018.

Manthan Shah is from Ahmednagar, Maharashtra. *Unstoppable*
is his first book.

UNSTOPPABLE

How Youth Icons Achieve
Extraordinary Things

MANTHAN SHAH

EBURY
PRESS

An imprint of Penguin Random House

EBURY PRESS

USA | Canada | UK | Ireland | Australia
New Zealand | India | South Africa | China

Ebury Press is part of the Penguin Random House group of companies
whose addresses can be found at global.penguinrandomhouse.com

Published by Penguin Random House India Pvt. Ltd
4th Floor, Capital Tower 1, MG Road,
Gurugram 122 002, Haryana, India

Penguin
Random House
India

First published in Ebury Press by Penguin Random House India 2022

ISBN 9780143454076

Typeset in Adobe Caslon Pro by Manipal Technologies Limited, Manipal
Printed at Replika Press Pvt. Ltd, India

www.penguin.co.in

MIX
Paper from
responsible sources
FSC® C016779

To all the young people who want to do something extraordinary.

*To celebrate the people who are shaping our communities,
25 per cent of all author royalties will be donated to local
non-profits, including Snehalaya.org.*

Contents

Introduction

Ajay was born into a middle-class family. From the age of twelve, he was enrolled in several tuition and coaching classes. He played sports and participated in debates. Anything less than topping the class was seen as a failure. After completing his twelfth standard, his parents insisted that he pursue engineering or medicine. He chose engineering. After graduation, he worked in a corporate job for a couple of years. Dissatisfied, he applied for a master's programme at a college in the US, and now he is working hard to find a job there.

Anam Hashim was born in Kanpur, India. Her mother was forced into a second marriage with a drug lord. Anam grew up in abusive circumstances. At seventeen, she ran away to Pune to live with her aunt. Anam loved bikes; she taught herself stunt riding. She dropped out of college and focused on riding bikes, and she soon became one of the best motorcyclists in the country.

Manthan was six years old when he discovered his love for table tennis. By the time he was eight, he was beating players twice his age. His family moved to Pune to take advantage of the better training facilities there so he could hopefully become a national champion and win international medals for India. He was home-schooled for a few years, yet his academic performance was above average in school and high school. But then, conforming to the norms of society, he left table tennis to pursue a safer career. Now, studying to earn a business degree, he experiments with both conformist and non-conformist routes to becoming successful in life.

The first story is a hypothetical one. It illustrates the typical path laid by society. It is a safe route for most of us. Broadly, in terms of life's milestones, it sounds like the standard path, but when you scratch the surface, many individuals don't find fulfilment in it. They often find themselves asking, 'Is this all there is to life or is there more to it?'

The second is a real story. Anam grew up in a patriarchal family. She was a woman in what was deemed to be a man's industry. She did not get there by following the path of others; she had to create her own path. I wanted to see if her experience was unique or part of a larger trend. What I found showed me a new approach to finding happiness and success.

The third is my story. While I am not as successful as I would like to be yet, I have observed that many who have done exceedingly well have not followed the path laid out in the first story.

Ajay is a typical conformist, following the rules of society. Anam was a non-conformist. While, finally, I have travelled both the conformist and non-conformist routes.

We live in harsh times. On a macro level, India is one of the unhappiest places on the planet. In 2020, India ranked 144 out of 153 countries in the World Happiness Report.[1] Now in the bottom ten globally, India also saw one of the largest drops in the happiness index between 2008–12 and 2017–19 due to a combination of economic, social and political stresses.[2]

With regard to education, due to lack of professional skills, only 46 per cent of Indian graduates are employable.[3] The degrees leave a sense of dissatisfaction within the students. The education system lags behind many in the world, and it doesn't train students to prosper in their professional lives.

If we look at employment, due to the absence of jobs in the formal sector, the informal sector absorbs large masses of workers. The portion of informal workers participating in the workforce has been increasing and now stands at around 92 per cent.[4]

In terms of income, India ranked 150 out of 194 economies in terms of GDP per capita.[5] The per capita income in India is Rs 1.45 lakh per year.[6] The average salary in India is incredibly low, even after individuals put many years into education. Many of my friends who graduated as engineers in India have had a tough time finding a reasonably paying job, which impacts their self-esteem.

The suicide rates in India are among the highest in the world[7] and on the rise among students,[8] particularly in the youth between the ages of fifteen and twenty-nine years, especially among females.[9]

Mrugesh Vaishnav, president of the Indian Psychiatric Society, says, 'Stress, anxiety disorder, depression, personality disorder—all these result in mental illness that leads a student towards suicide. This happens when the students are not familiar or satisfied with his or her surroundings.'[10]

Inequality is another factor contributing to discontent in the country. Before the COVID-19 pandemic, the richest 10 per cent of Indians owned around 80 per cent of the country's wealth, while the lesser privileged 60 per cent Indians owned less than 5 per cent.[11]

India is among the top five nations in terms of number of billionaires. The number of billionaires in India surged by 330 per cent over the last decade, outpacing the global average growth of 68 per cent, and the momentum will continue over the next decade.[12]

The new money dollar-billionaires such as Vijay Shekhar Sharma of Paytm and Ritesh Agrawal of Oyo Rooms did not earn their success by following the conventional path. Ritesh Agrawal was just twenty-four when his net worth was estimated at $1.1 billion (Rs 7800 crore).[13] Vijay Shekhar was thirty-eight when he broke into the billionaires list. While these two are the outliers, they must have taken some non-conformist decisions to achieve the great things that they did.

I often ask myself, how do young individuals who face everyday struggles crack these ceilings and achieve something great in life?

In general, South Asian society believes that success and happiness come from conforming to certain rules. The Indian school system requires one to learn whole textbooks by heart and recreate them in tests. The textbook then replaces the creative heart of a young adult. Following the norm, the majority of students choose engineering, medicine, law or charted accounting programmes in college to abide by their parents' wishes and follow their friends' choices.

One of the outcomes of this is that there has been an increase in mental health disorders, personal insecurities and feelings of isolation. The void that this generation feels comes from not understanding where one belongs in society.

There is a monotony in career and life patterns, with the majority trying to score the best possible grades in the tenth and twelfth standards, aspiring to work at consulting firms, tech companies, banks or starting their own business, then marrying and having kids. That's what society pushes one to do. The promise of a better future is prominent, yet the results are of discontent. There is no breathing space for those who feel or identify themselves as different.

Teens who are unable to speak English, come from a rural setting or do not follow the same customs as their fellow students are often bullied. One is often ridiculed for being too thin, too fat, too smart, not smart enough, too Indian or not Indian enough, etc.; patriarchy prohibits girls from wearing the clothes they want to wear; one's complexion is deemed to be more important than one's intellect; permission must be granted to see friends. One therefore tends to lose oneself in conforming to 'what society thinks'.

There is also a lack of meritocracy: you must know someone to get a job, admission in a private college or even fix an arranged marriage. If you do not, you are marginalized. When you graduate and start looking for a job, you may not be able to find good opportunities. Moreover, you need to come from a certain family background and identify your beliefs in a certain way to be happy. Often, who your family is becomes your matrix of success.

All this noise makes it difficult to understand what real success means for a young fifteen- to twenty-five-year-old in this society. How does one achieve it?

One of the first persons I spoke to when I was seeking direction for this book was Dr Achyut Godbole, a polymath and the author of twenty-seven books. He gave me a great insight: all the self-help and motivational books talk about the top 0.1 per cent of people in society such as Steve Jobs and Bill Gates. However, it is difficult to be like them. Given the structure of Indian society, 80 per cent of the people simply do not have the resources, infrastructure and external support to achieve what these top 0.1 per cent have achieved. So, their 'chapters to success' are baseless and even outrageous for normal people. Further, the fluffy talk about thinking positively and thinking big is nice and may motivate you for a day or two, but there isn't anything concrete about it.

In this book, I want to share the stories of people who are just like you and me. These are the stories of people with an average age of twenty-five. While some have become celebrities in their industries and made it to the Forbes 30 Under 30 list, others have travelled vast distances and have overcome some wicked problems, shaping the community around them in doing so. There are a few personal anecdotes that you may relate to. There are also a few research insights and tips for your personal growth.

As a young adult, I often ask, 'How can I as a young person go on to achieve extraordinary things and be successful?' After pondering over this question for four years, studying hundreds of research papers and articles on positive and developmental psychology, sociology, genealogy and motivational literature, reading more than fifty self-help books, speaking with thirty industry experts and mentors, interviewing forty of India's best and brightest young people, doing a primary survey of 300 students in January 2020, and speaking with hundreds of friends and acquaintances about their goals, ambitions, obstacles and the structure of this book, I want to share my findings on how to be successful as a young person in India.

Multiple instances in the last four years have inspired me to think deeply and to write this book. I feel there is a gap between what India's youth have the potential to achieve and what they aspire to or end up achieving. I saw there were not many meaningful non-fiction books that tell the story of Generation Zs who are crushing it. Further, there weren't any young voices writing about it. This gave me the inspiration to write this book, but the following incident in particular is what pushed me to start writing.

In 2018 I was in Colombo, Sri Lanka, working as a volunteer on a six-week project in support of United Nations Sustainable Development Goal 6, which is to provide clean water and sanitation for all.

I was sitting on the veranda of our guesthouse, looking into the deep purple evening sky and thinking about what I should do next with my life. It was one of the hardest phases of my life. I had recently taken the decision to hang up my table tennis racket, having been a former national champion, and move towards more standard academic pursuits. The reasons for this change were a combination of future prospects—one cannot make a financially sustainable career in sports other than cricket in India—due to lack of infrastructure and coaching, and a few personal reasons. For the first time I felt a burning void within me. I was giving up on my Olympic dream, which had captured my every waking hour and inspired me to wake up at 5 a.m. every morning and train six hours a day, every day. I felt empty.

I spoke to a friend on the purpose, potential and meaning of life. I felt life would be meaningless if one simply went through it without really experiencing it to the fullest. Something that many young adults feel deeply. Not having pursued a big goal early in life, most students are oblivious to their strengths, weaknesses and how society functions around them. She pointed out that not many people have the exposure to opportunities that push them out of their comfort zone and inspire them to achieve something big. Something that will make a difference.

I wished there was a book that told the stories of those who had made a difference and with whom I could relate to. I would often visit bookstores in our leisure hours, but I couldn't find anything aimed at young adults that talked about coming of age in a developing economy with its peculiar economic and socio-political challenges, mental health issues, and explored identity and reaching one's potential. I wanted to hear the stories of the sixteen- to twenty-five-year-olds from our background who overcame their struggles to create something of value.

Indian society, like many developing countries, revolves around a struggle to be mediocre. The prescribed path is to become an engineer, doctor, lawyer or accountant. For those who aspire to become something else, there is no conversation around growth and success. Most non-fiction and self-help books for sixteen- to twenty-five-year-olds are written by Western authors. The stories in them are not relatable at most levels. To produce the next Bill Gates or Elon Musk, India needs the same infrastructure, political will, social structure and other external factors present in the West, which we simply don't have.

'I should write a book,' I laughed. It was just an idea roughly based on the style of Malcolm Gladwell's book *Outliers*. 'You do not want to preach in a how-to book or write a motivational guide to achieve freedom or a presumptuous self-help book. It should just be a storybook, a buffet of individuals who have their own highs and lows, and written in a candid fashion,' my friend said.

With that in mind, I worked on this book for nearly four years in Singapore, Mumbai, Madrid, Dubai and my hometown in Ahmednagar, but by no means am I qualified in terms of number of years on the planet, professional experience and degrees to be writing a self-help book. So, please look at this book as a friend sharing his notes on life.

In my journey of writing this book, I observed ten common themes that are particular to and relevant for us youth:

1. It is not about finding your passion, it is about nurturing it by sticking with your goals over the long term.
2. It is not about being fearless, it is about going forth despite all the fears and anxieties you might face.
3. It is not about cribbing about the problems around us, it is about thinking creatively and making things happen and learning from doing.
4. It is not about conforming to what society thinks, it is about finding your own way and working hard to reach your destination.
5. It is not about your analytical skills, it is about your emotional intelligence and ability to deal with failure.

6. It is not about what you know, it is about who you know and building your social capital.
7. It is not about the talents you are born with, it is about having the right mindset to constantly learn.
8. It is not about micromanaging people and leading with authority, it is about enabling others to achieve a shared vision.
9. It is not about how well you can *fake it till you make it*, it is about having an inwardly looking, deep-rooted faith in your abilities.
10. It is not about how much you can take from others, it is about how much you can give.

This book is for younger individuals in the Indian education system; for those who want to achieve greatness and bypass the redundant conformity imposed by society but do not know how. Most of us young people and our ambitions are overlooked and underserved. And I want to change that.

1

Grit and Perseverance

'Grit is living life like it is a marathon, not a sprint'
—Angela Duckworth, founder and CEO of
Character Lab, MacArthur Fellow and a
New York Times Best Selling author[1]

If you are admitted into the National Defence Academy (NDA), you know you have made it.

The admissions process for the NDA is one of the most rigorous in the country. Getting into an Indian Institute of Technology (IIT) is insanely competitive too; I would never have cracked it even if I had tried. But unlike IIT admissions, to get into the NDA you have to pass academic, physical as well as psychological tests while competing against the country's best and brightest.

Every year, 4 lakh students appear for the entrance exams for the NDA, of which only about 8000 clear the exam. All these 8000 aspirants are called for an interview, and only 300 to 450 finally clear the Service Selection Board.[2]

After such an intense selection process, it is curious to note that 16 to 20 per cent of the selected candidates quit the course. Over 1200 candidates have dropped out of the NDA in the last ten years.[3]

Former cadets and several alumni of the elite military institution have cited ragda (similar to ragging), corporal punishment and unsanctioned training practices as among the main reasons cadets leave.[4] Other key reasons for such a staggering dropout rate have been a lack of physical fitness on the part of cadets, being boarded out on medical grounds, indiscipline, homesickness and realizing that the reality of serving in the forces is not the same as they had envisioned.

So, who actually makes it through the years of ragda and all the physical and mental challenges that come after one gets into the NDA?

When I spoke with Colonel Pagay, who excelled in commando training, he said the training is devised to toughen you mentally, physically and socially. In those gruelling training sessions, it doesn't matter how intelligent you are, how wealthy your parents are, what your connections are or where you are from. The people who make it through this training are the ones who have perseverance and a passion for serving the country.

This type of dedication is what an elite athlete, musician or researcher must possess to be successful in his or her craft.

In the dozens of interviews I conducted for this book, the successful individuals—young and old—weren't more successful than their peers because they were better at taking tests, had a particular IQ, connections, resources, and so on. Instead, they had an 'I never quit' attitude. Two main traits support their ferocious determination. Firstly, these outliers are unusually resilient and hardworking. Secondly, they have a deep understanding of what they want and how they will get there. They have a path laid out and an unshakeable determination to get through all challenges. This intersection of perseverance and passion is something we will discuss in this chapter.

An institution such as the NDA, like life in general, trains and tests your grit over your objective talents.

* * *

What is grit? Grit is having the passion and perseverance to achieve long-term goals.[5] Grit is having stamina. Grit is sticking to the dreams for your future, day-in, day-out. Not just for the week, not just for the month, but for years. And working hard to make that future a reality.

People with grit are unstoppable because they are passionate about their long-term goals and persistent in achieving them. One study of 702 American students of pharmacology showed that grit was a significant and an independent predictor of academic performance.[6]

In a study of undergraduate nursing students, researchers found a statistically significant positive correlation between grit and both course engagement and skill development. Higher grit in medical students was a predictor of better academic performance as well.[7]

So, what does grit mean to us in the Indian subcontinent?

Hye Won Kwon, a University of Iowa researcher, found that people in the lower social classes structures are gritter than the ones in the higher social classes. She notes, 'Grit has a within-culture variance: those from lower social strata are more likely to value grit as a virtue than those from higher social strata. Therefore, grit is not a class-free resource.'[8]

With the world's largest middle and lower classes,[9] Indians are well placed socially to value grit more. In societies where grit is valued, parents may seek to teach their children grit as an important skill or character trait. I remember when I lost a whole season of tournaments, my father was surprisingly not angry. He wanted to teach me the value of grit.

But at the same time, in a society like ours, social pressure can be paralysing. Living in a collectivist society, 'what will people think' can act as a tremendous force to derail us from our track. The notion of 'saving face' and '*log kya kahenge*' takes over, and our efforts to preserve our social status take centre stage in our lives as Indians.[10] This is one of the biggest challenges we must overcome to become unstoppable. This balance between being gritty and overcoming the pressure of 'what will others think' is perhaps an important thing to understand for us.

The young trailblazers have gone against the norms of society, time and again, on their journey to becoming successful.

Let me tell you the story of a young girl who ran away from her home in Lucknow to become India's leading motorcyclist and stunt rider. She was one of the first people I interviewed for this book back in 2018.

* * *

Anam Hashim is the face of stunt riding in India. She was the first woman ever to ride to Khardung La Pass, the world's highest motorable road, on a 100cc Scooty during a ride called Himalayan Highs, a feat that won her a place in the *India Book of Records*. In 2017, Anam became the first Indian to win a freestyle stunt competition on an international stage. She has been the brand ambassador for GoPro and Red Bull and has won multiple laurels for India in international motorcycling events.

At twenty-five, she has become one of the most recognizable people in this industry with a feature film to be released on her life story soon.

When I met Anam at her house in the suburbs of Pune, she came across as warm and timid. She has a slender frame. She speaks crisply, with a sense of urgency. Her responses have an innocence and simplicity. You cannot guess she is a legendary motorbike rider.

Anam was born in 1995. Her upbringing was very modest.

'We grew up in a very small house—just one small room and kitchen. I remember it was my paternal grandmother's house and she used to charge us rent.'

'Initially, my father was a taxi driver. My mom was a teacher, and I had no interest in studying.'

Anam's father encouraged her to ride bikes when she was just five years old; he would seat her in front of him on the bike and give her the control of the handlebar. He taught her to ride a bike on her own when she was around eleven years old. When she was twelve, she would steal her mother's scooter, go for rides and practice stunting. Her dad taught her to ride a geared bike when he realized her talent for control and balance.

Although everything was going well, when she was thirteen her world came crashing down. Her parents got a divorce. Her mother remarried, and her second husband turned out to be abusive.

After her tenth standard exams, Anam got a bike from her father after a lot of pleading. That's when her life changed.

She started going to school on her bike in the eleventh standard. She met a few guys who did stunts on their bikes and she was fascinated. She says, 'I really wanted to learn how to do that. I started a Facebook page and uploaded my stunt videos.'

However, the ordeal at home persisted. Not only was her stepfather abusive, he was dismissive of her stunt riding.

'My second father used to fight with my mom all the time. If there was anything I did wrong, he would beat her up. This one time I got so angry with him for doing that, I took a knife and put it across his throat.'

As things got worse, Anam left home to pursue stunt riding. After completing her twelfth standard she ran away from Lucknow and went to Pune to live with her masi (maternal aunt). This gave her the independence she needed. She lied to her parents, saying she was preparing for the CETs, the common entrance test for an engineering course. However, she was stunt riding and practising all the time.

'At the age of eighteen, after my twelfth standard, I had no idea what to do. Growing up with all the drama, we never had a conversation about what I should do in life. I moved to Pune [to live] with my masi. I saved money to buy a bike. I borrowed Rs 10,000 from my real father and bought a second-hand bike.'

Eventually, she didn't make it into an engineering college. She joined an all-Muslim girls' college in Pune to pursue a bachelor's degree in commerce.

Her aunt was handicapped, and as her health worsened, she had to leave Pune.

Somehow, by doing multiple odd jobs, Anam managed to make a living in Pune. Briefly for a year, she had a company that manufactured parts for stunt motorcycles, which did well. But she moved on to focus solely on her goal to represent India on the world stage and become the best rider she could be.

In May 2017, in Jakarta, she became the only Indian to win a medal at an international competition by bagging third place at the Gymkhana Stuntride Competition Series 1.[11] She stayed in Indonesia for two months, and the experience was life-changing for her. She had always known she wanted to be an accomplished stunt rider, but she was pleasantly surprised by the short time it finally took her to achieve her goal of winning an international medal.

In 2017, her aunt passed away, and it was very difficult for Anam to process this loss. Still, she persisted in pursuing her dreams, and in 2019, she made her debut cross-country rally at the Desert Storm. This race is known to be India's most difficult and involves navigating over 1000 kms in the heat of May. Although she had little experience in racing events, she performed as well as the top athlete. This boosted her confidence.

At the time of writing this book, Anam was preparing for the motor sport cross-country race, Indian National Rally Championship, a prestigious national-level sports race. In the next few years, her goal is to ride in the Dakar Rally, the world's longest and most dangerous race, which will be held in Saudi Arabia.

* * *

In the journey to develop true grit, the first step is to have a long-term goal.

I have lived two lives. One with a clear vision, and one where I am still exploring. As a table tennis player, I had a clear aim to win medals for India. Everything I did was to help me reach that goal. For example, when I was ten, my family moved from Ahmednagar to Pune so I could train at a professional academy. I was home-schooled, and I focused solely on training and competing. I prioritized table tennis over family functions and hanging out with friends for the eight years I played seriously. I trained with the national athletics sprinting and middle-distance team in Balewadi Stadium for physical fitness. In three years, I made it to the state team. Within five years, I was beating the country's best junior players. I became the captain of the under-seventeen (U-17) Maharashtra state team for the national school games in 2014. I won the 2014–15 School Games Federation of India National Championships in teams and individuals. And finally, I lived my dream when I won two bronze medals for India in the Pacific School Games in Adelaide, Australia, in 2015.

I was definitely not the most talented person on the circuit. But having a clear vision and putting in the hours enabled a random kid like me to achieve this milestone.

Now in my second life as a university student and future businessman, I do not have a clear goal yet, as I did formerly as a sportsman. I find myself being a promising beginner in multiple things such as writing, podcasting, researching and starting non-profits. It is not quite as satisfactory as being world class at something.

If someone asks me what I want to achieve, I would think for a moment and say something like, 'I would like to write books and positively impact a lot of people. I also want to study at a good university for my master's. I would like to try my hand at consulting or investment banking, as most finance students do. Then maybe I'll try starting something on my own. I am passionate about the non-profit world and would like to run an NGO one day.'

If someone probes further and asks me what exactly I want to achieve, and how I plan to achieve that, I would fumble and say, 'Um, I am pursuing a lot of things. I have a lot of projects I am passionate about.'

Honestly, I am all over the place, and I have no clue what I am doing.

If you are someone like this, who is still finding a goal, then give me a high five, because we are in the same boat. This chapter will hopefully help both of us.

One technique that I have learnt to get some clarity on goal-setting supposedly comes from Warren Buffet. His advice is to list twenty-five goals you have in your academic or professional life.[12] These should be in no particular order of importance. Next, circle the five that are the most important to you in the next ten years. These are your top-level goals. Identify the cluster of other goals that might be supporting goals that will help you reach the top five ones. These will be your mid-level goals. Understand the steps you will need to take to reach these mid-level goals, and these will be your low-level goals. Eliminate all the other goals as they will only be time and energy consuming.

At first, I couldn't think of more than a few goals. But when I started writing down all the projects I was working on, my academic and career aspirations, my list had over thirty goals. This exercise helped me gain a lot of clarity.

* * *

You can use the table below or use your journal to list your own goals. After that circle the five goals that truly speak to you. These will be your high-priority goals. Among these, try to identify one top goal that you would like to dedicate all your time to. That will become your north star or your high-level goal. After this, a cluster of supportive goals that will enable you to reach the top-level goal will become your middle-level goal. And the more urgent smaller steps you will need to do will become our bottom-level goals.

WARREN BUFFET'S 25/5 RULE

1.	10.	19.
2.	11.	20.
3.	12.	21.
4.	13.	22.
5.	14.	23.
6.	15.	24.
7.	16.	25.
8.	17.	
9.	18.	

THE GOAL HIERARCHY [13]

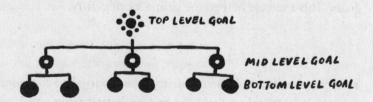

TOP LEVEL GOAL

MID LEVEL GOAL

BOTTOM LEVEL GOAL

After decades of her research, author Angela Duckworth describes Grit as holding the same top-level goal over the long-term. For people with true grit, such as those you will read about in this chapter, the mid-level and bottom-level goals are related and aligned to their top-level goals. People lacking grit tend to have goal structures that are all over the place.

In this goal hierarchy, the bottom-level goals are the specific tasks you would do, such as go to the gym every day at 6 a.m.; follow a nutrition plan; write in your diary and reflect on your training areas. These all work towards achieving a bigger goal, such as being the best table tennis player in the country. The lower level goals are a means to an end. And the top-level goal is an end.

The mid-level goals are separate still large goals that will enable you to reach your top-level goal. These are not specific tasks, but they are slightly bigger in ambition. For example, to become the best player in the country, your mid-level goal will be to the state-level tournaments in the next two years.

The above diagram is an oversimplification of course. There can be many layers of mid-level goals between a bottom-level goal and the top-level goal.

Having this clear vision is important to reach your target.

When I spoke to my friends about having top-level goals, I noticed a few of them had a clear vision, such as to become an investment banker (or even a Goldman Sachs investment banker in particular), to be the best free-style footballer in India, or to get on the cover of *Rolling Stone* magazine. They imagined how great life would be then. But they didn't know what short- and medium-term goals they would need to get there.

There are also people who have a lot of projects they are working on (like me), but they are not aligned to an ultimate top-level goal.

* * *

Once you have set a long-term goal, it takes grit and determination to achieve it. In the next story, you will see an Olympian who overcame various obstacles with grit to make the country proud on a global stage.

Dipa Karmakar is truly the pride of India and one of the most celebrated athletes in the country. She is one of the only five women in the world to have successfully landed the Produnova, also known as the death-vault, which is the most difficult vault of those currently being performed in women's gymnastics.

She is a recipient of the Padma Shri, the fourth highest civilian award in India. She was the first Indian female gymnast to compete in the Olympics. She was then twenty-two and participated in the women's vault gymnastics event at the 2016 summer Olympics in Rio de Janeiro, with an overall score of 15.066. She missed out on the bronze medal by a mere 0.15 points. For her performance, the Government of India conferred upon her the Rajiv Gandhi Khel Ratna Award in Sports and Games in August 2016.[14]

In July 2018, Dipa became the first Indian gymnast to win a gold medal at a global event, when she finished first in the vault event of the FIG Artistic Gymnastics World Challenge Cup in Mersin, Turkey.

Despite her grand success, she was one of the humblest and kindest persons I had ever met.

Dipa was born and brought up in Agartala, Tripura. Her father was a weightlifting coach at the Sports Authority of

India and formerly a national-level athlete himself. He liked gymnastics. When Dipa was only five years old, she showed an inclination towards gymnastics. Her father encouraged her to pursue the sport.

Her first coach, Soma Nandi, says, 'She was very serious about gymnastics. She wouldn't stop until she was satisfied with her practice.' In 2002, when she was only nine, she participated in the North East Games held in Agartala.[15] In spite of being the youngest participant, she won a gold medal after beating far more senior and experienced contestants.

There she was scouted by the Secretary of the Tripura Sports Council and then started working with her current coach, Bishweshwar Nandi, who is a Dronacharya awardee, India's highest honour for outstanding coaching in sports and games.

She was judged rigorously by him on her level of interest, grit and dedication. All of which she passed with flying colours.

Dipa's first challenge was that she had flat feet. When she was younger she was told that she could never be a great gymnast due to her condition. To overcome the defect, Dipa was put through many strenuous exercises. One of them included standing with her foot bent for long durations to create the desired arch.

Her first coach Soma says, 'She was average in the beginning, but I found her improving by the day. And she was, and still is, stubborn. I think that is why she reached where she did at Rio.'

Dipa dedicated all her waking hours to practising. As she persevered, her feet developed arches, and she started performing better.

In the 2007 Junior National Games, she won three gold and two silver medals. And that was her turning point. She then became unstoppable.

She won gold medals in all the four events she participated in at the 2011 National Games of India. Between 2010 and 2014, she continued to impress by bagging five national championships, winning five gold medals each in the Jharkhand and Kerala National Games editions. She won a bronze medal in the 2014 Commonwealth Games in Glasgow, secured fifth place in the 2015 World Artistic Gymnastics Championships and came fourth in the 2016 Olympics in Rio de Janeiro.

Her second biggest challenge was the lack of infrastructure and equipment that is required to perform in the Olympics. Only a handful of people know that the foundation of her skills was laid using equipment made from the second-hand parts of a discarded scooter.

'We initially had no apparatus and had to use our imagination to improvize,' Dipa's coach Bishweshwar Nandi told Reuters in an interview. 'For example, we stacked eight to ten crash mats on top of each other to make a vaulting platform. We bought second-hand springs and shock absorbers from discarded scooters, then asked a local carpenter to make some kind of a springboard with the bits.'

When Dipa first started to vault, she used to jump from this improvized springboard on to a pile of mats. To train for the Produnova, the most difficult vault jump, all she had was her grit and dedication to compensate for the lack of equipment.

'I am attempting the vault morning, noon and night so I can get it right for the Olympics. My goal is to produce my best performance,' she said.

She noted down her attempts over one week in a diary she keeps of the practice vaults she makes. The final tally: 127 vaults. In one week.

In comparison, American gold medal favourite Simone Biles attempts about fifteen complete vaults a week.

But then, Biles has had access to top-of-the-range apparatus from the start and did not have to overcome the challenges faced by Dipa.

'I don't think my rivals know what obstacles and hardships I have had to face to get myself to Rio,' says Dipa.

She became the first Indian gymnast at the Olympic Games in fifty-two years and the first-ever female from India to make an appearance in the sport. Now gymnastics and the state of Tripura have become synonymous with Dipa Karmakar. Furthermore, her accomplishments at the 2016 Rio Olympics have helped change the mindset of people towards the girl child and female athletes in India.

Dipa's story of struggle, grit and determination to overcome all challenges and imperfections is the stuff of legends.

To put things into perspective, Angela Duckworth's model from her book *Grit* comes in handy.

I have learnt a lot about the true meaning of grit by speaking with ultra-successful young people such as Dipa and reading scientific journals and books. There are four traits that make these successful people gritty, and you can develop them too.

Interest

Firstly, there is an element of obsessive interest. The ultra-successful have an undying passion for what they are doing. They intrinsically enjoy what they do.

It is true that 'follow your passion' is an over-used statement. Every great college commencement speech says something along the lines of 'find what you love and follow it'. I think most people would do exactly that if they knew what their passion was. The key lies in nurturing your passion. A lot of industry experts and paragons of grit in India say that they spent years finding what they liked and even more time cultivating it.

To find your passion is a lot of work. It is not like you are struck by lightning and you immediately know what you want to do for the rest of your life. In fact, you might need to expose yourself to different interests and see what sticks for you.

As children we are far too young to know what we want to do when we grow up. Our early interests tend to be fragile and fleeting. Finding our interests is not so much about introspection but it is about interacting with the outside world. This process can be time consuming, but it reaps more rewards in the end.

* * *

Kunal Pandagale, popularly known as Kaam Bhaari, is a famous Indian rapper, lyricist and poet. In 2019, he played a critical role in making the Bollywood superhit *Gully Boy*, starring Ranveer Singh and Alia Bhatt. Many of us have enjoyed his songs *Kab se kab tak* and *Kaam bhaari* from the movie. For his many original songs, Kaam Bhaari was nominated for the MTV Europe Music Award for Best Indian Act two years in row.

His social and economic circumstances have made him a passionate, spiritual and curious person. His obsession with writing and poetry found a new channel in rap music. He found his calling in this form of expression when he was in high school, and he hasn't stopped since.

Born in 1998, Kunal grew up in the ghettos of Kandivali, Mumbai. His father was the only breadwinner in his family.

'When I was ten years old, my father lost his leg in an accident, and we were never financially well-to-do.'

To help their financial situation, Kunal's mother had to work as a house help. Growing up with economic struggles, Kunal saw the life of Mumbai in all its colours.

He was a curious and sensitive child. Since his father was home-bound, he asked him all sorts of questions on how the world functioned. His father gave him streetwise answers, while his mother gave him a spiritual outlook towards life.

He started writing one-liners in English and Hindi when he was in the fifth and sixth standards. Kunal enjoyed the subjects of Hindi and Marathi, and felt encouraged to express himself in those languages at school,

Soon he discovered the American rappers Lil Wayne, Snoop Dogg and Eminem. Listening to their music inspired him and sparked an initial interest in rap music as a way to express himself.

In school, as a natural performer, he would make a ruckus, climbing up on the desks and rapping as his friends cheered him on.

He was expected to finish school, graduate from college and get a job. But his frustrations and financial condition were ever-present. So, he felt he had to do something soon, '*Uske pehle kuch toh jugaad hona chahiye.*'

He recorded and edited a few songs on his phone when he was in the tenth standard. All he wanted to do was express himself.

'I saw in my surroundings Bombay's [now Mumbai] nightlife, school life, college life, hood life, classes and family life. I don't know how it happened, but it was my calling that I fell in love with writing.'

Since he did not have his own room, he would sit at the kitchen table and reflect on his surroundings and create music. The inspiration for all his songs came from his personal experiences and encounters with poverty, oppression, heartbreak, loneliness and the language of Mumbai. In 2016, using an inexpensive phone, he started uploading his videos on a YouTube channel he created under the name Kaam Bhaari. Since he had started writing at the age of fourteen, he had a lot of material ready. He did not wait for someone to validate his writing; all he wanted to do was create.

Around the same time, Ranveer Singh was working on a jingle for the Jack & Jones clothing brand and announced a talent search for rappers. Kunal submitted his entry, uploading the video on his YouTube channel. His video made waves. His recording was identified by a leading musician and caught the eye of Ranveer Singh. Within four months of uploading it, he was invited for an audition.

Kunal went to the Don't Hold Back auditions. Out of the 5000 artists that applied, only four were selected. Kaam Bhaari was one of them. This gave him the opportunity to work on the jingle for the commercial Don't Hold Back 2.0.

After the commercial, Kunal got signed to Ranveer Singh's and Navzar Eranee's record label called 'IncInk Records', with three other artists. Thereafter, Kaam became unstoppable by producing electrifying hits one after the other.

After the campaign, Ranveer Singh began working on the movie *Gully Boy* with Zoya Akhtar. They wanted to work with Kaam Bhaari, and he played an instrumental role in making the story of the film and contributed to the movie's soundtrack. This marked his break into the mainstream market.

When I interviewed him in May 2021, he told me what artistry meant to him. With a broad smile and a child-like enthusiasm, he said, 'It is a process to really delve deep into any matter of life, and truly feel everything, and that is where the music is composed.'

I asked him what it was like during the months when he was uploading music but hadn't been spotted yet.

He replied in Hindi, 'I didn't think so much about the process and being selected. I was just going with the flow, reflecting on my surroundings, and writing. I still cannot believe I got selected and featured in a Bollywood film.'

We often like to try new things and move from one thing to another. But as Kunal's story suggests, once you find your passion, it is sensible to stick to whatever it is you like for a few years so you can cultivate your skills. This will open you to opportunities that you would never have thought of.

* * *

Practise

The second major contributor to grit is practise. All the successful people I spoke to for this book, be they musicians, athletes, academics, businessmen and even politicians, are always practising and improving their skill sets. They are the hardest working people in their respective industries. They constantly challenge themselves and try to become better than what they were yesterday.[16]

The people who are world class at anything not only practise the hardest, but also the smartest. These high performers are more deliberate in their efforts. They have ambitious goals, they put in tremendous effort with great concentration, and they constantly reflect upon and refine their work.

An ambitious goal is something that might be truly out of their league, such as winning an Olympic gold medal, being the best rapper in the country, or becoming the best motorsport athlete in the country. Then they pursue that goal with incredible effort and a laser-like focus. All of this goes on outside the spotlight. They love to seek feedback, especially negative feedback. And they find the pain and the challenge enjoyable.[17]

* * *

Sandeep Chaudhary is India's leading track and field para-athlete. He competes in the javelin throw event. At the age of twenty-two, he broke the world record in the Asian Games. In 2019, at the World Para Athletics Championships, he broke his own previous record by hurling his javelin 66.18 metres. He became the world champion and world number one in the same year. Although in the Rio 2016 Paralympic Games he came fourth with a margin of centimetres, when we spoke, he was preparing for the Tokyo 2021 Paralympics.

To reach where he is today, Sandeep practised very hard to overcome his obstacles and become a better athlete.

Sandeep was born in an army family in Gurugram, Haryana, in 1996. When he was twelve, he met with an accident and injured his left hip. Sandeep was a rough-and-tough kid, so he did not tell his parents about this injury. As a result, it went untreated, which led to pus formation in the joint. As a fallout, his mobility was affected, and he could no longer walk as easily as he once could.

He was sporty and used to play volleyball in his hometown. Then he realized his lack of mobility was an issue that was hurting the team more than helping.

'I didn't even know that the word or category of people with a disability existed,' he says. It was only when he went to college that he realized there was something called the Paralympics.

Back then people in his community would look down on athletes with disability. So, he did not want to participate in parasports at first. But later, his mentors encouraged him to think practically and shared how he could bring glory to the country by winning international medals in parasports.

Sandeep was introduced to the javelin throw event only in late 2014. With intense practise and hard work, he went on to make India proud by winning a gold medal at the 2016 FAZZA World Para Athletics Championships in Dubai. He followed that up with winning yet another gold in Germany at the Berlin Open the very same year. These impressive feats helped him qualify for the Rio 2016 Paralympics. In Rio, he finished at a commendable fourth position, but he felt devastated.

He remembers, 'In 2016, I had never seen such a big stadium in my life. Only in the movies. I felt no pressure. I got injured in the first round. I reached the finals and made one of the best throws, but lost the bronze medal by centimetres, finishing fourth. I was very disappointed and cried for half an hour.'

When he came back to India, everyone knew the four medallists. But no one knew who came fourth.

He said, 'In India, fourth and fortieth are the same. No one cares. No medals no glory.'

Sandeep feels that failures are the most formative events in one's life. He took his setback as incentive to practise even harder for his next tournaments.

'I stopped showing people that I was working hard. Silently I kept on working on my game.'

He took professional help to develop a standardized schedule and plan, and had the support of the GoSports Foundation, a non-profit venture that helps India's top talents in Olympic and Paralympic disciplines, through the athlete scholarships and other programmes. He went on to break the world record thrice.

When we spoke in late 2020, he was working towards making it to the Tokyo 2021 Paralympics.

Sandeep has only one quest—to reach 100 per cent of his potential. He says, 'I train and try to compete with the able-bodied athletes.'

To the people who have disabilities, or any shortcomings, Sandeep says, 'Don't make excuses for the little things. The one who wants to do it will do it. Problems become big when we allow them to become big. We can be patient and display the grit to overcome any shortcomings in the world.'

Sandeep's story reflects the value of practise in perfecting one's craft. He had an ambitious goal of winning a gold medal for India in the Paralympic Games. He pursued this goal with a laser-like focus, and on his journey, he reflected on his setbacks so he could get back better and stronger.

* * *

Purpose

The third contributor to grit is purpose. The grittiest people find purpose in what they do. This is related to the feeling that their work is important not only to them but also to the people around them.

The initial interest that they have nurtured is great, but that is only one source of passion. Another source of passion is purpose. And this comes when you reflect on how the work you are doing will make a positive contribution to society.[18]

Over the past thirteen years, as the founder and artistic director of Project FUEL (Forward the Understanding of Every Life-lesson), Deepak Ramola has built a global organization that documents and shares the life lessons and stories of people from each of the 195 countries around the world.

He is also the author of two bestselling books, *50 Toughest Questions of Life* and *Itna Toh Main Samajh Gaya Hoon*. He previously served as the Kindness Ambassador for UNESCO Mahatma Gandhi Institute of Education for Peace and Sustainable Development (MGIEP).

Thanks to his methodology, which empowers people to collect and document life lessons in their own geography, Project FUEL was recognized as among the world's top 100 innovations in education by Finland-based organization HundrED.

Forwarding the understanding of life lessons of the women of the Maasai tribe, young girls in Afghanistan and sex workers of Kamathipura, to learnings from earthquake survivors in Nepal and Syrian refugees in Europe, Deepak is a new age storyteller and artist who has worked with a wide range of people. Deepak grew up in a middle-class family in Dehradun. His grandmother pulled his mother out of school when she was only in the fifth standard. Nonetheless, his mother became a very active member of her community. Looking at his mother, Deepak realized that your value isn't attached to your money or fame, but to the knowledge you have and how you apply it in your life and community.

* * *

In school, Deepak was a great student. But he sounded a bit different, and that was a reason as good as any for his classmates to bully him. From the sixth to eleventh standard, he had a tough time at school and trouble making friends.

During this phase, he became introspective and turned towards reading and writing stories. Soon enough he realized that he had a knack for storytelling. He started participating in debate competitions, and with the same voice for which he was made fun of, he would take the stage and hold everyone's attention while presenting meaningful and beautiful ideas.

He was bullied so much at school that he thought he may never overcome those scars. But stories that he heard about other people's life experiences gave him a lot of strength and confidence. He felt he could overcome his own troubles.

So wherever he went, he would strike up a conversation, whether it was with people in his tuition classes, at school, at extracurricular activities, in his school bus or at train stations, and he started collecting their stories. He realized the stories he was collecting by speaking to so many people was helping him a lot. He felt that all this information had to be passed on to others.

Deepak remembers the power of sharing stories, 'I think when you tell someone's life story to people, they reflect it like the energy of the sun, and they store it. And they continue to glow in those stories in their dark days when creating their positive memories doesn't work.'

When he narrated these stories of life lessons learnt from day-to-day people, he would grab the attention of people, and many would tell him later how much the stories had helped them. The value of sharing stories helped him grow as a person and shaped his purpose.

He recalls, 'I started collecting life lessons at the age of fourteen. When I moved to Mumbai in 2009, I started teaching those life lessons that I had documented at theatre workshops, school lectures and college festivals. And that's when Project FUEL took shape.'

When he was nineteen years old, he saw a beggar lady sitting on the footpath outside the Andheri station in Mumbai. She was in her seventies, visibly aged and sick. He sat next to her and asked about her life story. At the end of their chat, he promised her he would share her story in a class. The lady was touched and surprised.

She said to Deepak, 'I sit here every day stretching my arms begging, thinking, what have I done for the world? And if you tell me what I have learned in my life is going to be valuable to somebody, I have no right to be upset with myself. I have been made able to make a difference.'

This was one of the thousands of stories from his journey, and this helped him think more intuitively and confidently about what he was doing.

To make Project FUEL a multinational organization required a lot of grit, passion and a strong sense of purpose. Deepak's vision with Project FUEL is to build a world wisdom bank. A global repository of life lessons and knowledge from common people's learnings that is as easily accessible as the stories of famous people. Anyone can understand what a Mongolian grandmother has learnt in her life or the struggles of a girl in Afghanistan. He wants to share the stories not of the rich and the famous, but of the common people who live their lives in such an extraordinary way that you can't help but pause and admire them, and hopefully absorb some of their wisdom so that you can grow in your life too.

Today, whenever anyone tells him, 'Deepak, I don't know what my purpose is, I need to find my purpose,' Deepak smiles and replies, 'Amazing, congratulations. It is a blessing to know what your calling is, but it is an equal blessing to know what your calling is not. Because then you can try as many things as possible and not feel guilty. If you don't know what you came here to do, then everything is an experiment to better understand that purpose.'

For Deepak, storytelling was his passion and his purpose. In his World Wisdom Map, a project that documents and shares the life lessons and stories of people from the world's 195 countries, he discovered the positive impact of stories. He says, 'For many people, the world might seem like a very bleak place, but when you study people's stories and learn the moral of their story, it leads you to a sense of realization and hope.'

* * *

Hope

Finally, gritty people have the unshakable hope that everything will turn out all right. The road to success is paved with rejections and failures. Every time one is knocked down, there is the unflinching hope that it will all work out.

'What doesn't kill me makes me stronger,' the German philosopher Nietzsche once said. People who are in pursuit of greatness endure tremendous pain on account of their own mistakes or their environment. Navigating through these obstacles by their own efforts makes them confident about their strengths. This makes them stronger in life.

* * *

Pratishtha Deveshwar is the first wheelchair user from India to study at the University of Oxford, and she is the recipient of the prestigious Diana award (one of the world's most prestigious accolades that youth under the age of twenty-five can get for social work), an ambassador for the *Beti Bachao*

Beti Padhao campaign appointed by the government and a TEDx speaker.

She overcame many personal obstacles to become a beacon of hope for girls from the rural areas in Punjab to the cities of London and Hong Kong.

Pratishtha was born in Hoshiarpur, Punjab, in 1998. She was a happy, outspoken and studious child. One evening, when she was thirteen, she met with a serious accident. Half her body was paralysed. With an only 3 per cent chance of ever walking again, it was a lot to process.

For the next five years, from 2011 to 2016, she was completely bedridden. She had to stop going to school and lose out on her social life. School and the public places are largely inaccessible for a person with disability. The disrespectful and stereotypical attitude that the society had towards people with disability affected her self-esteem and hampered her growth in those early years.

Imagine the frustration of not being able to move even your toes. The helplessness you feel when you are thirsty, and the glass of water is kept on the table right across your bed, but you can't reach it. You try and you fall only to injure yourself. As a person with a disability, wherever she went in the society, she was challenged with the lack of accessible infrastructure. These early experiences made her question the lack of inclusion in the world and set her on a path to do something about it.

For a long time, Pratishtha had a fundamental longing to get her old self back.

In her time of adversity, when everyone—her doctors, physiotherapists, and government—failed to give her a ray of light, she found her solace in prayers, meditation and journaling.

She says, 'I would write to God saying that you have deprived me of the social life of a teen. I would then detail my dreams and aspirations of what I would want to do if I got my old self back.'

One day when Pratishtha was feeling particularly dejected, her father told her a story from the Indian epic Ramayana that helped her see opportunity in her adversity.

The day before the coronation of Sri Ram, his father, the king, sent him on a fourteen-year exile. His mother, Queen Kaushalya, was heartbroken, but Sri Ram kept his calm and composure. He smiled and said, 'Father was going to make me the king of our great kingdom. But now he has made me the king of the whole jungle and there is so much more opportunity for me to work there and bring about a change.'

Much like this story, Pratishtha learnt to reframe her anguish into an opportunity for action. She felt that God had given her an opportunity to make an impact on the wider world.

For several years after her accident, it was hard for her to share her story with other people. She did not want people to see her flaws, her scars or see her in the wheelchair because of lack of societal acceptance of people with disabilities and the prejudice that comes along with it.

One day, her parents were going out for a get-together, and she asked herself how long she would hide away from the world just because she was a bit different. She decided that this fact wouldn't stop her from living her life to the fullest.

Pratishtha recalls, 'I started accepting myself and embracing the fact that okay, this is my identity now, and I don't have to hide anymore. Accepting my imperfections and focusing on my abilities has been my biggest accomplishment.'

That was when she decided to get out of the house in a wheelchair. Having topped her class in the eleventh and twelfth standards, and with the encouragement of an angel-figure, she applied to Lady Sri Ram College, Delhi University, on the last day of applications. She got in. And she went.

The next three years at Lady Sri Ram College transformed her life completely. From learning how to live independently to becoming a feisty voice advocating for inclusion internationally, her prayers had been answered.

She started sharing her story and soon realized the power of it. It had a tremendous impact on people.

Most people think that happiness comes from the people around them, their circumstances, their family background or material riches and success. Pratishtha believes that happiness comes from appreciating the small things in life. Happiness comes from an intrinsic confidence in oneself, so when you ask yourself what is the worst that can happen, your answer will be that come what may, I will survive it.

She says, 'I had never even gone out with a friend to have a cup of coffee in my life, something most people do daily. And now that I am finally able to do it too, along with many other things that people take for granted, I feel immensely happy, grateful and content.'

In the two-hour call for this interview, I learnt a lot about Pratishtha. She has the candidness of a young girl, but it is backed by an Olympic-level confidence. Her confidence and sense of hope come from a very deep-rooted experience.

When she was much younger, her doctors and parents would often tell her all the things she could not and should not do. It became very difficult for her to find her own voice.

But she developed the habit of writing in her journal, which came in exceptionally handy for her to realize her self-worth. She would write down her thoughts every day, and the journal became her most trusted and reliable friend and helped her get rid of all her negativity.

In 2020, Pratishtha demonstrated that nothing is impossible for those who are courageous in the face of adversity by becoming the first wheelchair-user from India to study at University of Oxford. At the age of twenty-one, she smashed all the stereotypes that the society imposed on her growing up. She overcame various hurdles of inaccessibility and exclusion to pursue a master's degree in public policy from Oxford. She was the youngest person in her class, where most students were thirty-five or above.

There can come a point in your life when you feel you are close to breaking. In that moment, if you see somebody who refuses to give up, it changes things for you. This is the inspiration Pratishtha has been for me, and for many of the young people she has spoken to on her journey.

In July 2020, as an ambassador of the *Beti Bachao Beti Padhao* campaign, she addressed a group of tenth standard district topper girls from the rural areas of Punjab.

After her speech, Pratishtha realized that these top-scoring girls did not have their own dreams. They were dependent on their parents to show them the way after they completed school too. They did not even have the hope for a future that they could prosper in.

Because of her disability, she could resonate with girls who thought they were only good enough to stay at home and eventually get married. She reflected on her own life story and inspired them by saying, 'I am so much more than what people have thought about me and my capabilities. You too can dream big and live a life much beyond what society expects of you.'

For a girl with a disability who was dependent on her mother for everything, from combing her hair to bathing to moving, for someone with no visible future, to go on to speak at international forums, work for disability rights and inclusion and study at Oxford would have been unimaginable. So how did she do it?

'Thoughts are things. If you can dream it, you can be it! All it takes is hard work, grit, courage and hope,' she says.

Now that her inspiring journey is internationally recognized, she gets a lot of opportunities to impact lives of people. She advocates for inclusion, mental health and disability rights at platforms big and small, public and personal in an attempt to ignite a ray of hope in every life she touches.

She says, 'My story is now ten years long, and it is a journey long enough for people to see and understand that no matter how now feels like, their tomorrow is going to be much better.'

* * *

If you have been reading closely you would have noticed that all the individuals described in this chapter epitomize grit. They have achieved success by having a surplus of interest, passion, purpose and hope.

As we saw in the beginning, if you are admitted into the NDA, you know you have made it. Similarly, in sports like table tennis, if you get on the national team as an amateur player, you know you have made it.

However, while every year dozens of new athletes make it to the national team, only a few go on to achieve greatness on the global stage.

I would like to leave you with a story of two table tennis athletes whom I looked up to while growing up. They have taught me what grit means.

Manav Thakkar is a twenty-year-old table tennis paddler from Surat, Gujarat. He wears rectangular spectacles and speaks deliberately. Each word and every pause is measured. And while he may be only five feet five inches tall, in a table tennis arena, his presence can cause a six-foot-tall world champion to sweat.

In January 2020, at the age of nineteen, he was the first Indian to be ranked number one in the world junior (under eighteen) and youth (under twenty-one) table tennis rankings.

Manav's father is an ENT doctor in Surat. His mother is a doctor of Ayurveda and a yoga instructor. Manav was the rebellious single child. He started skating at the age of six. However, given the rashness of the sport, his parents encouraged him to pursue another sport. Although cricket was six-year-old Manav's first choice, they had a table tennis table in their house. Manav was shorter than the table, but he wanted to try it. He took three steps back from the table, looked up at the edge and hit the ball randomly. In the first rally of his life, he played five balls. Talent right there.

His parents enrolled him in a local table tennis academy. He played for two hours a day, five days a week for the next four years. At the age of ten, he became India's under-twelve number two. Then, he was scouted by Petroleum Sports Promotion Board (PSPB), a government-run academy for sports development in India for young talents.

He went to Ajmer, to PSPB's table tennis academy. They provided better schooling, a Chinese coach, equipment and all the infrastructure to train an athlete. He decided to become an international athlete in table tennis.

That was the turning point. In 2014, he became India's number one in the sub-junior category (under fifteen). And from then on he was unstoppable domestically. Although his grades in school dropped from the 90s to 80s, then to the 70s and down to the 50s, his performance in table tennis kept improving. He became the under-fifteen national champion and won the nationals not only in his under-fifteen age group but also in the under-eighteen and under-twenty-one categories. He was challenging the biggest names in the national circuit.

But now, as he graduates to an older category of senior-men at the pro level, he is struggling to perform well.

He said, 'In 2019, I was performing well in junior events, becoming world number one and winning the pro-tours in my events. But in the seniors, I am still struggling. I am world number 142 currently in the men's category.'

He was working hard with the world's best coaches, and even using artificial intelligence to improve his game, but his performance was still lacking. So, he sought advice from one of the living legends in the table tennis fraternity, Achanta Sharath Kamal.

Sharath Kamal, who is now a four-time Olympian and a nine-time Indian national champion in the senior's category, never made it to the Indian team in his junior years. When Sharath Kamal was in his teens, he worked incredibly hard for five years, but he didn't shine at the national level. He was looking for a break, and in the 2003 National Championships, he emerged victorious.

Just like in education, where we spend twelve years in school before going to college and specializing, in sports too it takes time to become a champion at the global level.

Sharath Kamal reflected on his early years of performance and his eventual breakthrough. His goal from a young age was to win at the international level, and he stuck with that goal for decades to achieve what he has achieved today.

'It takes time,' Sharath Kamal told Manav. 'The junior to senior transition is very difficult. Everyone has a different mental level. Since you have achieved so much in the junior circuit, you are expecting too much from yourself in the senior circuit. Give it some time and build your game tactically.'

Sometimes, for all of us, even if you are the grittiest, most talented and do all the things right, all it takes is a bit more time. So despite the challenges, and obstacles you will face, keep putting in the effort, and stick with it.

* * *

Once you overcome the barriers of 'what will people think' and decide a top-level goal that you want to accomplish, nothing will stop you from reaching there, as we saw in Anam's and Dipa's story.

To become successful, you will have to be gritty and keep the same top-level goal for a long time. This will involve finding your interests and nurturing your passions, as Kaam Bhaari's story tells us.

Practise and a laser-like focus towards your goals and seeking constant improvements will help you master your craft, as we saw in Sandeep's story.

If you feel that your work is benefiting not only you but also the people around you, that will help you feel great about yourself, and continue putting in the hustle, as Deepak's work truly personifies.

Finally, in everything you do, a hope that everything will be alright will be a source of light for you in your darkest days, as Pratishtha in being a beacon of hope truly illustrates.

2

Courage

'"Be not afraid" does not mean we cannot have fear.
Everyone has fear, and people who embrace the call to
leadership often find fear abounding. Instead, the words
say we do not need to *be* the fear we have'

—Parker J. Palmer,
an American writer, speaker, and activist [1]

Do you know what Mahatma Gandhi, Nelson Mandela,
Savitribai Phule, Jagjit Singh and Muhammad Yunus have
in common? They all challenged the status quo, which proved
to be transformational and unprecedented. By questioning
the strict segregation of races, how women were supposed
to relate to their sensuality and identity in public, what folk
music was supposed to be or how banks operated, these icons
courageously clashed with the times in a way that made them
relevant and memorable.

But it is worth noting that these icons weren't necessarily born fearless. In fact, they had a life full of experiences that shaped their character and gave them the courage to create change.

For example, I would have thought Mahatma Gandhi, as a leader who united India through the Satyagraha movement and accelerated India's freedom movement, was born courageous. But in his autobiography *The Story of My Experiments with Truth*, it appears that Mohandas Karamchand Gandhi was a shy, meek and fearful child, as he writes, 'I used to be haunted by ghosts, serpents and thieves. I used to be very shy and avoided all company; books and lessons were my sole companions.'[2]

His various experiences and low points in England, India and South Africa propelled him to start a four-decade-long fight against oppression. And on his journey, he became a courageous, confident leader and one of the most recognizable figures of the twentieth century[3] by marching on despite the resistance, anxieties and fears he might have felt.

Earlier, in our grandparent's generation, the definition of courage was more along military lines, such as 'having no fear of death' and showcasing bravery in the battlefield.

But today the meaning of courage has changed from an 'absence of fear' to 'going forth despite the fear'. Stanley Rachman, in his wonderful book *Fear and Courage*, offers one such alternative view that courage is the 'quality of mind or spirit that enables a person to face difficulty, danger and pain despite anxiety or fear.'[4]

As an athlete, my friends and coaches would tell me to be courageous. But they would usually point to two forms of courage: physical and moral. This was the equivalent of having the courage to jump off a cliff, and standing up against injustice. However, after reading dozens of books and articles, I learnt that there are four types of courage: moral, physical, social and creative.

Moral courage is about the righting of wrongs, taking the risk to speak the truth to those in power, demanding change and facing the consequences.

When she was eleven years old, Malala Yousafzai began advocating girls' education rights in Pakistan. As an anonymous writer, she wrote a blog on the British Broadcasting Corporation's (BBC) site titled 'I am afraid', describing her fear of the war that was breaking out in her hometown in Swat Valley, and her fear of going to school because of the Taliban.[5]

The Taliban issued a death threat against her, yet she continued to speak out. When she was fifteen years old, she was shot by Taliban gunmen, but she survived. In 2013, on her sixteenth birthday, when addressing the United Nations General Assembly, she said, 'The terrorists thought they could change our aims and stop our ambitions. But nothing changed in my life except this: weakness, fear and hopelessness died. Strength, power and courage was born.'[6]

People like Malala and Mahatma Gandhi expressed moral courage that brought about visible change and inspired everyday people to stand up for themselves. Moral courage comes from ordinary day-to-day things too, when you stand up for yourself and what you think is right.

Although nothing as world changing as Mahatma Gandhi and Malala, I had a small bout with a moral courage that shaped my personality to what it is today.

In 2015, the School Games Federation of India's national under-seventeen table tennis championship was held in

Medak District, Telangana. I had won the same national championships the previous year, and our Maharashtra state under-seventeen team was the favourite to win as the reigning national champions.

Usually, every team has a state-provided manager and a coach. While these titles are impressive, these guys are usually low-level bureaucrats who have never played a sport in their lives. The government has a provision to provide tracksuits, travel allowances and food stipends for all athletes. Although it is not a big amount individually, cumulatively for each age group and category of athlete and sport, as well as for male and female teams, it adds up to a sizable figure.

The normal practice of these managers, exploiting the ignorance of the teenage athletes, is to get them to sign the required paperwork by giving out the t-shirts and tracksuits, but pocketing the funds allotted for the athletes. Most sports people are not aware that they are entitled to an allowance as they usually just trust the management, don't read the regional language in which the paperwork is written, or don't wish to speak up and seek trouble. Further, arguing with bureaucrats might cost an athlete their spot on the team for upcoming tournaments, given how political team selection can get.

On one of the final days of the tournament, I managed to get hold of a file of team-related official documents from the managers and read through what we had signed. I realized we had been cheated off a few lakh rupees. I declared that our team would not play in the next round until this issue was addressed. We eventually received our money. While this event was of minor importance, it was my first experience of standing up for what I felt was right despite the fear of consequences. And this made me realize that common people like us too can engage in small acts of courage and affect change in our communities.

* * *

The second type of courage is physical courage. It comes when we push our bodies to go on bravely, whether it is to battle a chronic illness or to do more than what is normally expected of our physical bodies. It comes from a willingness to risk pain, injury or death for the sake of another or for the sake of our own survival or growth.

Physical courage is commonly associated with military heroism or valour in the face of the enemy. However, it is not brashness or bravado, that form of derring-do that may have more to do with feeding your ego or being afraid to look less than what you are.

It can be the courage where you push your physical boundaries and strive for growth.

Vedangi Kulkarni is an Indian endurance cyclist who pushed through physical and emotional obstacles to cycle around the world, unassisted. This journey not only led her to new places around the world, but also made her realize that her capabilities were limitless.

In 2018, at the age of twenty, she peddled 29,000 km around the world in 160 days to become the youngest woman, the first Asian, the first Indian and the fourth fastest woman to circumnavigate the planet on a bicycle.

Vedangi was born in 1998 in Dombivli, India. She grew up in Mumbai and Pune. Her father worked in the petrochemical industry and her mother was a teacher.

Growing up in India as an only child, with only her mother at home and her father travelling for work six months a year, it was hard.

'Back in middle school, I was the lonely kid with no friends. I felt like there was nowhere to go,' she says.

She had major self-esteem and self-confidence issues.

'The phases between thirteen and fifteen, I didn't know what was going on with me. I had major issues with self-esteem. There are phases of me going, fuck, I am not good enough and I cannot make it . . . I had very little confidence in my abilities. If someone told me I was not strong enough, I would probably have believed it.'

Vedangi was good at sports and studies. But she had her own teenage angst.

'Until my tenth grade, I was above average in the class—in the top ten. After tenth, I played for Pune FC [football club]. The whole dynamic in football was not working well for me. I was good enough to be on the team, but I did not feel confident to be there. I was always chosen last. The coach always yelled at me and that reminded me of my mum, and I was like, fuck you.'

Vedangi used to ride her bicycle to school and football and back, as a form of cross-training. She really liked it, and as a getaway, her father offered her to take on a trip to Manali.

In April 2016, Vedangi and her parents went on an excursion, in Manali, where she completed a 60-km ride. There they met Sumit Patil, an Ultra cyclist, who was the field director of the cycling expeditions through the Youth Hostel Association of India. He suggested that she could even ride the longer route that goes between Manali and Leh.

But as a seventeen-year-old, she was too young to join the Youth Hostel Association of India's Manali-Leh-Khardung La expedition. So they left the conversation at that.

In July 2016, at the national football camp, she didn't like it very much there. While she was at a national camp in Bandra, her dad who saw Vedangi unhappy at the football camp, and asked her whether she wanted to go on a ride from Manali to Khardung La with just him and his mother for a change, although she wasn't eighteen years old and eligible to join the Youth Hostel Association of India's expedition group yet. He asked, 'Do you want to do a ride across the Himalayas? The season is now. Do you want to go now?'

That was the last time she played football in India. When she rode her first Manali to Khardung La Pass expedition, she loved it.

'Riding your bike in the mountains really makes you realize how little you and your problems are. Because it gives you a unique perspective. And I think that perspective changed a lot for me.' She was only seventeen then.

Vedangi had a dream to study abroad, get an international football coaching qualification and return to India to start a goalkeeping coaching centre. So she started applying to colleges in the United Kingdom. She was accepted at Bournemouth University, in southern England, where she pursued a bachelor's degree in sports management on a 50 per cent scholarship.

When Vedangi was a college freshman, she did not have many friends. But she loved riding her bicycle and decided to go on a cycling trip from her town in southern England to London. On the way, in the town of Bentley, she met a family that invited her to stay at their place for the night. Over dinner, in the spur of the moment she casually mentioned that she would like to cycle to the northernmost point of the UK—John o' Groats. So she skipped going to London, and instead undertook a 1600-km ride from Boscombe to John o' Groats, which she finished in three weeks

Successfully completing her first long-distance cycle ride in England, covering the length of the country, boosted her confidence, and she decided to cycle from London to Edinburgh and back. It was a total of 1400 km, which she completed in five days. But on this ride, she had a bad accident. She crashed into a tree and dislocated her knee.

'Many people had their turn persuading me to not continue. But I was confident. I was so slow. I was in agony. It was disgusting, but it was fine, I finished riding London–Edinburgh–London on my cycle.'

This ride made her dream global. She gained the confidence to do a world tour expedition.

'In 2016-17, after my London–Edinburgh–London ride, I wanted to go around the world. Because I truly felt I got this. And I wanted to go on an adventure at a global scale.'

The dream was big, and so were the challenges. She decided the route, trained physically and had a cycle custom made. Yet there were still many uncertainties.

'I was not getting any sponsors. Everything was super late. People were not taking me seriously. The visa issues as an Indian were prominent. It was a tall climb.'

With incredible persistence, hard work and plain hard-headedness, she rode through all the difficulties.

Her expedition around the world was filled with adventures and misadventures. She grew stronger and more confident over the duration of this journey as she did through her life in India and in the UK.

She started her race in Perth, Australia, in 2018.

Given her tight budget, she once stayed with an indigenous aboriginal family. They were sweet to invite her to stay with them for the night. The problem was they did not speak English. For dinner, they laid out a four-course meal with great hospitality. The meal tasted a little too meaty. Vedangi was curious about what she was eating. Through a lot of hand gestures, she asked what the dishes were. The parents looked a little hesitant. However, their child, with great excitement, ran to get his English alphabet book. Opening it and pointing to the letter 'K', he then did a little kangaroo hop. The delicacy she was eating was in fact their national animal. With a nervous laugh, Vedangi continued eating.

These incidents were not uncommon on the road.

After she finished her ride across Australia from Perth to Brisbane, she flew to New Zealand to ride the length of the north island. She covered the distance of 700 kms from Wellington to Auckland in four days, averaging just three to four hours of sleep a night.

The next leg of her journey was to start in Alaska, but due to visa issues (the first of many), she decided to ride across Canada instead of the US, as she had originally planned.

It was a 7500-km commitment in this country. She rode through British Columbia, the prairies, the western mountains, and the beautiful landscape of Quebec and the Atlantic region.

'In the Glacier National Park, at around the 8000-km mark of the whole journey, I was up in the mountains. I was listening to the audio book *Mind of a Survivor* and eating an energy bar. Riding steadily, I saw three grizzly bears on my right. It was a proper family. The big daddy bear had eye contact with me and suddenly started chasing me. It was super massive. They run surprisingly fast. I started riding zig-zag to make him stop chasing me. I had earphones on. A lorry was zooming in from my left and honking. I only heard the screeching of brakes when it stopped in front of me. If it weren't for the bear, the lorry would have killed me. The bear ran away. The driver gave me the finger.'

After several of these misadventures, running into a family of bears, riding 600 km in the wrong direction, running out of water in a ghost town and narrowly missing a thunderstorm, she made it to the capital, Ottawa.

In Canada, Vedangi was on a tourist visa. To apply for a visa to the Schengen countries, you have to be in your country of residence or origin. So, when she applied for a visa at the embassies of various Schengen countries in Ottawa, they rejected her applications. Fortunately, after considering all Vedangi's documentation, which included a letter from the prime minister of India, the Danish ambassador granted her a Schengen visa which allowed her entry into mainland Europe.

'I had just cycled through a forest fire and got a lung infection. And I did not have the visa to go to the Schengen countries to start the next leg of my journey. I was in the French embassy telling them the whole story. I collapsed. Two men carried me out. I was basically kicked out of the French embassy. I was not getting any visas. Every embassy was rejecting me. Then on the tenth day, the Danish embassy came in like an angel and gave me a visa. It happened to be my twentieth birthday.'

She started her leg of the Europe tour in Iceland. But after being hit by a mini-bus, she couldn't continue her ride there So, she had to move on to the next country on her route. She decided to start from Portugal and cycle up to Finland. After cycling 200 km across Portugal, she entered Spain.

Later, at the 19,000-km mark, while still in Spain, she had the worst incident of her life. She was mugged at knifepoint and pushed into a ditch. She suffered a major concussion.

'I could have died. I woke up and checked to see if I could move my arms, legs, but nothing was working. I saw my bike—which was luckily all right. I carried myself to the nearest shop a few kilometres away. The guy immediately closed his business and took me for a coffee to find out what had happened. Then we went to a hospital. I had a concussion. It affected my digestion, coordination and performance. I felt bad for myself. I screwed up. I felt I should not have ridden the bike that late in the evening. Bad decision.'

In spite of that mishap, she decided to continue. However, the distance she usually covered in four hours was now taking her sixteen hours. Her dream to ride around the world in 100 days seemed to be fading.

She rode another 4000 km to reach Finland from Madrid. She wanted to cross the border from Finland into Russia, but had an issue getting into Russia.

At the Russian embassy in Finland, she had to pay the visa fees, but she was unable to transfer the money from her account. So, the ladies at the embassy paid for her visa on immediate basis.

Then when she arrived at the Russian border, she had a major problem. The border officials asked her for a bribe.

Showing great presence of mind, she fake-called her lawyers, which rattled the border police and they allowed her to pass.

Given that the expedition was self-funded, Vedangi was committed to camping outside, irrespective of the weather.

'Russia was really cold. And I was serious about not spending money in hotels. So I would camp everywhere. At that time, I used to sleep for four hours and cycle for sixteen hours. It was hard but it was fun.'

After cycling 3120 km in eleven days in Russia, she flew to India to do the last 5000 km. Between 4 to 28 December 2018, she rode from Ahmedabad to Bangalore to Kolkata.

To qualify as having cycled around the world one must end where one begins. Vedangi flew to Perth on an early morning flight to cycle the last 15 km to finish her journey around the world.

'You know what, after this journey I know that if anything happens to me at any point in my life, I can take care of myself. And that is all I need to know. That's what I tell myself when I have issues with imposter syndrome and self-esteem in my day-to-day life too.'

Vedangi is an embodiment of a courageous person who constantly pushes her physical limits. Over the past five years, Vedangi went from knowing nobody in the UK to have ridden her bike around the world (29,000 km in 160 days, mostly solo and unsupported, at the age of 19-20). She has now started her own business with a goal to make adventure accessible for everyone and she is also writing her book. Pushing her physical boundaries, in 2023 she plans to again circumnavigate the world, that too in 100 days by bike, solo and unsupported and become the fastest woman to do so.

* * *

The third type of courage is social courage. Social courage pushes you to stand tall and be comfortable in your own skin even if it means not conforming with society's expectations.[7]

This type of courage is about overcoming shame, embarrassment and sorrow. It involves risking one's self esteem in the eyes of others while still standing up for yourself.[8]

Imagine you are one of India's top athletes. As a part of the prestigious Indian national team, you are in Glasgow to compete in the Commonwealth Games. And a few days before your event you are dropped from the team.

Dutee Chand was dropped from India's contingent for the Glasgow Commonwealth Games and the Asian Games in Incheon after her naturally occurring testosterone levels were found to be in breach of the International Association of Athletics Federations' (IAAF) guidelines.[9] She went on to challenge the world athletics body, compelling them to re-examine and rewrite their rules in a hard-fought legal battle.

Dutee started athletics when she was five years old. She comes from a village called Chaka Gopalpur in Orissa. Her family had nine members. Her father was the single bread-earner in the family. His monthly income was Rs 200. Yes, only two hundred rupees a month.

Dutee took up athletics because of the job prospects that might come from the sports quota. Her older sister was an athlete. Coming from a backward village, for a girl to participate in sports was in itself a matter to be frowned upon.

In the winters, she used to train on the concrete streets. She had no shoes and few clothes to cover her body. From this abject poverty, Dutee rose to become the only Indian woman, after P.T. Usha in the 1980s, to become an Olympic track sprinter.

Her only motivation was that to get a better life and improve her family's situation, she would have to work hard and secure a government job. Running was her key to success, and she did remarkably well. She has won over 2000 medals, ranging from the state to international levels.

But in 2014, three days before the Commonwealth Games in Glasgow, she was set aside as tests showed that she had more testosterone in her body than the levels set by IAAF.

This was a very hard phase for Dutee. The people around her, the media and fellow athletes, started looking down on her. Even for normal things such as going to the washroom, she was asked if she should go to the male or the female bathroom.

At that point she felt the loneliest she had ever felt. She had to fight her battles on the track and outside too.

Although she was forced to sit out for over a year, she continued training every day. Her training regime involved waking up at 5 a.m. then training from 6 a.m. to 10 a.m., followed by another session from 4 p.m. to 7 p.m. She had to maintain a strong mindset to fight her athletic, legal and social battles simultaneously.

Growing up in poverty, she and her family were always treated poorly. So, she was conditioned to have a thick skin to others' opinions. But now, even when she was in the sporting spotlight in India, she faced some controversy or the other.

Many people told her that her career was finished. The IAAF had an international regulation regarding hyperandrogenism, a condition wherein the body produces high levels of testosterone. Female athletes with this condition, such as Dutee, could not compete in the women's category.

No one had ever dared to challenge a regulation like this in an international court.

In a similar previous case, in 2006, an Indian athlete called Santhi Soundarajan was stripped of her silver medal at the Asian Games. She was forced to leave sports and work as a daily wage labourer, earning Rs 200 per day to make ends meet.[10]

With great courage, Dutee chose to challenge this rule in the Court of Arbitration for Sport, a Switzerland-based independent institution that settles all sports-related legal disputes.[11]

To challenge a policy like this literally meant going against the world. It meant challenging the Sports Authority of India, IAAF, and many of her competitors who would have loved to see her gone.

In July 2015, the Court of Arbitration for Sport ruled in her favour and allowed her to compete.[12]

Dutee, after the court ruling, went on to win a silver medal in the women's 200-metre event at the Kazakhstan National Athletics Championships in Almaty, set an Indian national record and qualified for the Rio 2016 Olympics.

In May 2019, she also broke another boundary, coming out as India's first openly gay athlete.[13]

When we spoke in 2020, Dutee was training for the Tokyo 2021 Olympics.

Dutee has become a role model who gives courage to many young people. By standing up for herself and her rights, she has become a paragon of social courage.

* * *

The fourth type of courage is creative courage. It means leading with new ideas and creating things that are unknown to the rest of us.

This type of courage means overcoming the voice that asks us, 'who do you think you are?' when we try to create something new. Despite all the self-doubt, creative courage means creating something meaningful, beautiful and unique in spite of the risk of failure and rejection being high.[14]

Creatively courageous people look at life like a canvas and paint it with their choices and legacy.[15]

Ritviz is a twenty-four-year-old artist from Pune, India. With four million monthly listeners, Ritviz is one of the most iconic musicians in India. He is one of the most-streamed indie artists on Spotify, with over 200 million streams. His songs *Udd gaye, Pran* and *Jeet*, amongst many others, are a fusion of traditional Hindustani and Western pop music.

During the two-hour call I had with him, Ritviz made it clear that he was obsessed with music. While creating music, Ritviz feels that he is his true self. He often gets into a special 'zone' where he feels like an instrument of the universe.

His parents are musicians—his mother is a classical singer, and his father is a tabla player.

As a child, Ritviz would wake up hearing his mother practising her singing. He started learning gayiki, Indian classical vocal music, when he was six years old. By the time he was eleven or twelve, he was practising for five to six hours every day.

He grew up in a healthy environment at home. Music was neither forced on him nor was he was expected to make music.

He was learning Dhrupad, a style of Hindustani classical music, by following the guru-shishya parampara—the teacher-disciple tradition that we have in India. In those early years of learning, he was constantly surrounded by musicians.

Around this time, he was also watching VH1 Top 40 and Western music videos on television. He was influenced by the freedom of pop culture. It had no conventions or rules to follow.

Ritviz recalls, 'I was attracted to the West purely because of the freedom that I saw that I didn't see in Indian classical music.'

Traditionally in India, we respect, follow and polish our roots. In Hindustani music, one stays within the traditional confines of classical music. But Ritviz had a strong desire to express his own voice.

He says, 'I didn't want to sing and confine myself to only the given notes. I felt a strong need to express myself. I wanted to do something else. So, I started composing music in the fifth or sixth standard.'

At the age of twelve, Ritviz had started producing original music. He dreamt of becoming famous by the time he was in the ninth standard. So, he worked nearly sixteen hours a day from an early age to realize his dream.

In the ninth standard, unlike his friends who were worried about things such as friends, tests and games, Ritviz was dreaming about 'breaking into the scene'.

When he was fourteen years old, he participated in a competition, the winner of which would be signed with a record label. He was devasted to finish third. And that made him re-evaluate his music and work even harder to bring out new songs. At the peak of his creative self thereafter, he would create seventy songs in a week.

He was a good student at school and scored 86 per cent in the tenth standard. He then opted for the commerce stream, but after a month, he moved to humanities. Still, the system of mugging everything, even for practical exams, was suffocating for him.

So, he decided to take science in IB with the aim of becoming a sound engineer. However, he didn't enjoy that either as he was frustrated by the teaching style. He felt school was like a prison, and he was unable to unleash his creativity.

Finally, he decided that school truly wasn't for him, so he dropped out when he was still in the eleventh standard and focused on creating his own music.

His parents were supportive. His mother created a shield around him and told him, 'You only focus on creating your music,' despite the disapproval of his extended family and friends. He put his head down and continued honing his creativity.

'Every time I am singing, writing or composing, I feel closer to myself. So, it became like an addiction at a very young age.'

With each song he created he got into his true element, his zone. Philosophically, each song brought him closer to his true self.

If you listen closely to his music, you will notice that the content is Indian, but the format is Western. In making all his songs, his early childhood impressions of listening to his mother, to the many singers around him at home and to the VH1 Top 40 songs stuck in his memory. All the listening that happened in his childhood has morphed into the music that he makes today.

It took courage for him to not only drop out of school to pursue his creative calling, but to also break away from the confines of classical Hindustani music and create his own original pieces.

He says for creative people to be successful, they should learn about themselves first and not worry too much about the rules. If they reflect and discover their story and calling, and if they have a burning desire to share it with the world, they will figure out a way to do it. They don't need to stick with the conventional norms of society.

Ritviz says, 'We are not slaves to grammar. We should be slaves to literature. People forget that knowledge is only a tool. The true power comes in what you have to say.'

He candidly shares that one of the trade-offs of this creative courage is the loneliness one can feel. When he is in the zone while creating music, he feels euphoric. However, there is a negative side. 'Every time I get a creative block, I hate my life. I see the negative comments, I tell myself that, oh, I don't know what my next two years are going to be like. I start worrying, I get anxious.'

In his journey of creative expression, Ritviz made a symphony from all his life experiences that tens of millions of people enjoy today.

There is a lot to unpack from the stories of Malala, Vedangi, Dutee, and Ritviz. They moved past barriers and made landmark achievements at a very young age through courage.

But even in our day-to-day lives, we all need the courage to make our lives more rewarding and fulfilling.

* * *

It appears that at the end of our course of life, we wish we had had more courage to do things and live a fuller life.

> *No one has looked back sadly on a life full of experiences, but many look back wishing they had had the courage to do more.*
>
> —*Anonymous*

Bronnie Ware is an Australian nurse who spent years working in palliative care and caring for patients in the final weeks of their lives. She recorded their most common regrets and collected them in a blog and later a book titled *The Top Five Regrets of the Dying: A Life Transformed by the Dearly Departing.*

'When questioned about any regrets they had or anything they would do differently,' Ware says, 'common themes surfaced again and again.'

These themes provide an invaluable insight into what really matters in our lives.

One of the most common regrets is not having had the courage to live a life true to oneself, but living the life others expected of one.[16] When people realize that their life is almost over and look back on it, it is easy to see how many dreams have gone unfulfilled. Most people do not honour even half of their dreams and die knowing that this was due to choices they made or did not make.

Another common regret is not always having had the courage to express one's feelings.[17] Many people suppress their feelings to keep peace with others. As a result, they settle for a mediocre existence and never become who they are truly capable of becoming. Many develop illnesses related to the bitterness and resentment they carry as a result.

We need courage in everyday life, to try and honour at least some of our dreams. Only that will make our lives well lived.

Years of schooling and growing up in Indian society has instilled in us one thing: fear. Fear of getting a poor grade. Fear of not getting into the right college. Fear of not getting a job right out of school. Fear of not fitting in. Fear has almost become a tool to keep us compliant.

Fear feels bad. But to live life to the fullest and have no regrets at the end, one must be courageous. You need to actively teach yourself courage. The following exercise can help.

Firstly, keep a journal and reflect on all your past experiences. A track record of all the courageous things you have done in the past will serve as an inspiration to you.

Secondly, use micro-opportunities or challenges to expose yourself to new environments. Don't shy away from challenges. Instead, be mindful of your anxiety or fear, if any, and still go ahead and give it a shot. Once done, irrespective of the outcome, it will feel rewarding. Finally, remember that having a new experience in overcoming your personal fears and anxiety is more important than the outcomes.

To illustrate, here is one of my personal stories from 2019. I was studying in Madrid, Spain, on a student exchange programme at IE University. I was a shy Indian student who wanted to explore the place as much as possible.

At the beginning of the semester, all the university clubs put up stalls to showcase what they did, and students were invited to join any of them. The clubs were engaged in activities ranging from sports to social work, and from debating to beatboxing. I was dead set on joining the outdoorsy clubs such as sailing and rock-climbing.

I had recently lost a bet over a football match outcome to a friend. Jokingly, he said, 'Manthan, I challenge you to join the cheerleading club.'

I must reiterate, I was as shy as any Indian kid could be. I am terrible at dancing. This was going to be as cringe-worthy and awkward as anything could get. But with much hesitation, I decided I would join the club for a day and pay my dues for the lost bet as soon as I could.

I signed up for the cheerleading club, and as I walked into the gymnasium on the first day of practice, I was the only boy in a room full of girls. Although they looked pretty okay with my being there, I had never felt so uncomfortable in my life.

Anyway, I enjoyed my time in Madrid, and it was a fun experience making friends in the cheerleading club too. Sometimes I laugh at the experience, but it propels me to try new things wherever I go.

We have seen how well-known figures such as Mahatma Gandhi, Malala, Vedangi, Dutee and Ritviz challenged the status quo and led transformational lives in their respective fields. Moral, physical, social and creative courage are essential to achieving greatness in life. But in everyday life, sometimes courage is also about doing things with integrity. When many others use questionable means to maximize their benefits, staying true to one's values is also an act of courage.

* * *

Dr Rajeev Gowda is a successful former member of Parliament in the Rajya Sabha from Bangalore South and a national spokesperson for the Indian National Congress. He also served as the Director of the Central Board at the Reserve

Bank of India (RBI) and was the chairperson of the Centre of Public Policy at IIM-Bangalore. His is a story of having the moral and social courage to follow a righteous path and maintain his integrity despite the trials of Indian politics.

He recalls his early days: 'I grew up in a very inspiring public service-oriented environment. From the time I was a child I heard stories about India's freedom movement. So, I grew up wanting to make a difference.'

When he was twenty years old, he got a scholarship to pursue a master's degree in economics in New York.

'I got a scholarship to go abroad after my BA, and found myself eventually at the Wharton School, where I did my PhD.'

After his PhD, he did his post-doctorate fellowship at the University of California at Berkeley, and later became an associate professor of political science at the University of Oklahoma. When he achieved tenure and had settled his brothers, cousins and in-laws in the US, he felt he had fulfilled his responsibilities.

'I was married, and my second child was born. Then I told my wife, remember we always talked about going back to India and entering politics? Why don't we go back now?'

He was thirty-seven years old then and had been in the US for seventeen years when he decided to return to India in the year 2000.[18]

He started teaching at IIM-Bangalore. His father was a speaker in the Karnataka Legislative Assembly. The Congress party nationally was in the opposition. Dr Gowda was active in politics since his arrival from USA in 2000, and the leaders were happy to have an Ivy League-educated person contribute to the party.

Smt. Sonia Gandhi invited him to participate in the Vichar Manthan Shivir in 2003. There he had the opportunity to engage with many of the top leaders including Dr Manmohan Singh before he became prime minister.

Soon after this, Dr Gowda launched the Congress Party's youth-focused campaign in Guwahati ahead of the 2004 Lok Sabha elections,[19] and everything went well. However, when he wished to contest from the difficult seat of Bangalore South, the party didn't give him a ticket. This saddened him.

Still, throughout his political journey, Dr Gowda has been idealistic. While money and power play a significant role in politics, Dr Gowda remained true to his morals and refused to play that game.

After organically creating campaigns in Bangalore against moral policing and for the safety of women, he became a 'Super Citizen'. However, the party still denied him a ticket to contest the elections from Bangalore South. He learnt that there is no point in getting bogged down by such setbacks.

Reflecting on all the obstacles he has faced, he says, 'One has a very deep commitment to the country. All these ups and downs should not matter in the larger mission of making a difference in India.'

Because of the delimitation of the constituency, he shifted to Bangalore North. He did all the groundwork campaigning and built a buy-in from the public. But in the internal party elections to get a ticket to represent the party in his constituency, he lost. All the office holders held allegiance to the chief minister and party heads who had their own favourites.

In 2014, the Congress chose him to be the director of the Central Board of the RBI.

And in the same year, the Congress Party was attacked consistently by the media and other political parties. When Narendra Modi became the prime minister, Dr Gowda was given a break to become a member of Parliament in the Rajya Sabha at the youthful age of fifty in a smooth and unanimous election.

He went on to build and serve as the chairman of an internal think tank called Congress Research Department, which helps in the central decision-making of the party.

In his political career, Dr Gowda has strived for freedom. He explains, 'Amartya Sen has a concept called development as freedom, where he says what we achieved in August 1947 was political freedom, the right to run our own lives and to elect our own leaders and governments. But his concept of freedom is much larger. Although we are beyond the political freedom we got in 1947, we must strive to abolish the "unfreedoms" of poverty, famine, starvation, poor economic opportunities and intolerance among others.'

Many politicians have used the argument that they must remain in power in order to make a difference to justify money-making and creating a big empire. But it appears they tend to do good for themselves and their offspring rather than for society.

Dr Gowda has stayed away from this and has maintained his integrity. After sacrificing his academic career in the US, he has spent the last few decades focusing on abolishing Amartya Sen's 'unfreedoms' in India, and he continues to do so with moral courage and rigour. Although this path was difficult and paved with many setbacks, his character has been a source of inspiration to me and many others.

In an interview for this book, his advice to young Indians was, 'Be true to yourself in finding your calling. Be honest and maintain integrity. Do not take shortcuts. Do not fall victim to criticism. Do not lose your humanness, empathy and compassion. Stay grounded and stay humble in pursuit of your dreams and making a difference.'

3

Creativity and Innovation

'We can't solve problems by using the same kind of thinking we used when we created them'
—Albert Einstein

Anirudh Sharma is not your everyday genius. Instead, he is one of the few inventors who took the unconventional path to build world-changing social innovations.

A designer and an inventor, Anirudh is currently the chief technology officer at Graviky Labs, where he leads a team of engineers and scientists to build the future of turning carbon into new products.

His work at the intersection of technology, design and environmental impact has won multiple awards and has been featured on TED and in *Time* magazine. In 2012, he was also one of *MIT Technology Review*'s 35 Innovators Under 35. In the past, Anirudh led a wearable tech start-up that created navigational shoes for the visually impaired. Anirudh is interested in fusing design and technology in ways that impact people's everyday lives. Anirudh is a graduate of the MIT Media Lab and his journey so far, just like his inventions, has been unconventional.

In 2010, as a typical backbencher engineering student, he stumbled upon a TED video by Jeff Han on a cheap, scalable multitouch and pressure-sensitive computer screen.[1] Jeff's talk was on what has today become the basic touchscreen technology that is used for our phone screens, tablets and computers.

Before the iPhone era, the way we interacted with devices with a screen and a keyboard was outdated and hadn't evolved much over the last forty years. Anirudh was fascinated by this new interface and was introduced to the NUI group, an open-source community that wanted to simplify interaction with computers.

'I was sitting in this small town in one room and thinking how can I learn from this. I wanted to create my version of Jeff Han's reality.'

He assembled a team by inviting two of his friends from different fields of engineering. They started building what would become India's first multitouch table called Sparsh. And it was built very unconventionally as compared to its Western counterparts.

He and his team started travelling the country to participate in dozens of tech competitions including those held in IIT-Bombay, IIT-Kanpur, BITS-Pilani and so on. Without exception, they won all these competitions.

The other two friends went on to pursue advanced degrees in design. But Anirudh had accumulated over seventeen backlogs, the number of subjects he did not pass due to absenteeism. So, in the final year of college, he decided to drop out.

'I went to a government engineering college in the town of Bikaner, Rajasthan. I had too many backlogs, so I didn't finish college.'

Hewlett Packard (HP) Labs were working on something similar to Anirudh's college project. So, he reached out to a scientist there and got an opportunity to intern in HP's Bangalore office.

In Bangalore, he saw a lot of people with visual impairments. To minimize their problems, he designed Le Chal, a smart shoe to help the visually impaired find their way around. In 2012, Anirudh won the prestigious *MIT Technology Review*'s 35 Innovators Under 35, and also the Innovator of the Year award.[2]

This exposed him to the MIT community. As a dropout, he couldn't apply to any other schools in India or globally, but he could apply to MIT Media Lab—one of the world's most prestigious and selective institutions, which values learning by doing.

'The style of innovation in modern times has changed. If you want to solve a problem, let's say in my case blindness that I addressed using haptics or vibrations, you do not need a PhD in electronics for that. You need to be able to spot the right problem, collaborate with the right type of people, and create a solution. So that whole idea of collaborating with different disciplines is what MIT Media Lab was about.'

Our generation is growing up in the fourth industrial revolution marked by a combination of technologies that blurs the difference between the physical and digital world. At the rate at which technological breakthroughs are happening today, in twenty years we will be living in a significantly different world from the one we are living in today.[3]

However, our current education system is still fixated on the first and second industrial era that required mechanical, repetitive and mass production-related skills. Today, we need to learn new skills that will help us innovate and thrive in the new world. These skills will arise from collaboration, empathy, creativity, execution and constant improvement, which are at the core of any innovation and creative process. In my survey of 300 students, Generation Zs indicated creativity as the crucial trait that will enable them to be successful today. And these skills will allow students to find solutions to complex and open-ended problems that persist today.

* * *

As young adults, we all try to find our place in the world. We often look to our elders or to professionals for guidance, but it is not always helpful. In fact, looking outwards for direction can be very confusing and misleading.

When I had just passed my tenth standard, my parents took me for an aptitude test. This test was supposed to tell me what education and career choices I should make. The counsellor suggested that I would be great at computer engineering. But unfortunately, I disliked coding, and every effort I made at it that summer was a failure. So, I did not even take science for my eleventh and twelfth standards and focused on my table tennis. I eventually got into business and finance, dabbled with creative writing and worked at various non-profits. Finally, I decided that I would use my skills at the intersection of social work, finance and storytelling in the field of climate finance and help India's transition in reaching net-zero carbon emissions.

Although software engineering would have been a promising career, it didn't feel like the right fit for me, and taking the initiative to find my own way helped.

For one of my friends, Siddhi, finding her way was even more confusing. She took a dozen aptitude tests, consulted various career counsellors and even took a biometric test, in which they scanned her thumb.

The results from all these tests pointed in multiple directions, suggesting careers in everything from architecture to medicine. Some results even indicated that she was not good at maths, whereas she liked maths and statistics. After much consideration, she eventually pursued an undergraduate degree in economics and got a CFA charter. Her test results did not even mention the economics, CFA and finance fields that she followed, excelled at and said, 'I think my passion is here.'

Looking outwards for answers when we are stuck in life can thus often fail miserably. Answers emerge when one looks within and experiments with many things wholeheartedly. Creativity and innovation start with finding a problem statement that excites you. Once you identify this problem, it is important to start where you are and with what you have.

It does not matter where you come from, which school or college you went to or what your job is right now. It is never too early or too late to start anything. Time and again, the stories of the young overachievers have proved that they have found a way forward from wherever they are. Regardless

CREATIVITY AND INNOVATION
IN LIFE
=
FINDING PROBLEMS
+
SOLVING THEM

of their problems, creative thinkers always find a way ahead. They love problems. They turn their anguish into action through creativity.

Once you decide to do something exceptional, creative and innovative, you should not wait for other things to fall in place. You must start right away from where you are, with what you have, reflect on your surroundings, and start creating things.

As we saw in the chapter on Grit, Kaam Bhaari's story is one of overcoming obstacles, nurturing his interests with a few resources he had and dropping ground-breaking hits.

Kunal Pandagale, popularly known as Kaam Bhaari, is a young Indian hip-hop rapper, lyricist and poet. He was instrumental in making the 2019 Bollywood movie *Gully Boy*, starring Ranveer Singh and Alia Bhatt.

His story is of a boy who overcame many financial, emotional and structural obstacles, and made use of what little he had to become the superstar that he is today.

'When I was ten years old, my father lost his leg in an accident, and we were never financially well to do.'

Kunal's father was the sole breadwinner in the family. After his father's accident, his family faced severe financial issues. So much so that his mother had to work as a house help. She would bring back the discarded clothes from the houses she worked in for Kunal, his siblings and his father.

'I used to wear those clothes and flex as if they were my own! I remember, we did not have chappals, and I used to play barefoot for weeks till we could buy a new pair.'

The non-profit Save the Children India helped Kunal and his siblings by supporting their school fees.

Kunal was a sensitive boy and would seek his mom's support in everything that he did. There were many low points in his life. During the heavy rains and floods in Mumbai, the toilets in their community would choke. They could not afford to hire a sewage cleaner, so his mother had to clean those herself. Memories like these were deeply imprinted in Kunal's mind. Yet, despite their financial problems, his family always tried to provide for him and his siblings.

These early struggles shaped Kunal's worldview.

'My creative process was always about the things I saw in my surroundings: Bombay's nightlife, school life, college life, hood life, classes and my family. I didn't know how it happened, but I would empathize with the world around me, and I fell in love with writing.'

Eventually, he started making music based on his life experiences. Then, in 2016, using an inexpensive 10,000-rupee phone, he started uploading his videos on his YouTube channel under the name Kaam Bhaari.

He applied for a talent hunt competition called Don't Hold Back 2.0. Within four months of uploading the video, he was scouted by a talent manager.

Kunal confesses, 'I didn't know what they saw in me.' His background, upbringing and daily struggles, which were a source of inspiration for his music, became his unique identity.

He eventually became an instrumental part of the record-breaking Bollywood film *Gully Boy*. And today, his songs *Kab Se Kab Tak* and *Kaam Bhaari* have been a significant source of inspiration to millions globally. After the movie, his other songs include *Zeher, White Collar, Ayo Burn and Vichaar*, which nominated for the MTV Europe Music Awards (EMA's) for Best Indian Act two years in row 2020 and 2021 for his original music that reflected on the life and struggles of a common person.

* * *

There are hundreds of ideas and iterations that go into making a song. In life, too, if you want to find solutions to unique problems and unstick yourself from your current situation, you must ideate as many solutions as you can before you arrive at your final answer.

We live in a world where the problems we want to solve can be complex and multifaceted. To solve these problems, we need to be very creative. And creativity comes easily to children because they don't hold on to the constraints of society. In your process of finding solutions, it is essential to let your horses loose first.

Ideo's Divergent and Convergent Thinking model

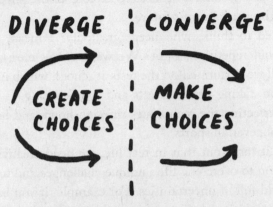

Diverge and Converge[4]

In the first stage of diverging with some crazy ideas, ask yourself, 'How can I make things better?'

Once you have several impractical and even wild ideas, the next step is to combine these ideas and select a few important ones. You should narrow them down to two or three solutions.

After choosing a few of the best ideas from the lot, the most crucial part is to create a product prototype rapidly. You shouldn't spend too much money or resources on it. Just make the product as quickly as possible and share it with others for feedback.

> 'They slow us down to speed us up. By taking the time to prototype our ideas, we avoid costly mistakes such as becoming too complex too early and sticking with a weak idea for too long.'
> —Tim Brown, CEO, IDEO

Most people think that they need to find *one* right idea. But actually, you need a lot of ideas to explore all the possibilities that might arrive in your future.

I used to think, who needs creativity? I mean, success is all about repetition, right? We were always measured on how well we performed on the tests at school, which involved repetition, taking practice tests and rote learning. It was all about perfecting the techniques through hours and hours of repetition, even in sports.

But it turns out that in real life, we need creativity and innovation to overcome life's unique challenges and to thrive in a world full of uncertainties. For example, if you have tall personal ambitions, you need to use creativity to get to your desired goal.

* * *

In 2019, I had a very inspiring flat mate in Singapore. He is one of the youngest people in India to lead a team building a near-space micro-satellite.

Sanket Deshpande is now a PhD student at the University of Wisconsin–Madison and develops hardware for quantum computing and networking. As an undergraduate, he studied physics and electrical engineering at BITS-Pilani in India. In college, he spent most of his time outside classroom working on projects that fascinated him. He helped build an affordable Braille learning device, which is now known as Annie from Thinkerbell Labs (you've probably seen it on Shark Tank India). He headed Project Apeiro, India's first student-led near-space microsatellite mission. He was also a part of 'Hyperloop India' team that was a finalist at the SpaceX

Hyperloop Pod Competition, where he met Elon Musk in person. His journey of sending a student-made satellite into space involved out-of-the-box thinking and innovation that was a stratum beyond his age.

Sanket grew up in Aurangabad, India. Both his parents are doctors.

He says, 'While my parents would have liked me to become a medical doctor, they never stopped me from pursuing my interest in physics and engineering.'

He wanted to create something new. He wanted to make something that would go into space, 'the final frontier', and not stay on the ground. To reach this goal he had to explore many ideas before arriving at something great.

He recalls, 'As an eighteen-year-old first-year college student who wanted to make something, we had absolutely no idea how to go about it. So, we tried to see the ISRO [Indian Space Research Organisation] student space missions, but it turned out that ISRO's timelines for a rocket launch were way too long.'

Most student satellite projects of other universities were multigenerational; they took nearly five years to complete, which was longer than Sanket's undergraduate degree. Sanket and his team were too impatient to wait that long. They wanted to create something that mattered, and they wanted to do it quickly.

They thought of many wild space-related project ideas that they could develop independently.

First, they thought of sending up a camera to take images and make earth observations, but there were many regulations around deploying cameras. Also, a lot had already been done in this field and this wouldn't have led to any new science.

The second idea was that they could relay satellites. This involves sending information to a satellite, which then relays it to someone on the other side of the planet. As undergraduates, they felt they could do something newer and more unique.

Their third idea was inspired by work of NASA Gravity Recovery and Climate Experiment (GRACE). GRACE measures changes in the local pull of gravity as water shifts around Earth due to changing seasons, weather and climate processes. [5] It does this by deploying a pair of satellites orbiting the earth and separated by 220 km in space. However, this project turned out to be very technologically challenging for a team of undergrad students.

Finally, they stumbled on a critical challenge faced by astronauts and global space missions: cosmic rays. The main challenge of long-term space missions is cosmic ray exposure. Cosmic rays are high-energy particles that are known to be carcinogenic when humans are exposed to them for long periods. Even the electronics that go into space are prone to errors caused by cosmic rays. The challenge was so pertinent that their project could impact humanity and the future of space travel.

They thought it would be more purposeful to identify materials that could shield the capsules and astronauts from cosmic rays.

Therefore, they chose to develop a device that could compare the shielding ability of various materials against cosmic rays. They wanted to test aluminium and high-density polyethylene as a potential shield from cosmic rays.

Unfortunately, soon the team realized a fundamental flaw. To extract any meaningful data, they would require at least a 20-metre layer of aluminium and polyethylene – which is simply not possible for a space mission due to the size and weight constraints. They had to pivot, and they had to pivot quick.

Local resources and guidance were lacking. So, they tried to figure things out on their own and studied various cosmic-ray experiments happening worldwide.

Eventually, they came across a NASA mission that was developing a model for predicting cosmic ray exposure during commercial aircraft travel. Inspired by this mission, they decided to build an instrument to measure cosmic ray flux incident on earth from outer space.

Their instrument would measure cosmic ray flux at two different altitudes—something that had never been done in India before. This was possible due to the flight control experts at the Tata Institute of Fundamental Research in Hyderabad.

Sanket recalls, 'We were stupid and naïve. We thought if the math says it can work, then it must. So, instead of using expensive machines, we bought cheaper substitutes from eBay to put them together and make things work.'

Most of Sanket's learning in aerospace came from failing.

The team often thought they would be able to launch on a particular date, but then something would blow up and they would have to postpone it. A few days before their final launch date, their data acquisition board (the device's CPU) blew up in an electromagnetic radiation test. The shielding wasn't excellent, so the crucial component of the device failed. To stick with the launch date, overnight, they hand-soldered everything, and the next day they did all the tests. Luckily, everything worked.

Their launch was finally a success.

Sanket reflects that, 'People have standard practices and ideas in engineering, and usually don't want to try out new things. We had no option but to use first-principles and try out new things.'

Now Sanket is pursuing his PhD from the University of Wisconsin in a field that he failed classes in during his undergraduate programme. 'I had a D grade in my quantum mechanics courses in college. My professors were disappointed in me for sleepwalking through their courses. Today, I am a student leader for a US-government funded centre for developing quantum computers. Nothing really stops you from doing what you like,' he says.

* * *

I learned a lot from Sanket's story about having a goal, converging to have many ideas, and then rapidly pursuing the idea into reality. Sanket did so by actively questioning every assumption he thought he 'knew' about his selected problem—and then creating new solutions from scratch with few resources he could get his hands on. At some level, I wanted to use these learnings in my own life.

In June 2019, during the same time I met Sanket, I was exploring various internship opportunities in Singapore. I finally landed an internship at the global non-profit organization Ashoka: Innovators for the Public. The organization has a network of over 3000 impactful changemakers globally, each with an inspiring story of how they are changing their communities. But these stories weren't being told to the young people in a palatable way. I thought of various we could close the gap, by either starting a newsletter or starting a college summit.

In one of the Tuesday team meetings, I suggested starting a podcast series to tell the stories of these changemakers. Sumitra, my boss, encouraged this idea. So the next day, I borrowed microphones from friends and the music room of my university. I quickly learnt how to use audio editing software, build a website and set up a distribution account with an RSS feed.

We got the Planet Impact podcast running that same week.

In the process of rapidly getting it started, I made some blunders. But it was all worthwhile.

The process of finding social entrepreneurs to tell their stories introduced me to inspiring people. I had conversations with them that shaped my life.

One of the guests on my podcast was Kiran Bir Sethi, a pioneer in design thinking and the field of education. She is the founder of Riverside School in Ahmedabad and Design for Change, a worldwide design thinking and education movement. She is also an Ashoka fellow.[6]

In the interview, I learnt about the FIDS design thinking framework that she developed. This model helps to develop the much-required 21st Century Skills in children, builds their social and emotional competencies and promotes their employability skills.[7] This FIDS model, which stands for feel, imagine, do and share, is now taught to tens of thousands of students in over sixty seven countries.

The design thinking model that Kiran ma'am developed starts with 'feel'. This is the ability to put oneself in another's shoes. It asks you to slow down and understand the problem, before jumping on to solve it.

It is essential to always keep the community of users in focus while developing an idea. This helps you to move away from assumptions into insights. In empathizing with the community, you should not overthink whether your teacher, parents or boss will approve of an idea or not.

The second step in the process is to 'imagine' and brainstorm solutions, that will improve the situation or solve the problem. You must be intentional in creating something, and take full responsibility of changing the current situation. This might even involve breaking away from the constraints of the real world.

Thirdly, the most important thing is learning by 'doing'. Making things rapidly instead of just sticking to the idea is critical. Just by acting on your thoughts, you become an outlier. An intention that is followed by action creates an impact.

Finally, the most powerful part is 'share'. This inspires others to be more empathetic, and it helps you to create an abundance mentality. It's really about *completing* with others, and not competing with others.

This philosophy has changed how I look at the world and find my place in it. The design thinking model has transformed my previous feeling of restlessness into a sentiment of empowerment. And I think it will help you too.

After the interview, I asked her if I could get the opportunity to work for her. Luckily, she said I could work in their Madrid office as a volunteer for an event they had planned with His Holiness Pope Francis in Vatican City.

This internship in Madrid provided me with the ultimate design thinking and creativity experience.

The project entailed organizing the world's biggest children's event, the I CAN Children's Global Summit. Four thousand children and their teachers from seventy countries came together in Rome for a three-day summit at the end of November 2019. This event was also given a private sitting by His Holiness Pope Francis.

I was stationed at Pio XII, an old Catholic school in Rome. It was a beautiful winter day. The school's ancient Roman architecture, its exposed brick walls, the surrounding apple trees, and the reverent Catholic vibe created a serene atmosphere.

A contingent of students from eleven countries was seated in their allotted areas. They were all between six to sixteen years old.

One by one, these children walked on the stage in groups of five to sing, dance and present their ideas. I would never have imagined the things they had accomplished.[8]

Thirteen-year-old Ivan and his friends from Colombia realized that burning waste tyres pollutes the environment and affects people's health. To prevent such pollution, they made creative furniture from used tyres. Further, they gathered support from environmental groups to raise awareness.

A group of eleven-year-old children from Israel saw that students in their school were not interacting during lunchtime, so they selected an area, painted the benches and walls there to resemble a colourful bus stop and posted someone on duty to get people talking, interacting and making friends. They called it the 'Friendship Station'—where kids now go during lunchtime to socialize.

A group of twelve-year-olds from India found the stench from their school toilet unbearable. So, these students from a government school in Trichy district designed low-cost urinals using twenty-litre plastic bottles that were cheap and easy to install.

Listening to these children made me realize that using creativity to solve problems has no prerequisites.

The students taught me that 'DO' was the most crucial design thinking component. It made me feel that 'design thinking' as a term is actually more about doing than thinking.

One does not need education, experience and resources to change the world, but rather the desire to make one's ideas a reality. All you need is the ability to empathize with the community, imagine a solution, implement the concept quickly and share it with the world!

'Don't procrastinate. Start building immediately. Just keep the old lady in mind.' So said the eight-year-old girl from Sudan who was building toys for a home for the elderly in South Sudan to me.

* * *

I found these traits of rapidly making solutions in a few young entrepreneurs too. Let me tell you a story of a young Indian serial entrepreneur who rapidly designed solutions to every problem he saw. Akshat Mittal is a student at Amity International School in Noida. As an eighth grader, he would regularly see the Akshardham Temple while returning home from school. However, for a few days in winter, the smog got so thick that he could not even see three metres away.

It is said that breathing in Noida is equivalent to smoking forty-four cigarettes a day. To solve this, the Delhi government declared an odd-even rule. So, on odd dates, only vehicles with odd number plates can be on the roads. Likewise, even-numbered cars are allowed only on even dates. This created difficulties for people with only one car or two cars, both with either even or odd numbers. Akshat quickly solved this problem by creating Odd-even.com at thirteen years of age.

He created the portal to help connect odd-numbered car owners with even-numbered car owners. The website saw 30,000 users in the first week itself and was later acquired by Orahi. This made him the world's youngest entrepreneur to sell his website.

Creative problem-solving combines three human gifts that we all have: critical thinking, creativity and practical abilities. Integrating these three skills makes it possible to identify solutions that don't yet exist, imagine new ways to solve a problem, and appropriate actions that can take us closer to desired outcomes.

> 'If a picture is worth a thousand words, then a prototype is worth a thousand meetings.'
>
> —*Jennifer Aaker, Professor at*
> *Stanford Graduate School of Business*

Akshat used these creative problem-solving skills to solve another big problem in India. At the start of the COVID-19 pandemic, Akshat empathized with the issues faced by the migrant community. He says, 'Imagine a pregnant lady walking thousands of kilometres with a suitcase on her head only to reach the boundary of her home state to get quarantined for fifteen days, or even jailed.'

The impact of the nation-wide lockdown was most felt by the migrant and marginalized community. Over 100 million of India's migrant workers became jobless and felt the wrath of the pandemic. [9]

To help solve this, Akshat started Bharat Shramik with the vision to create India's largest blue-collar employment platform.

'I want to reach a place where if a carpenter or a construction worker loses his job, he knows that it's okay. I know Bharat Shramik exists. I can just call the helpline and get myself registered. And within a week or two, I will definitely get a job in my area.'

In just a month, Bharat Shramik received over 3000 registrations and connected migrant workers to contractors.

Over six years, Akshat attempted to solve two systemic problems with two creative solutions. The theme of his work was relatively constant. He always started by empathizing with the beneficiaries' pain points, defining their problems and ideating solutions. Then, he quickly prototyped a minimum viable product and tested it right away.

Akshat thinks that we all have great ideas occasionally. The fundamental difference occurs in converting these ideas into reality.

'I thought of the idea on 8 June. And I started working on it on 9 June. I did not create a financial plan or business plan. It's important to focus on the most important thing, which is the product, and get it out as quickly as possible.'

At the time of writing, Akshat was eighteen years old and was planning to pursue a bachelor's degree from the University of California, Los Angeles (UCLA).

Something that his dad told him rings a bell: 'You don't need to work at Google. You have to work to create the next Google.'

You don't have to follow the conventional route. You don't have to wait until you finish school and college, get a job for ten years, and finally, start a company. Children who are just ten or twelve years old have also begun small initiatives and launched applications. All you must do is experiment and try.

* * *

Design thinking is not merely an intellectual exercise. It is about making things that can be used to test the presumptions grounded in society and one's community.

This journey of designing solutions and making things can often lead to setbacks or failures. Your initiatives might not always work as you would have planned. But it turns out that failure is actually important.

A lot of people think that creative people don't fail. However, a University of California professor, Dean Keith Simonton, wrote in his book, *Origins of Genius*, that all creative geniuses ranging from artists like Mozart to scientists like Darwin were quite extraordinary in terms of several failures. They just didn't let their losses stop them.[10]

His research found that creative people did significantly more experiments than ordinary people. Therefore, their eureka moments came along more often than those of others not because they were exceptionally talented, but because they tried and failed repeatedly. They simply took more shots at the goal.

Thomas Edison, for example, is one of the world's most renowned inventors. He understood that an experiment that ended in failure was not a failed experiment—it was simply a learning experience in disguise. As the famous story goes, he tried a thousand times before inventing the lightbulb.[11]

Looking at the life stories of numerous creative geniuses, it appears that early failure is crucial to success later in life. The faster you fail and find your weaknesses, the better you will innovate and thrive.

For example, the Wright brothers are best remembered for inventing the motor-operated aeroplane and taking the 'first flight' in December of 1903. But the focus on that accomplishment often overlooks the hundreds of failed experiments they faced in the years that led to their first breakthrough.[12]

Another example of someone who experienced many failures on his path to success is Anirudh Sharma, who we met in the beginning of this chapter. Anirudh is now trying to solve the problem of the climate crisis by developing climate technologies to address carbon emissions.

He says, 'I don't have a background in chemistry, but I have a background in making sure that we build good teams and solve hard problems.'

He started with many ideas such as building low-cost carbon sensors, but they didn't work as a concept. What did work was creating something quickly and putting it out there for feedback and making constant iterations to it.

Through observations and talking to people, he arrived at the idea of converting carbon emissions into ink.

Anirudh's innovation with Graviky Labs makes paint and ink from India's polluted air by capturing carbon soot through its KAALINK unit, a retrofit device fitted on vehicles or chimneys. Their invention showed the world that 'recycled pollution can be as powerful as plastics and paper'.[13]

But through all these inventions and accolades, failure was a constant. He shares, 'On a weekly basis, whatever we try, we see failure.'

From failing at the conventional education system, that was college, to his day-to-day failures in inventing technologies that will solve the climate crisis, Anirudh has faced a considerable dose of setbacks. But he says, 'College was big failure. But instead of cribbing about it, I understood what worked and what didn't. Then I tried to leverage what worked and built my career. My early failures were something that shook me, but also made me the person I am today.'

He shares his mantra of *tod phod jod*, which roughly translates to breaking things and putting them together. 'If you want to learn anything,' he says, 'get your hands dirty, share it with other people so the idea gets better and you can constantly iterate.'

I think there is a lot to learn from the above stories. And now, after speaking with all these highly successful people, I see opportunities to use creativity everywhere. Growing up in a society like ours, we all have a lot of opportunities to create solutions that will leave a meaningful impact.

In India, where I am writing this book, we are surrounded by things that don't always work too well, slow or inconvenient services, and poor infrastructure. If we really look at our society, many things are just plain wrong or could be done so much better. These range from not having wheelchair access in one's school to having an unpredictable public transport system. When you start noticing things that might be broken, you start your creative journey.

Making a list of things that annoy or bug you about the world's current state can allow you to apply your creativity. Whether you use a piece of paper in your pocket or record ideas on your smartphone, keeping track of opportunities for improvement can help you engage with the world around you more proactively.[14]

When you write down the things that bug or bother you, you become more mindful of them. But instead of focusing on the negatives and complaining, ask yourself, 'How can I make the most of what I have and how can I improve this situation?'[15]

When you tackle your next project, remember to feel the problem and understand it deeply, before you jump on a solution. Next, brainstorm as many solutions as you can and start building immediately. Finally, share your solutions with the world and see where that takes you.

4

Hard Work over Talent

'Freedom began on the day the first sheep wandered away
from the herd'
—Marty Rubin, author of *The Boiled Frog Syndrome*

In 2006, a thirteen-year-old started selling SIM cards at his
family's kirana store in Odisha to help make ends meet.

'In my family, it was a big opportunity for me to run
our grocery store,' he says, 'and an even bigger opportunity
would have been for me to become an engineer and join an
IT company.'[1]

As a teenager, he decided to opt for the road less taken
and chose to travel across India. He didn't have a lot of
money, so the budget was tight. On his travels, he discovered
an opportunity in the hospitality industry.

In 2011, at the age of eighteen, he visited over a hundred
hotels in India and convinced their owners to let him stay for
free to study their operations. In his study, he discovered that in

India, the key problem was that there was no standard quality of service in budget hotels. And he wanted to solve that. Soon he dropped out of college to pursue his entrepreneurial dream. He started a website that helped travellers book hotel rooms called Oravel Stays. In 2013, his company was rebranded as OYO Hotels and Homes, which focused on assisting owners in bettering their operations.

In 2019, OYO operated over 12 lakh rooms globally across 800 cities in eighty countries.[2] They raised $1 billion or Rs 7,400 crore from SoftBank and others and within a year their valuation increased to as high as $10 billion or Rs 74,000 crores.

The name of this entrepreneur is Ritesh Agrawal. He was born in a lower-middle-class family in one of the poorest states in India, Odisha. He became one of the youngest billionaires in the world, and his journey has been an unlikely one.

Ritesh was a non-conformist, and his convictions were backed by hard work that only a few of us can imagine. In this chapter, let's look at each of these two traits that appear to be common among ultra-successful young people.

Non-conformist, n, *someone who lives and thinks in a way that is different from other people.* [3]

There are two ways to accomplish anything—conformity and non-conformity.

Conformity means when your thoughts, ideas and ambitions align with the path laid out by society. Whereas non-conformity arises when one thinks out of the box, holds opinions and beliefs different from those of society, and does things that don't abide by society's expectations.

Growing up in India, we believe that we must follow a linear path to be successful in life. That means scoring well in school and entrance exams, getting into a good college, securing a high-paying job and then settling down. Eventually, you may consider starting a business or doing something of your own after the whole cycle.

I felt this linear progression was suffocating. I wondered if going through all these milestones was all there was to life. I felt like another scared sheep in the herd.

I wanted to learn what choices and paths successful young people had followed to reach where they are today. So, I reached out to several mega-successful young Indian entrepreneurs, musicians, sportsmen, politicians and scientists. It was interesting to find that a majority of them refused to conform to the societal norm of following a linear progression in life. Instead, they had found their own paths and shaped their own destinies. And in their journeys, hard work played a more critical role than their innate talent in reaching their ambitions.

In his late teens, after dropping out of college, Ritesh Agrawal became one of the first Asians to be selected for a Thiel Fellowship. This is a prestigious and highly selective fellowship that gives start-up founders $100,000 or Rs 74 lakh and mentorship from Silicon Valley entrepreneurs. It opened many doors for young Ritesh.

A youth icon, Ritesh has definitely made a mark in entrepreneurship and youth ambitions in India through his journey.

Young people in India today are very entrepreneurial and determined to do things that make a difference. So, I surveyed 300 students between the ages of fifteen and twenty-five from urban and rural areas, with family incomes ranging from below Rs 1 lakh a year to more than Rs 1 crore a year, and with an equal gender distribution. I wanted to know what their life aspirations and barriers were.

Our generation appears to be much more inclined towards risk taking, multitasking and entrepreneurship than the previous generation.

It was fascinating to observe that 78 per cent of all respondents strongly agreed that they want to start their own businesses. And roughly 60 per cent strongly agreed that they are more competitive and strive to multitask more than their older siblings and parents. Furthermore, 60 per cent agreed with the statement, 'I value taking risk more in my life than stability'.

This makes them well-suited to follow what they think is right and not care as much about social norms as the older generations.

I could relate to the respondents of my survey. As a teenager, I didn't want to follow a safe path of pursuing engineering or medicine, get a job and get settled; that was expected of me, and I wanted to do something different.

I was sure I would not make a sound engineer or a doctor, even if I tried. I wanted to continue playing table tennis. So, I took the commerce stream for my eleventh and twelfth standards.

I scored 85 per cent in the twelfth standard, excluding the additional 5 per cent allotted for winning two gold medals at the School Games Federation of India Under-17 National Championships and two bronze medals for India at the Pacific School Games held in Adelaide, Australia, in my high school academic years. I wanted to pursue table tennis and become a pro international athlete, but that wasn't working out. I needed some time to decide my next steps.

I took a gap year after finishing school just to experience the world and get some work experience before starting college. This was massively frowned upon by our relatives, neighbours and friends. It was uncommon to take a gap year, and usually, it was only students who failed or got poor grades that took a gap year to reappear for the exams.

In my gap year, I solo-backpacked across India for a month; volunteered at multiple non-profits; started two of my own small non-profit initiatives; wrote a research paper; created an online course on corporate social responsibility; and worked at a fitness start-up for eight months to gain experience. This real-life experience really opened me to the world around me. Moreover, it gave me a pulse of Indian youth, their ambitions, frustrations and opportunities. This gap year experience was life-changing and eventually translated into this book that you are reading.

While it was hard to go against society's norms, the perspective that I gained from opting for the road less taken gave me an edge among people of my age. Moreover, not blindly following the path laid by society made me more confident in my own skin.

In my first bout with non-conformism, I learnt that it is okay to carve my own path, even if it is frowned upon by people around me. The world will not come crashing down if you don't strictly follow what is expected of you. You will not miss out on an education if you set constructive objectives, milestones and processes. Rather, you will learn more than the average student.

Let me tell you the story of someone who failed to get into a business school yet emerged as one of the most successful entrepreneurs in India. At the age of only twenty-four, he was making millions.

* * *

Praful Billore, founder of the iconic tea brand MBA Chai Wala, went from not getting into any MBA colleges to establishing a multi-million-dollar business selling tea. He has been a non-conformist through and through.

Praful is from Ahmedabad, India. He was born in Indore. His parents had a small business selling incense sticks. His aspiration while growing up was to get a good education, a well-paying job and have a stable life. He failed his CAT exams (the entrance exams for MBA) twice. After that, he worked in McDonald's for a few months. Then, in 2017, he started his chai-ka-thela (tea stall) in Ahmedabad. Today, he speaks at IIM-Ahmedabad and other prestigious colleges where he didn't get admission. At the time of the interview in 2020, his brand MBA Chai Wala is worth Rs 15 crore ($2 million), with a presence in fifty cities in India. He plans a global expansion.

'Growing up, I was curious about the world, and the global economy. I am from a Brahmin family. Not a business family. Life in a corporate cubicle or a government job would have been my natural choice.'

Many Indians aspire to get a government job or a stable high paying corporate job. That is what Praful wanted. As a student, Praful considered himself average in terms of grades. He scored some 72 per cent in the tenth standard.

'There were sixty-five students in my class. Sixty of them chose physics, chemistry and maths [a popular choice among aspiring engineers]. And four chose biology. I was the only one to choose commerce. I knew I wouldn't survive science after the twelfth grade.'

After completing a bachelor's degree in commerce, getting an MBA from a prestigious college was his goal. He prepared rigorously for the Common Admission Test (CAT), an exam for admission in graduate management programs. However, he did not make it on the first attempt. He studied even harder for a re-attempt. But the second attempt's result did not make a mark. His grades were disastrous. Settling for a local private college with astronomical fees did not make sense. He started to study again for his third attempt; however, he threw away the books in a couple of months and started travelling.

After travelling the length and breadth of India, he visited Ahmedabad and instantly fell in love with the city.

'I travelled for two months, and there was nothing else left for me to see. So I wanted to do something on my own. The only thing that came to my mind was McDonald's. I read that a lot of American billionaires had worked at McDonald's. Jeff Bezos is one of them. I didn't want to work there for the money or job stability. Learning, engaging myself and starting somewhere was my intention.'

In the first two months at McDonald's, he learnt about consumer behaviour, how to talk, how to deliver, how to place orders, how to flip burgers, how the menu and pricing work, how to arrange seating in the food industry etc. It was a formative experience, but he wanted to start his own thing after that.

'I thought I should start something of my own. The first thing that came to my mind was selling burgers and cold coffee. But it didn't seem that would scale in India. In my travels I observed chai was the connector in India. Everyone in India drank chai.'

It would cost him Rs 15 lakh to start a chai café, including the rent, interiors etc. He could have asked his father for the money. But he thought that risking that amount did not make sense. Having failed to get into a prestigious college for an MBA, he felt he should start small. So he started a roadside thela.

'Dream big, start small. Starting small is important to gain confidence,' is his advice to young students wherever he goes to give a guest lecture now.

It took him fifty days from the initial idea to start the business. His biggest fear was what family, relatives, friends and society would say. What would people think of someone who came from a relatively well-to-do family starting a chai stall?

'Marta kya nahi karta. I didn't get into an MBA college. I thought I wouldn't be able to get a job in the future. So I thought, why not sell chai. Things would work out somehow. It will be better than a low-paying job.' He reassured himself that something would work out, so he blocked out the noise.

On the first day of setting up his tea stall, no one stopped by. So, he approached people in parked cars, saying, 'Sir, I make awesome chai, would you like to try it?' Drivers were surprised to see an English-speaking chai wala (tea seller). On the first day, he sold only five cups of tea.

In the initial days, he used to work at McDonald's from 9 a.m. to 6 p.m., then run the tea stall from 7 p.m. to 11 p.m. But after three months, he left McDonald's and worked on the tea stall full time.

To create a brand, he would use board games, run entrepreneurship, poetry and shayari nights, install a whiteboard to create a networking platform and more.

'We did everything with passion. We didn't just sell tea, we sold our concept, we sold our emotions.'

However, surviving on the streets was not easy. Starting a roadside tea stall was tough for someone privileged enough to have never made tea at home. When he began his chai-ka-thela on the road, many people threatened him, demanding he shut down. A few incidents involving local gundas and the municipal corporation deeply disturbed him.

'Initially, people used to ridicule me for selling tea. But today, MBA Chai Wala is a nationally recognized name.'

What drove him through the crisis of societal pressure was the battle of roti (Indian bread). 'Let me explain,' he says. 'If you have dal [lentil] and chawal [rice] to eat, you will not go below that standard. Then you will aspire to eat some sweets and desserts. But, if your target is to be a crorepati [a multi-millionaire], then you need to take steps accordingly . . . If I would have taken a Rs 1 lakh per month job, I would make Rs 12 lakh a year. And it will take me nearly nine years to make a crore. Without even calculating for expenses.'

Praful believes that if your goal is significant, you can't walk or cycle there. Instead, you have to change the vehicle or the road, or shorten the goal. And in this process, you are responsible for your own success. It is not your parents', siblings' or friends' duty to help you reach your goal.

'Ambanis gave us Reliance. Howard Schwartz gave us Starbucks. Steve Jobs gave us Apple. Today when one buys an iPhone or a Starbucks coffee, they feel privileged as if they made it themselves. This inspired me to create value for the customers. We are delighted to be the customers today. But what have you given to the world that has made the consumers proud?'

Praful notices that today's youth is still afraid of others' opinions and the fear of failure. It is time for them to burn those bridges and start afresh.

Today, MBA Chai Wala, which stands for Mr Billore of Ahmedabad Chai Wala, regularly serves chai at significant corporate events, glamorous Indian weddings and on the street sides of fifty cities around India and is expanding.

Praful still makes tea, and he won't stop until every Indian has tasted his chai. So the next time you are walking down the streets in your city or town, if you see a bright board saying MBA Chai Wala, you will know the person behind it and his story.

Praful says, 'Either your way or of the world. Just do it because fear is temporary, but regret is forever.'

Praful truly has a fire in his belly. I have the deepest respect for all the hard work he put in to build his brand and a chai empire. I learnt from him that it's our responsibility to shape our own destinies and hustle their way through.

This trait of not following a linear path laid by society and working incredibly hard to reach your goal appeared to be true not only for entrepreneurship but any chosen field. Let me give you another example.

I used to think politics and being at the top of a political party was the best way to create a lasting impact. But I used to often wonder how does one reach that level of influence without coming from the right backgrounds and having those connections.

I would like to share the story of someone who achieved just that by shaping his own destiny.

* * *

As you would have guessed, the road to becoming influential and affecting positive change might not be a straight line.

For this book, I spoke to Krishna Allavaru, who at the time of writing this book was the Joint Secretary of the All-India Congress Committee and national in-charge of the Indian Youth Congress. He did his LLM from Georgetown University in Washington, D.C. Today, he is a well-known strategist for the Indian National Congress and close aid to Rahul Gandhi. In terms of age, Mr Allavaru is young as compared to his counterparts, and he says he was not destined to be where he is today. His story shows that there is no linear path to success.

His father was an army officer. So, his mother brought him up. His dream was to be a general in the Indian army. He got into the NDA after the twelfth standard, but his perspective changed, and he chose not to join. Instead, he studied economics and law. Then he practiced law in the high court and Supreme Court in New Delhi for a year. He also worked at one of Asia's most innovative law firms, Nishith Desai Associates, for three years in Mumbai. Then he set out to do his own thing as an entrepreneur, which didn't work out very well.

It was not easy for a lawyer to switch gears and join a consulting firm in those days. But, after a lot of effort and persuasion, he joined Anderson Consulting and worked there for four years.

After that, he did an MBA from the prestigious INSEAD and started working with Boston Consulting Group in Singapore.

In 2010, he decided to return to India. Initially, he wanted to start a hedge fund, but then he saw the interesting new initiatives Congress was undertaking, especially with the National Students' Union of India. Their intent seemed to be well placed. So he started working with the youth and student wing.

He observes that today's young millennials and Generation Zs in India are agitated and frustrated with their economic prospects.

When I asked him what it takes to bring about positive change, he said, 'I think it's not a big deal to change the world. I think all of us change the world every day, in a small way. However, the youngsters should keep in mind that the change they are making should have a positive vision, outcome, outlook, and it has to be sustainable. Furthermore, the positive means in achieving the outcome are more important than the outcome in itself.'

Mr Allavaru believes that to do good sustainably and through suitable means should be our goal. And this might take us on paths that are outside the norms of society. From his experiences, he shares a great insight in setting goals and taking the path less travelled.

Mr Allavaru says, 'My one suggestion for you would be for you to challenge your definition of success. I think that is in broadening, widening and deepening it beyond the conventional definition of success. As a result, you will probably get some fascinating insights, which are not already existing in the conventional wisdom.'

Most importantly, once you have decided on a goal and being a non-conformist, it takes a lot of hard work to reach your destination.

Mr Allavaru's advice on this is, 'The youngsters should have the persistence, conviction and tenacity to see things through despite all the challenges.'

Once you realize that you have to follow the path you have carved for yourself, you need to understand that hard work is way more critical than talent to achieve your desired goals.

* * *

In the book *Outliers*, author Malcolm Gladwell popularized the idea that to achieve mastery in any field it takes over 10,000 hours of practice.[4] Among the examples he cites are Bill Gates, who used to sneak out of his parents' house at night to go and code at his Seattle high school. The Beatles went to Hamburg five times between 1960 and 1962 and performed for more than 250 nights in those two years. When they finally arrived in the US in 1964, before they became mega-successful, they had already practised their performance over 1200 times, which is more than what most bands do in their lifetime.

While Bill Gates and the Beatles became true outliers and shaped the world through hard work, it appears that our generation needs to put in those hours to be successful in any field today. Studies have shown that people could reach world-class levels more quickly in the nineteenth and early twentieth centuries than they can today.

In the recent few decades, it appears that the bar for excellence to reach international heights in any field, especially at a young age, has increased significantly. For example, today's high school swimmers and amateur marathon runners do better than the Olympic medallists of the early twentieth century. Today all fields have become so competitive that it is impossible to beat the 10,000-hour rule.[5]

Like his examples, Malcolm Gladwell spent thirteen years in journalism working at prestigious publications such as the *American Spectator*, the *Washington Post*, and the *New Yorker* before writing his debut bestseller, *The Tipping Point*. So the global success and recognition for all his seven bestsellers and his podcast Revisionist History that followed were not surprising at all. Success is truly a function of hard work more than innate talent.

Similarly, coming back to Ritesh Agrawal, by the time he started his venture in his late teens, he already had seven years of experience selling things such as SIM cards, running the family kirana store, and doing other side hustles through school and college. He had the knowledge gained from travelling and studying hundreds of hotels in India, and the exposure from the Thiel Fellowship. And finally, it took him five years, from 2013 to 2018, to perfect and scale the OYO model across India.

The number of hours of experience he has (calculating quite conservatively for a five-day work week), if you calculate from when he was thirteen and working three hours a day, increase it to six hours when he was between seventeen and twenty years old and further increase it to the twelve hours a day he worked from the age of twenty-one to twenty-six, is *28,000 hours*. When he started OYO Rooms at the age of around twenty, he had 9360 (nearly 10,000) hours of work experience!

Hard work was one trait that was so obviously visible among all the young outliers I spoke to for this book. Yet, in my peer group, and in the survey of young college students, I noticed how easily and frequently they mentioned the lack of talent or a natural gift as a reason for not achieving their dreams.

* * *

I often hear my friends saying something on the lines of 'I have zero talents. Therefore, I will never reach exceptional levels of achievement.'

Regularly, we stress needing the talent to be successful and discount all other factors.

Collectively, we believe that talent leads to achievement. But I disagree.

Dr Daniel Chambliss, the Yale-trained sociologist and winner of the American Sociological Association's award for best dissertation on medical sociology, defined what we all think of talent as a 'substance behind the surface of performance, which finally distinguishes the best from the rest'. He also said that some great athletes 'have this special gift, almost an invisible thing inside them that is denied to the rest of the people—something to do with physical, genetic, psychological, or physiological traits. Some have it, and some do not. Some are naturally gifted, and some aren't.'[6]

That is an excellent description of talent as we collectively see it. But he concluded his research paper *The Mundanity of Excellence* by saying, 'Talent is a useless concept. Varying conceptions of natural ability ("talent," e.g.) tend to mystify excellence, treating it as the inherent possession of a few; they mask the concrete actions that create outstanding performance.'

Further, it was insightful to learn from his paper that the high performers didn't simply do the grunt work, and do more of the same thing. Instead, he mentions that excellence comes from deliberate practise and the qualitative phenomenon, which means not doing more things, but rather doing *different kinds of things*.

He wrote that 'excellence is accomplished through doing small, ordinary actions, consistently and carefully. These small actions might be different on a qualitative level. Still, they are neither unimaginable nor difficult when taken one step at a time.'[7]

In terms of swimmers, whom he was studying, it meant practising their strokes differently, but the same can be applied to life at large.

* * *

I could connect to my life as an athlete while reading his work.

I used to be a try-hard type of athlete. From the age of ten to seventeen, I was obsessed with table tennis. Every waking hour, I used to think of playing table tennis, improving my footwork, strokes, service and so on. As my coach put it, I had 'no ounce of talent'. But I overcame that and achieved a few titles nationally and internationally through sheer hard work and determination. However, I often think I didn't reach my desired level of achievement because I put in the wrong kind of effort and was routinely misdirected, as many Indian athletes are.

I once attended a junior national table tennis camp held in Indore, Madhya Pradesh. A former world table tennis champion, Peter Karlsson, was the head coach there. Playing in the stadium with the best Indian paddlers and being coached by an international athlete opened me to a whole new world.

I could see that the most accomplished table tennis players worked hard but they didn't necessarily put in the most number of hours on the ground and in the arena. They didn't believe so much in simply repeating the training and strokes umpteen number of times. But they did small things differently; they modified their techniques slightly.

I could relate this to the trends I observed when speaking to successful young adults across fields. For example, I spoke with super successful musicians such as Ritviz, Kaam Bhaari and Achyuth Jaigopal. It was apparent that they were not only hard working but also, they tried different things such as mixing Indian classical with electronic music or narrating their struggles and life in Mumbai through poetry and rap or fusing various instruments and languages to create original indie music. Not only did they work harder than the rest of the lot, but they also put in efforts slightly differently.

Talent that follows efforts helps you quickly acquire the skills required for success. Achievement occurs when you take your skills and use them in all the opportunities that you are exposed to and do things slightly uniquely. Let me share another story of a Forbes 30 under 30 scientist, who showcases how hard work, tenacity, and doing things uniquely leads to astronomical achievements.

I saw a TED talk in June 2021 that greatly inspired me. It was titled 'Listening to the Universe'. It was about a young Indian astrophysicist who made a ground-breaking discovery and proved Einstein's general theory of relativity right. I contacted this fascinating scientist with a cold email requesting an interview for this book. He replied promptly, and we spoke within a day of the email. I was taken aback by this accomplished man's humility and generosity.

* * *

Dr Karan Jani is a world-renowned astrophysicist who works in the nascent field of gravitational-wave physics. He was part of the team that worked on the Nobel Prize-winning experiment, Laser Interferometer Gravitational-wave Observatory (LIGO), and he is currently on the research faculty for physics and astronomy at Vanderbilt University in Tennessee, US. His research is at the forefront of understanding black holes and testing Einstein's General Theory of Relativity with gravitational-wave experiments on earth, the moon and in space.[8]

He is a recipient of various research and innovation honours. Jani is on the Forbes 'all-star alum' list of 30 Under 30 that also includes Olympian Simone Biles and Grammy winner Billie Eilish. He was voted CNN-News18's Tech Personality of the Year and was awarded the Postdoc of the Year by Vanderbilt University. In addition, he received the Sam Nunn Security Fellowship funded by the MacArthur Foundation and the Special Breakthrough Prize in Fundamental Physics from the previous recipient of this prize, Stephen Hawking.

With such outstanding achievements under his belt, one would assume that he was always a genius at school and destined for greatness since childhood. Instead, he humbly says that he was only an average student growing. He scored 84 per cent in the twelfth standard, which is above average, but not something that would make newspaper headlines. But he reached scientific heights through hard work, perseverance, and doing things uniquely.

'I grew up in Baroda, in a quintessential Gujarati family,' he says. 'I was surrounded by Narsinh Mehta's bhajans. There was a heavy Gandhian influence in the family. There was always an undercurrent in the house of not being materialistic or capitalistic.'

His family had a spiritual outlook towards life, which later translated into his interest in physics as a young adult.

Dr Jani was born in a family with four generations of teachers. There was no flesh and blood scientist in the family. No one knew what it meant to be a scientist.

He had no pressure to score well and succeed while growing up. His parents were supportive of his scores and gave him the space to explore his personal interests. This made his childhood remarkably accessible, and it is impressive how much creativity got built in that free time.

His mother was a computer teacher. So she put him into NIIT camps to learn computer languages such as C and C++ in the seventh grade. As a result, he picked up programming very early on. This skill would come in very handy in the later years.

When he studied eleventh-standard physics, he was inspired by the fundamental truth exhibited in Newton's equations, which could explain the motion of the stars and planets all the way to a cricket one fundamental truth that held everything together. It was a universal truth that was beyond our own existence. So, learning physics was a very spiritual exercise and he was naturally drawn to it.

After his twelfth standard, he knew he didn't want to do engineering or medicine.

He says, 'I knew that I would never crack a JEE or NEET exam. It would be an absolute waste of time for me to even attempt. Of course, I don't say that out of my snobbishness. Still, I genuinely mean that I do not think I can solve any problem in science in a matter of few minutes.'

He wasn't particularly curious about engineering or pharmacy. He had found his passion for research in physics, and he wanted to pursue that.

Following his interests, he started studying physics at the Maharaja Sayajirao University of Baroda in Gujarat. He finished his first term there. To learn more about what his future could look like, he asked his seniors about life after graduation. It became clear to him that in India, it would be challenging to start an early career in research. He started exploring more rewarding avenues to honing his passions, but he had to overcome many obstacles in doing so.

He started thinking of applying to universities in the US. But unfortunately, it was too late to sit for the required tests and complete the application process for that academic year. Further, the exam centres had no slots left. So, he called the US office of College Board which conducts SAT examinations across the globe. They told him that he could take a gamble by going to the exam centre, and if a test-taker was absent, he could take their seat.

He took that gamble and got to take the test. His SAT scores were decent.

He applied and got into various public colleges in the US. Finally, he chose to go to Pennsylvania State University, where he then got a research assistantship.

Even then, he had to work hard and overcome obstacles to make his mark at the university. At Penn State University, in the first physics mid-term examinations, he scored a D. In the class's histogram, he could see himself at the very bottom of the curve.

He recalls, 'That really shattered my dreams. I came to the US to study physics, and I couldn't even get a decent grade in the easier physics test.'

From that moment on, he dropped everything else. He put in the effort and solved all the problems in the textbook and even took on additional study material. Eventually, he scored more than a 100 on his test. Through sheer perseverance, he was slowly mastering the subject of Physics.

The professor asked him to become a teaching assistant for the subject he had previously failed.

In four years, he received two bachelor of science degrees in physics and astronomy-astrophysics and a minor in mathematics. In addition, he did an extensive amount of research in gravitational waves throughout his time at college and was a visiting scholar at the Albert Einstein Institute, Germany and Perimeter Institute for Theoretical Physics, Canada.

After his undergraduate degree he applied for various PhD programmes. He got into a few universities including Lieden in the Netherlands, which offered a prestigious fellowship to study cosmology. Something that was promising, and an already well-established field in science.

He was also accepted for a PhD programme at the Georgia Institute of Technology (commonly known as Georgia Tech) to study gravitational waves. To help decide between the two, he spoke to a Nobel laureate who was visiting his university. The Nobel prize winner advised him to go to the Netherlands and stick with a known field.

But instead, he opted to study gravitational waves at Georgia Tech, and what happened next changed his life.

Through sheer perseverance, he finished his PhD in four and a half years, and was the second fastest in his class to do so. And it just so happened that his PhD thesis was titled, 'Journey of Binary Black Holes: From Supercomputers to

LIGO to Universe'. This involved solving Einstein's equations and black holes on supercomputers and all that programming he learnt years earlier in school just found a natural course of action.

'I worked on the LIGO experiment which detected these gravitational waves after 100 years since Einstein first predicted in 1915. Our first gravitational wave detection came from the collision of Black Holes, which also nicely matched with my supercomputer simulations. Now, I also develop algorithms to hunt for massive black holes that may have formed from the very first stars in our universe.'

In 2017, for his contributions with the gravitational wave experiment at the LIGO lab, and being instrumental in detecting the first gravitational wave that in turn proved Einstein's general theory of relativity, he was the co-recipient of the prestigious Special Breakthrough Prize in Fundamental Physics.[9]

Reflecting on his work, Dr Jani says, 'Putting yourself there every day, and not giving up on your dream was important for me. That consistency and stick-to-itiveness is the single most important characteristic for success. As exciting as astrophysics sounds from the outside, the life of an astrophysicist can be very mundane. This day-to-day resilience and hard work is where the magic happens.'

* * *

In 1953, the Harvard psychologist Anne Roe published *The Making of a Scientist*. She found that what predicted outstanding achievement in science was not so much the individual differences in intellectual abilities but rather the capacity for endurance and concentration and a commitment to hard work. This shows that high achievement is more a function of tenacity than one's innate talents.[10]

Another significant study of adult experts in piano, violin, chess, bridge and athletics done by K. Anders Ericsson of Florida University demonstrated that levels of achievement reached in these domains correlated strongly with the sheer amount of deliberate practise in which these individuals engaged. That is, those who spend more time working on complex problems over and over to perfect them (deliberate practise) are the ones who reach the highest levels of achievement. Furthermore, he noted that in music, ballet and chess, the higher the level of attained performance, the earlier the age of first exposure to the domain, and hence the earlier the onset of deliberate practise.[11]

We often notice that popular self-help books are usually full of stories about people who became famous overnight, seemingly because of innate talent—they're 'naturals', people say. Some even say they manifested success by simply thinking about it. However, when examining the developmental histories of experts, we invariably discover that they spent a lot of time in training and preparation.

* * *

As observed in the study by Ericsson, deliberate practice over a long period helps one truly reach the highest levels of achievement. While it was great to hear that in theory, I was lucky to speak with one exceptionally accomplished young swimmer who has been a personification of this study.

In 2018, one of the first interviews I did for this book was with Prabhat Koli. He is the Guinness world record holder for the youngest person to swim across the North Channel from Northern Ireland to Scotland. He was only nineteen when he accomplished this feat. In 2019, he was awarded the prestigious Tenzing Norgay National Adventure Award by the president of India, Ram Nath Kovind. In addition, the government of Maharashtra awarded him the Shiv Chhatrapati Award, the highest prestigious sports award honoured annually to the sports people from Maharashtra, in 2018-19.

Prabhat has swum across channels and completed marathon swims in India, England, South Africa, Denmark, Japan, Scotland, Spain, California, Hawaii and New York. He was the fastest, youngest and the only Asian to complete most of these swimming marathons.[12] One of the longest swims he did was in Moloka'I Channel, Hawaii, in 2017, which took him seventeen hours. This swim is also the most gruelling of the Oceans Seven challenge, a marathon swimming challenge consisting of seven long-distance open-water swims across the most dangerous sea channels in the world.

Most people think that Prabhat is a natural swimmer. They don't see the hard work, perseverance and sacrifices behind his success.

Prabhat comes from a humble lower-middle-class family in Mumbai.

He started swimming when he was eight years old in a tank near his house. He learnt swimming a bit quicker than the rest of his group of friends. He soon reached state-level competitions, timing in a few of the fastest laps in his age category.

His coach saw that Prabhat had the patience and aptitude to endure long periods of training. This made him well-suited for long-distance open water swimming.

His first event was a 14 km race in the Hooghly River, Kolkata, when he was twelve years old. He became the youngest person to swim that race that year. Swimming in the freezing December cold, against the current, and competing against people twice his age, he found his passion in this adventure sport.

After that race, he decided to participate in the world's longest open water swimming competition, an 81-km race held in Murshidabad, India. To prepare for this race, he started training for twelve hours a day on weekends. His regime entailed swimming from 6 a.m. to 6 p.m. every weekend. In addition, eating and resting also had to be done in the water. As a result of his hard work, at only thirteen years of age, he completed the eighty-one-kilometre swim in a record eleven hours and forty-two minutes.

A natural succession to his ultra-swimming career was to compete in the English Channel race between England and France, which is also known as world's most historically significant and iconic marathon swims. At fourteen years of age, to train for this prestigious race, he started swimming for three hours every weekday and for twelve hours every weekend. To get access to swimming pools for such long periods of time was a struggle. When he finally got permission, he had to work around the schedules of the pools, which meant he had to start swimming at 2 a.m. to finish his routine before 3 p.m.

To compete in his first international swim in the English Channel, he struggled physically, and his parents had to work hard to finance his participation. They took out personal loans, sold their property and borrowed money from friends and family so Prabhat could swim in the race.

After his swim in the English Channel, he discovered the Oceans Seven challenge. It is the ultimate test for extreme swimmers—the equivalent of climbing the seven summits in mountaineering.[13] Only a handful of people have completed the challenge.

Just before the English Channel race, he also completed the 66 km swim around Jersey Island, in ten hours and eleven minutes. He became the only Indian to swim such a long distance of 66 km in cold water.

One of his first races was swimming across the Catalina Channel in Los Angeles, US. He was seventeen at the time. He completed the swim in ten hours and thirty minutes.

To train for his next race in the Moloka'i Channel, Hawaii, he had to acclimatize himself to rain, headwinds and a choppy ocean. So he trained during the peak of the rainy season in India. He went to Alibag for the tricky natural waters there and had a rigorous gym schedule.

Right after this event, he swam around Manhattan, New York. Then, when he turned eighteen, he went for his fourth swim to Tsugaru Strait, which is a twenty-kilometre swim between the Japanese islands of Honshu and Hokkaido.

His next challenge was to conquer the Irish Channel. This race is considered the most brutal of the seven races, given the freezing water temperature. Furthermore, vibrant sea life such as the lion's mane jellyfish, basking sharks, dolphins and killer whales—which often swim alongside relay swimmers—live in these waters.

To train for this race, he went to Nainital and started a gruelling routine of ten hours of training every day.

On the race day in the Irish Channel, this training helped him survive the cold temperatures. However, eight hours into the race, he was stung by a few of the most dangerous jellyfish on the planet. No amount of training could have prepared him for this; it was his mental strength that enabled him to push ahead. He became the youngest person to swim the Irish Channel, winning the Guinness world record for his achievement.

He finished six of the Oceans Seven swims in record time.

His next and final challenge is to swim the Cook Strait between New Zealand's North and South Islands. After that race, which he plans to do in 2022-23, he will become the youngest person in the world to complete the Oceans Seven challenge.

He is now pursuing an MBA and wants to secure a government job. And whenever people tell him that he is a naturally gifted or a talented swimmer, he simply smiles. Only a few people will understand the deliberate practice and sacrifices that accumulated over the last fourteen years, nearly 14,000 hours in training, to make him 'gifted'.

* * *

If you have the passion to solve big problems, create an impact and lead an ambitious life, you often have to make choices that don't conform to societal norms as we saw in Ritesh, Praful and Mr Allavaru's life journeys.

In the journey to be successful, it takes far more effort than your innate talent, as reflected in Prabhat and Dr Jani's stories.

5

Emotional Intelligence

'It is with the heart that one sees rightly; what is essential
is invisible to the eye'

—Antoine de Saint-Exupéry,
author of *The Little Prince*

In the ancient Indian epic the Mahabharata, the Pandavas
were humiliated and stripped of their wealth, belongings and
kingdom. To regain what they had lost, the Pandavas had no
option but to fight their own relatives and brothers. Arjuna,
the third of the five Pandava brothers and a master archer,
was the only hope for the Pandava's army.

As the war was about to begin, Arjuna asked his
charioteer Lord Krishna to position his chariot so he could
see everyone who had joined the enemy camp. There he saw
his great-grandfather, Bhishma, who had practically raised
him, his gurus, Dronacharya and Kripa, and his brothers the
Kauravas.

Arjuna said to Krishna, 'I can't fight these people. They are my relatives and teachers. What will be a kingdom at the cost of their lives?'[1]

Bhagavad Gita, one of the most important religious texts of Hinduism, was essentially Krishna's response to Arjun's moral dilemma.[2]

The opening verse of the Bhagavad Gita has the words *'Dharmakshetre Kurukshetre'*, which can be interpreted as a place where dharma was established and the Kurus fought. The battle at Kurukshetra can be symbolic of the struggle that all individuals face in varying degrees at various stages of their lives.[3]

Arjuna's dilemma embodies the fear, anxiety, uncertainty and desperation a person feels. As Arjuna battles with his emotional turmoil, one understands a person's struggle for clarity of thought. Krishna's guidance to Arjuna gives a practical solution.

Krishna clarifies that one must fulfil their duty. But, in doing one's duty, one should not get attached to the results of their tasks. And one must do one's duty without any second thoughts.

Our world is much like this. In our journey to foster our passions and become successful, we find ourselves fighting our own small battles on multiple fronts. And in doing these duties, dealing with these emotional dilemmas, we emphasize our academic intelligence, analytical skills, and even school grades more than the emotional element of the journey. However, it appears that success in today's world doesn't depend on your academic intelligence, but it does depend on something more interpersonal.

* * *

A different kind of intelligence

Today, our society considers academic excellence to be the best predictor of success in the social, educational and professional spheres of life. However, success in today's world appears to be rooted in our ability to understand and manage our own emotions, while influencing those of others. This is known as emotional intelligence, and this concept has been deeply researched in the field of psychology.

One of these researchers, the world-renowned psychologist Dr Daniel Goleman, found that IQ and technical skills are only 'threshold capabilities'. They are only the entry-level requirements that help you get your foot in the door. According to his research, it is emotional intelligence that is necessary for success in life and leadership.[4]

IQ levels do not really show why people with similar backgrounds, schooling, opportunities and intelligence perform differently in life. For example, in the 1940s, ninety-five Harvard students with diverse IQ levels were followed through their lives for a study. This research found that the students with the highest scores in college were not more successful either in terms of their earnings or their status in their chosen field than their lower-scoring classmates. Nor did the higher-scoring students have more life satisfaction, better relationships or happier families than their lower-scoring counterparts.[5]

Similarly, in 1981, two professors studied eighty-one high school students who were the first and second rank holders of their batches. These students continued to achieve well in college and get good grades. Of these eighty-one class toppers, fifteen students went on to earn PhDs, six got law degrees, three received medical degrees, and twenty-two earned master's degrees. However, in their late twenties, they achieved only average levels of success in their lives, as compared to their classmates. These students who had excelled in school were now working in financially secure companies, but they were not exceptionally outperforming their lesser-scoring peers.[6]

Looking at that outcome, researcher Karen Arnold concluded, 'We have discovered the "dutiful" people who know how to excel in the set system. But these valedictorians [students with the highest academic standings] struggle as surely as we all do. A valedictorian reflects that the person is exceedingly good at getting grades. However, it doesn't explain at all how they react to the ups and downs of life.'[7]

Therefore, it is safe to say that academic excellence offers no training for the turmoil of real life. A high IQ level does not guarantee success, happiness, prestige and prosperity in a career. But still, our society and schools are fixated on getting the highest test scores and neglect emotional intelligence.

In the new world where the rules are changing, we are all still measured by the same benchmarks. Studies of tens of thousands of individuals across diverse fields show that in a workplace a person is no longer judged by their smartness or the number of technical skills they possess. An employer sees those as given. Instead, in the workplace, a person is measured by how they handle themselves and other people around them. The soft skills associated with emotional intelligence determine who gets promoted, passed over and even laid off.[8]

I too agree that academic intelligence is a poor determinant of success in life. From all the interviews I did for this book, it appeared that a majority of the young successful people from diverse backgrounds did not necessarily score the highest grades in their school or college. But they often did have one skill in common that they attributed to excellence. They all had enhanced people skills. Specifically, they showcased superior self-awareness, empathy and comfort in fostering connections with other people.

Today's successful leaders are not necessarily the most technically qualified people, but they are the ones who can create buy-in from their followers. This is because they have a strongly developed sense of empathy, and enormous emotional intelligence.

Now let me tell you the story of a young changemaker who overcame her ailments and built a community that has impacted tens of thousands of people who suffer from the same condition. Although a bright student, she chose to drop out of university after only a year. And it was her empathy that drove the movement she launched.

* * *

Jazz Sethi is the founder and director of the Diabesties Foundation, a type 1 diabetes advocate, and a performance artist.

In middle school, Jazz used to be a midfielder on the football team. Over a few weeks as she was practising to play her first game against another school, her parents noticed she was feeling unusually thirsty and was losing weight—symptoms they thought resulted from her football training. Still just to be safe, they took her to get a blood test done.

One Saturday afternoon, when Jazz was thirteen, she was peacefully watching *The Suite Life of Zack & Cody*. The doctor called her parents and told them that she had to be admitted to the intensive care unit immediately as her blood sugar was 1050 mg/dL, while a normal sugar level is between 80 and 130 mg/dL.

At the hospital, the doctor declared, 'You have type-1 diabetes.' And she heard her mother gasp.

At that moment, her life changed.

She didn't realize then that she would never be able to eat French fries without first injecting herself with insulin. She didn't know then that she was always going to need a needle in her, or that excessive stress would upset her sugar levels. The long-term affects her body will suffer due to the fluctuating sugar levels are still unknown.

Initially, she struggled to understand that she was always going to be *different*. She was the only one in school who had to check her sugar levels, who had to think before eating anything, and who was constantly afraid of what would happen next. This incredible sense of loneliness stuck with her through her teenage years. Finally, about a decade after her diagnosis, she realized that being different could help her make a difference.

Now Jazz says, 'Diabetes is something I've accepted, and it is like my invisible friend now. It has always been there but now instead of fighting the friend I'm embracing it.'

Jazz realized that there was a serious need for a community for people with diabetes. She made their very 'difference' a factor to bring people together. She tried to turn that invisible friend into visible friends.

She says, 'Most people with type-1 diabetes never meet another person like them in their lives. And it's a deep feeling of loneliness, and "why me?" So, the community support makes people feel less alone.'

Diabetes is a chronic disease that is not talked about enough. During the first ten years of suffering from type-1 diabetes, Jazz didn't know anyone else with that condition. She imagined that other people with diabetes would be feeling isolated too, so through her doctor's contacts, she reached out to about thirty other people with type-1 diabetes to start a community.

That first meet-up opened up a whole new world for Jazz. It showed her that there were people out there just like her, with similar stories and similar struggles. It also showed her that there was a wide gap in the health sector that needed to be addressed. The Diabesties Foundation aimed to bridge that gap.

Jazz says, 'Every time I meet a new person with diabetes, I am born again.' Many new projects were initiated from those interactions, and education has become an enormous focus area for her foundation. The healthcare system in India is overburdened and doctors don't have enough time to explain treatment techniques in detail. So, her foundation has been filling this gap.

Jazz's mother, who is a celebrated designer, taught her to design 'with' the user and not 'for' the user. So, the foundation's mission has been person-centred. Consequently, Jazz has always looked through the lens of sensitivity and empathy to drive her community.

Her experience as a person with type-1 diabetes and understanding the pain and suffering of others in the community have been at the core of her initiative.

Sharing her lived experiences and empathizing with each individual enabled Jazz to make Diabesties Foundation a nationwide movement. Jazz now leads a forty members team, and her Diabesties chapters are now present in fifteen cities and expanding as we speak. They are in Ahmedabad, Punjab, Kerala, Karnataka, Maharashtra, Madhya Pradesh and Uttar Pradesh among other regions, and will soon be starting internationally in Dubai and Jeddah too. Their marquee projects include running education projects through comic books, organizing international conferences and the weekly Dia-meets. Their *Back to Basics* project, in 2021 alone, helped over 450 people with type-1 diabetes through one-on-one conversations and person-centered counselling.

Instead of pursuing lofty business degrees, Jazz drove change through empathy. She says, 'I had no formal education. Instead, emotional intelligence driven by empathy taught me about leadership, networking and building a buy in from important stakeholders.' She also believes that living through adversity in her personal life, made her more resilient to face challenges in the workspace without ever making excuses.

When Jazz receives messages from newly diagnosed children or caregivers that tell her that her work has made them feel less alone or has comforted them, she believes she has succeeded.

Jazz has lived a life filled with ups and downs, with a condition that she neither asked for nor did anything to deserve. But she used her setbacks to create change, and she marshalled her emotions to help other people with type-1 diabetes 'take pride and . . . accept their condition, live happily with it, and let it live with you.'

In the next five years, she and the Diabesties team aim to reach the rural areas to spread awareness and education and increase access to insulin and blood glucose testing strips.

* * *

Overcoming our biggest obstacles

Today, everyone is running behind getting the best grades, preparing for college entrance tests, and earning a better GPA for a more stable job. In our journey towards our goals, we face obstacles. Unfortunately, most of these obstacles are self-imposed.

Studies have found that self-esteem and levels of emotional intelligence are strongly correlated.[9] Further, a study conducted at the Osmania University in Hyderabad showcased that foreign students between the ages of twenty and twenty-five had higher self-esteem than Indian students.[10] Across all categories such as undergraduate students, postgraduate students, students who are outgoing and those who have siblings, Indian students had lower self-esteem than their peers in the developed countries. This indicates that we have a lower level of emotional intelligence compared to our foreign counterparts.

I was curious to learn the key drivers of and barriers to success for under-twenty-five-year-old Indians. So, in early 2020, I surveyed over 300 college students in towns such as Ahmednagar and Nashik; cities such as Pune, Mumbai and New Delhi; and even internationally in Singapore, Dubai and Sydney.

When I asked these students about the single biggest obstacle to achieving their goals, more than 60 per cent referred to emotional issues (an even bigger factor than financial, educational and exposure-related issues). Upon further interviewing these students, they opened up to me about their self-doubts, lack of self-confidence, bouts with anxiety, fear of failure and a few clinical mental health issues. In India, mental health challenges faced by students are truly a 'health epidemic'.[11]

Often, these issues emerged due to family circumstances or childhood experiences.

At a personal level, I could relate to the people whom I had interviewed.

When I was ten years old, we moved from my hometown in Ahmednagar to Pune so I could get better coaching in table tennis. I was a skinny, awkward, maladjusted child, trying to settle in a big city. My mother and I lived in a small apartment near the training centre.

I was home-schooled for three years. It was hilarious for my peers to hear me speak in my poor English with a stammer. The bullying and a few ragging incidents in my first few national tournaments left a mark on me.

My table tennis coach had these military-grade humiliating strategies that would involve daily public belittling, for which I was a go-to target. It was a difficult environment, and I felt rather lonely growing up.

Psychoanalyst Harry Stack Sullivan has studied the importance of close childhood friendships in learning emotional intelligence.[12] I did not have these early close friendships. Therefore, empathy and soft skills did not come easily to me. With ridiculously little self-confidence, I never believed I could do anything of value. But I met very inspiring people who had overcome terrible childhoods and unspeakable traumas to become globally renowned for their work. One of them is Reshma Qureshi.

* * *

Reshma Qureshi was the victim of an acid attack when she was seventeen years old. She battled tremendous pain and depression to overcome her trauma. She started a fashion blog called 'Being Reshma', which got her immense attention and appreciation globally. Since then she has walked on the ramp of New York fashion shows and spoken at various international forums.

Reshma Qureshi was born in Allahabad. She was the youngest and the most loved amongst three sisters and two brothers. Reshma's father was the only bread-earner in the family.

Being a Muslim, she had to adhere to strict rules in the family and society. Marriage was usually the only way out. Her older sister was married young to a man who turned out to be abusive. During their divorce, her sister got custody of their baby.

When Reshma was seventeen, she was grabbed by three men as she was walking to a class at 7 a.m. They held her down and splashed acid on her face in broad daylight. These men were her own brother-in-law and his associates, who wanted to take revenge for her sister gaining custody of the baby.

'Acid is corrosive to metal. When it was spilt on my face, it was unspeakably painful. There were people around, but no one came to help me,' Reshma recalls.

She was unable to see, but when she reached the hospital, instead of treating her, the hospital staff sent her to a police station to register a first information report (FIR). The police questioned her for four hours while she still had acid on her face. It took a seven-hour surgery to stop the acid from further destroying her face. Her face was completely distorted in the process, and she lost her left eye due to the delay.

In overcoming the trauma, her family was a significant source of inspiration. All the mirrors in the house were removed. In today's world, your face is your identity. Your face is what you are. When it was literally melted due to acid, she felt emotional and physical pain that most of us cannot fathom.

'I felt like I wanted to end my life. The face is the main thing there is. I lost it for no fault of my own. I felt cheated. I tried to run away.'

She came across the organization Make Love Not Scars and met its founder, Ria Sharma. Over several hours-long calls, she gave Reshma a lot of encouragement and support.

Slowly Reshma tried to engage herself by starting a fashion blog, 'Being Reshma', where she would dress up and give fashion tips to people—irrespective of their complexions. Today the blog has 5000 weekly visitors. And in 2016, at nineteen years of age, she was one of the only eleven Indians selected to walk during the New York Fashion Week in New York City.[13]

In our patriarchal society, if a girl suffers an attack or accident, society discards her. It is always assumed that it must be the girl's problem, which is wrong. Reshma too faced these obstacles. But when others tried to pull her down or showed pity for her condition, she decided to grow.

'Beauty doesn't lie in physical appearance but in being strong from inside.'

Today, two of her three attackers are serving time in jail. On revenge, she says, 'I gained strength from knowing that my attacker wanted to ruin my life, and I got the sweetest revenge by living an accomplished, successful and happy life.'

While before the attack she would not go out alone without permission or an escort, she now travels independently to cities around the world for her talk and fashion shows. She walks with a self-assured stride; she speaks with glowing confidence.

'Life is a series of tragic events for many, yet I truly hope to show that at the end of the tunnel, we can always choose to switch on a bright light—from within ourselves,' she says.

Reshma advises women to stay strong, raise their voices and be confident in their own skin.

What is emotional intelligence?

When I was nineteen years old, I was volunteering at Entrepreneur Live event hosted by the Entrepreneur Magazine that got start up founders and investors of the region together at Marina Bay Sands in Singapore. There I met the author of *Elephants Before Unicorns*, the CEO of FORWARD, and the globally renowned leadership coach who helps create emotionally intelligent organizations, Ms Caroline Stokes. She generously spoke with me for this book and shared her ideas on emotional intelligence and millennials and Generation Zs.

The ability to recognize and manage our feelings and recognize and respond effectively to those of others is known as emotional intelligence.[14] Research shows that 90 per cent of the top performers have high levels of emotional intelligence, which is what sets them apart from their peers.[15]

Daniel Goleman's Emotional Intelligence Quadrant[16]

Various researchers have developed the emotional intelligence model. But for this book, I chose Daniel Goleman's model with four domains: self-awareness, self-management, social awareness and relationship management.

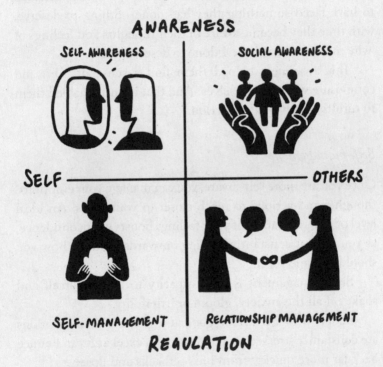

Self-awareness

Knowing our emotions and recognizing a feeling as it happens is the keystone of emotional intelligence. Self-awareness basically means to be aware of both your mood and your thoughts about that mood.[17]

People who are more certain about their feelings are in greater control of their lives. Otherwise, the inability to know your feelings might leave you at the mercy of how other people treat you.

Jazz and Reshma both faced the lion's share of setbacks, traumas and adversities. While at first they both felt cheated to have faced something they had done nothing to deserve, with time they became aware of their thoughts and feelings of 'why me' and 'what have I done to deserve this?'

This awareness helped them find a sense of calm and composure within themselves. And that in turn enabled them to turn their adversity to action.

Self-management

Once you are more self-aware, you can manage your emotions, thoughts and actions to reach closer to your goals. An ideal level of self-regulation of your feelings boosts your confidence, as you are not constantly looking outwards to know how you should feel and react.

Self-management is your capacity to calm yourself and shake off all the anxiety, gloom or irritability.

People who are not too good at regulating their emotions are constantly stressed, while those who excel at it can bounce back far more quickly from life's setbacks and upsets.

For the first few years after she found out she had diabetes, Jazz cursed herself for being different from the rest, but eventually, she recognized that being different could help her make a difference. Similarly, Reshma overcame her emotions by starting her blog 'Being Reshma'.

It did not come easily to them. Jazz and Reshma both had multiple setbacks. Both mentioned their moments of self-doubt, anxiety and even moderate depression. But they were able to bounce back from those setbacks stronger and excel in their chosen fields. And today, their initiatives have inspired and impacted tens of thousands of individuals around the world.

Social awareness

Once you are able to manage your emotions, you will become more aware of what is happening around you. Social awareness means the ability to empathize. It means sensing what others are feeling, reading situations appropriately and trying to see things from their perspective.

In starting Diabesties, Jazz designed her foundation after understanding the pain and suffering of other people living with type-1 diabetes. Her foundation's mission is person-centric and she looks through the lens of sensitivity and empathy to drive her community.

Similarly, Reshma empathized with thousands of other acid attack victims and advised women to stay strong, raise their voices and be confident in their own skin.

Relationship management

Being a leader always involves people. And your relationships with them cannot be transactional. They have to be friendly relationships, with a purpose. You need to be sociable to get the desired response from people. The skill of building strong bonds with others, influencing and inspiring them, arises from your self-awareness, self-regulation and social awareness abilities.

In Jazz's and Reshma's examples, they managed teams. They leveraged their relationships to open new chapters in more states in India and collaborate with NGOs around the country. And they did so very successfully.

Measure your emotional intelligence

Now that you know what and how important emotional intelligence is, try this exercise to gauge your own emotional quotient (EQ). Reach out to someone you trust. They could be your mentor, teacher, parent, boss or anyone who is neither too close to you nor too distant. They should be someone who has your best interests at heart. Ask them to rate you on the following assessment.

If you cannot find such a person, estimate how you would place yourself in the eyes of your peers as honestly as possible.

Rate on a scale of one to four, where four represents *always*, and one represents *never*.

This emotional intelligence assessment and the guidance that follows were developed by Dr Bijal Oza, psychologist and emotional intelligence expert, based out of Dubai.

No.		Never (1)	Sometimes (2)	Most of the time (3)	Always (4)
1	I am always aware of the emotions I go through.				

No.		Never (1)	Sometimes (2)	Most of the time (3)	Always (4)
2	I believe I am in control of my emotions.				
3	I am aware of the emotions people around me experience.				
4	I can form healthy relationships with people around me.				
5	I am aware of my emotions' impact on my thoughts, feelings and subsequent behaviours.				
6	I can regulate my emotions using effective tools.				
7	I can empathize with people around me.				
8	I can resolve conflicts effectively.				

To calculate your emotional intelligence score, add up all the numbers. The maximum score you can get is 32 (extremely emotional intelligent), and the lowest possible is 8 (not emotionally intelligent at all). A score below 24 would indicate a problem. Even if your score is low, don't worry. You can improve your emotional intelligence with practise.

Remember that your score at present is only a reflection of yourself right now. How emotionally intelligent you are right now might be different from how you were a few years ago, and how you will be a few years later.

As we saw previously, emotional intelligence has four components: self-awareness, self-management, social awareness and relationship management.

For your self-awareness score, add up questions 1 and 5; for your self-management score, add up 2 and 6; for your social awareness score, add up 3 and 7; and finally, for your relationship management score, add up questions 4 and 8.

As I mentioned before, don't worry if your score is low because you can improve your emotional intelligence with practise. To illustrate, let me share my own story.

I had a tough time socially in high school and during my early college years. If I would have taken this emotional intelligence test then, I would have probably gotten a low score of 10 or 12. I had very little empathy, and no willingness to discuss anything related to feelings.

After discovering this personal shortcoming over the last couple of years, I read a range of books on this topic. I did a lot of journaling and even took some counselling. Now I feel better equipped emotionally to take on the challenges around me. I improved my self-awareness, empathy and optimism, which made me foster many healthy and deeper relationships. This boosted my confidence and helped me succeed in my projects, which aim to help me make a significant positive impact in the world.

Many of the impactful people I met use their emotional obstacles to propel themselves towards a fulfilling and purposeful life full of achievement and influence.

> *Emotional intelligence can be learned, and in fact, we are each building it, in varying degrees, throughout life. It's sometimes called maturity.*
>
> —*Daniel Goleman, author of*
> *the best-selling book* Emotional Intelligence

Sometimes circumstances force people to develop emotional intelligence. Other times, emotional intelligence becomes a necessary skill that you need to learn to succeed in life.

A significant difference between analytical skills, IQ and your emotional intelligence is that your IQ is relatively stable over time as it is determined by genetics and environment. But your emotional intelligence can improve with dedication and guidance. Studies by neuropsychologists suggest that, with adequate training, people can become more pro-social, altruistic and compassionate.[18]

Just like working out at the gym, your brain is a muscle that can be trained to become more emotionally intelligent. As I shared earlier, I took deliberate steps to improve my empathic skills in my personal life, and I could see some personal improvement.

Once you identify your strengths and weaknesses, the first step would be to monitor yourself.

If you have scored low on self-awareness, reach out to a range of people you trust and seek feedback from them on both your positive and negative aspects. Ask them what they see as your strengths and weaknesses. Try to identify how you respond in a positive and a negative situation, during critical feedback, and in times of crisis. Don't tear yourself down or judge yourself too harshly, just try to analyse and become aware. Secondly, to help become aware of your emotions, practise mindfulness exercises.

Mindfulness is an ancient method that helps you in building attention and connecting with your environment. You need to engage with all your five senses to really become mindful. For example, you can practice a mindful coffee moment. When you make your morning coffee or tea next, completely immerse yourself in the process and focus on the sensations coming from it. Smell the coffee beans or tea leaves and notice the warmth rising from the steam. When you sip it, pay attention to the taste and the aroma. Focusing on the coffee can help you get in touch with your own feelings and sensations.[19] Alternatively, you could practise mindfulness in any of your day-to-day activities. It could be doing a colouring activity with a child, or simply while exercising at the gym.

If you have scored low on emotional regulation, start writing a journal and identify your stress triggers. Recognize how your body reacts to things that activate your stress, and notice how you usually deal with that stress.

Next, identify healthy and effective ways to deal with the stresses. Since dealing with stress is a personal thing, it can range from taking a deep breath or doing yoga, to talking to a loved one, listening to music, or journaling. You should avoid unhealthy stress management practices such as smoking and drinking.

The pandemic has truly normalized mental health conversations. Seeking therapy is not a bad thing. You can use it to improve your emotional intelligence.

If you think your social awareness components need help, you should work on your communication, listening skills and understanding of body language. Find a mentor who can help you understand body language and non-verbal cues of yourself and of others.

A mentor can be a professional one or a loved one you trust. Ask them to tell you what your body language tells them. Ask them what you are feeling without actually telling them. You might get feedback such as, when you are not up to it you slouch, you don't make eye contact or you are distant.

Finally, if you have scored low on relationship management, you should know that this component is about empathy and effective conflict resolution. Therefore, you can mindfully practise empathy. Don't practise empathy only with people you love, but with people you disagree with. It is not about understanding someone's journey as you have experienced but it is about how they are experiencing it.

People experience traumas, abuse or depression for causes that we know nothing about, so when empathizing with them you should truly put yourself in their shoes, and don't try to relate it to your own stories. We need to understand the emotions that they are feeling, and what it means to them.

Also, in addition to each of the four emotional intelligence domains, sometimes you need to stay strong and be open to seek professional help.

Often when you try to do exceptional things, life can become truly enduring. In pursuit of your goals, you may get flak from not only your peers but also the people you admire. Then, not your academic excellence but your emotional intelligence will shape your life outcomes.

Let me share a story of one of my favourite young authors and young leaders, Gurmehar Kaur. She has been one of the most courageous people I know who strongly advocates for peace among countries and religions and stands strong in the face of challenges.

I came to admire her not only for her great achievements, but for the emotional strength she displayed in times of adversity, and unwarranted criticism at a very young age.

* * *

Gurmehar Kaur is the bestselling author of *Small Acts of Freedom* and *The Young and the Restless: Youth and Politics in India,* published by Penguin Random House in 2018 and 2019, respectively. In her latest book, she followed the journeys of eight young political leaders. She explored their aspirations for the country's youth, themselves and the nation at large.

She is also a social activist and an ambassador for Postcards for Peace, a global youth-backed campaign that aims to help eliminate all kinds of discrimination. Kaur co-founded Citizens for Public Leadership (CPL), an independent, non-partisan movement focused on advocating progressive public policy in India. CPL's objective is to strengthen the capacity of Indian youth to take up leadership challenges in the public sphere.

In 2017, Gurmehar was listed by *TIME* magazine as a Next Generation Leader, a global listing of ten young men and women making a difference in the world. She graduated from Lady Shri Ram College in Delhi in 2019. After that, she joined Somerville College, University of Oxford, to pursue an MSc in modern South Asian studies.

Gurmehar was born and brought up in both Jalandhar and Ludhiana. She lost her father, a captain in the Indian army, when she was only three years old. Captain Mandeep Singh was one of the seven Indian army personnel martyred in terrorist attacks in Jammu and Kashmir in 1999.

She writes in her debut book *Small Acts of Freedom*, 'Everyone remembers the day of his funeral when he was wrapped in the tiranga (tricolour), decorated with strings of marigolds, saying goodbye to all of us. The few memories that I have of him were very difficult to write and even more difficult to share.'[20]

From a very young age, she had to overcome her feeling of loss, and navigate her way through the world. Early on, she started reading books voraciously. She found her solace in books as they taught her about love, life and forgiveness, while TV highlighted hate and discrimination among religions, genders and communities. In books, she felt the comfort that she missed elsewhere.

As a student, Gurmehar confesses she wasn't a top scorer. She couldn't focus and sit through eight hours of classes. She recently discovered that she suffered from attention deficit hyperactivity disorder (ADHD), which made it difficult for her to study.

Among all the flaws of our Indian education system, one of them is that teachers can be very mean to lower-performing students. When an authority figure such as a teacher normalizes shaming, the students think it is okay to bully the weaker performing students. As a result, students who are not at the top of the class are often belittled.

Gurmehar says, 'I hated school. I was never the best-scoring kid or the favourite one in the class. I was always the one who "has a lot of potential but doesn't study".'

When she was in the fifth standard, she used to train for tennis at the Harvest Tennis Academy in Ludhiana, a fancier school that had better facilities than her school. She and her sister were both talented tennis players. As a ten-year-old, she asked the sports teacher at the Harvest Tennis Academy if he liked the game of the Kaur sisters. The sports teacher said yes and that it would be great to have Gurmehar and her sister Bani on the school team for the upcoming national games.

So Gurmehar told the sports teacher, 'I will convince my mum to put us in this school if you give us a 100 per cent scholarship.' And that is how she and her sister changed schools on a full scholarship.

Gurmehar did her tenth standard from the same school in the IGCSE board, and her twelfth standard from an open school in the CBSE board.

'I flourished. I loved reading, studying and learning in an open environment. And I liked the grind of the athlete.'

At the peak of her career, she represented her state in three national championships. Pursuing professional tennis taught her about discipline and perseverance. She knew that if she put in the hours, she would get the results.

Unfortunately, at eighteen years of age, owing to an injury, she had to stop playing tennis professionally.

'I had so much anger and energy in me when I had to leave tennis. As an athlete, you always have a purpose. In the long term, you want to become India number one, you want to win all the tournaments in the season, and in the subsequent training sessions, you want to improve your forehand strokes. But when you leave sports, your purpose also collapses.'

After tennis, as she was exploring other avenues, she saw discrimination in the society that deeply unsettled her. Just like the humiliation, she observed lower-scoring students faced in the class, she felt something similar happened when the current government came into power.

She says, 'They would make policies and actions that would reduce minorities and say Muslims are impure or evil people. Then the population feels enabled to hate and bully the minorities too.'

She felt most passionate about telling stories. In the summer before college started, she took part in the Profile for Peace campaign that promoted peace between India and Pakistan, started by Ram Subramanian, founder of Handloom Picture Company. When Gurmehar met him in Mumbai in a café, she wrote a script of the story that was closest to her heart. She shot the video, which later went viral.

She had one important story to tell, and she told that. She appeared in a video holding a placard that read, 'Pakistan did not kill my father, war killed him.'[21]

That video, which no one paid attention to at first, suddenly reappeared and went viral on social media. More than 3 lakh people watched her video on YouTube, and it was widely shared. But, her innocent story was manipulated to show her as being 'anti-national'. People she respected including many celebrities, cricketers, politicians and media people, went after her with such hatred that she could not comprehend it at first.

She received numerous death and rape threats, which took a toll on her. She would feel anxious to be in a public space. More than the politicians' tweets and the politically orchestrated trolls, the feeling of being misunderstood was the hardest to deal with.

She had put out a heartfelt, meaningful and innocent campaign for peace by sharing her story. She genuinely believed that war was cruel, pointless and unnecessary.

Yet her innocent story of standing for peace between two countries and religions was misunderstood and misrepresented to show her as malicious, anti-national and disrespectful to her father's death. This was the most hurtful for her.

Gurmehar's family is very patriotic. 'I was born idolizing Bhagat Singh,' she recalls. 'Our patriotism isn't your ultra-right-wing patriotism, but the patriotism of Bhagat Singh.' But the people were taking away what was right in her bones and misinterpreting it as something nasty.

For three weeks, the media constantly followed her. Once, on her way back to her hostel from college, her rickshaw was chased by the media guys.

'Tennis really toughened me up. I learnt how to block out the noise and how to survive alone.'

But the public was discrediting her father's sacrifices for the country, and that was very hurtful.

'I've been trolled, mocked and bullied. I've had people call me names. And I've been frightened for my life. But I emerged from all of that more determined than ever to never be silenced.'

6

Growth Mindset

'Whether you think you can or think you can't, you're right'
—Henry Ford, founder of
Ford Motor Company

In 1985, in the cold mountains of Ladakh, a nineteen-year-old college student started tutoring students in the tenth to the twelfth standards. He wanted to support his personal educational expenses. So, although he did not have any money in his pocket, he leased a whole building and employed staff to help him run the tuition classes.

His tutoring was so successful that soon students in the hundreds started arriving at his doorstep. Moreover, his innovative teaching methods significantly improved the performance of otherwise failing students.

Within two months, he had earned enough money to cover the fees for the next three years of college, where he was studying for an engineering degree.

In the whole drama, she had to be emotionally strong. A week before the mid-semester break in 2017, she came home from Delhi in the middle of the political drama. She thought she would get a proper scolding from her grandfather, as the media was standing outside the house. Instead, her youngest uncle shook his head and started laughing. Her grandfather said, '*Khun ne to bolna hi hai.*' One's blood will definitely speak. He told her that she had proved she was her father's daughter. Rebellious, carefree and able to take a *panga* with people twice her size.

And to her, this meant so much that her faith in herself was reaffirmed.

'I am someone who loves agency. People love and worship the success and the rise of someone. And they will look down upon you when you are low. That's when I realized that I would never put myself in a position where people look at me with pity. I will keep achieving things so that . . . India and Pakistan can have peace. People say you are so successful that you must be right. And that is why I want to become everything.'

When she was at Oxford, she met Malala, who she says has a heart full of kindness. Such friendships changed the way she looked at the world. 'People to people, there is no hate.'

After her time at Oxford and because of the COVID-19 pandemic, she faced PTSD and went through a year of depression that she had to overcome. She couldn't get out of bed and lost a bit of her steam.

Whenever she has low phases, she takes guidance from professionals at Children First, an organization that helps with mental healthcare among adolescents. She has built structures and routines that accommodate her emotional health, and make her feel happy. She also practices Vipassana, one of India's most ancient techniques of meditation.

'I think I was emotionally intelligent to step back. Sometimes, stepping back and delegating work to someone to take care of you, and seeking help when required is emotional intelligence.'

* * *

One can see striking similarities between Gurmehar, Jazz, Reshma and Arjuna as emotionally intelligent people. They might not be always perfect, but they realized their emotional limits and used them to be leaders, inspiring tens of thousands globally. In doing so they used intelligence that was different than the academic.

As we saw earlier through Jazz's and Reshma's examples, the first step towards emotional intelligence is self-awareness. When one is self-aware, they move on to the next step of managing their emotions. After which the person becomes aware, empathizes with the things around them and that leads to better relationships.

Gurmehar too overcame many adversities with courage, maturity, and emotional intelligence. She also sought help when she needed it.

Similarly, Arjuna also signifies the traits of an emotionally intelligent person as he is aware of his emotional turmoil. He empathizes with himself and others for being in a place where they must fight their own dear ones and he feels pity for his cousins, who have brought their entire clan to this sorrowful state. Then he clearly shares his dilemma with Krishna and seeks his help to overcome it.[22]

It is in response to this that Krishna discusses the that lead to these disturbances, and offers a practical s that one should do their duty without any attachme results and second thoughts. Thus, Krishna's advice bec more practical. The course of action that he advises Arjun be followed by anyone at any place. The guidance is unive in nature and holds meaning even today.[23]

Therefore, even in your journey to becoming a leader, a doing extraordinary things, you will face emotionally charge situations. You must deal with them intelligently and strive t improve your emotional quotient. In doing so, do not hesitate from seeking help. After all your maturity, and EQ will make a great difference in your life outcomes.

This nineteen-year-old was himself a victim of an alien education system. When he first moved to Srinagar, Kashmir, from his hometown in Ladakh for his education, he was addressed in a language different from his own. As a result, he was labelled stupid due to his lack of understanding of a unfamiliar language.

Hindi and English were the official languages for instruction in primary schools in Ladakh. However, neither of these languages was spoken by the children in their everyday lives. Students would learn English only to take their tenth standard exams and were clearly weak in the language. As a result, a staggering 95 per cent of the government school students failed their tenth standard exams.[1] These students were stamped as failures for the rest of their lives. In fact, it was not they who had failed the system, but rather the system that had failed them.

At the age of twenty-two, he started the Students' Educational and Cultural Movement of Ladakh (SECMOL) with the goal of reforming the education system in Ladakh. They would only accept school dropouts and turn them around.

Over the next thirty years, he made these so-called failures into stars. Students are given vocational classes and experiential learning opportunities. Interestingly, the students are responsible for running their own schools, which they run like mini countries. Students elect their own government and a leader who delegates roles and responsibilities.

This changemaker taught the students the natural application of science and languages in vocational classes. For example, in winter, the temperature in Ladakh can fall below -15 degrees Celsius. After using only high-school-level science and locally available materials, his students built rooms that remained at 12 to 15 degrees Celsius inside when it was below freezing outside.

The name of this trailblazer is Sonam Wangchuk, and he found gems in the people who were branded as rejects. Students in his system too worked hard to overcome their initial failure tag. As a result, SECMOL graduates have become successful film-makers, businessmen, administrators and original-thinking citizens.

In his journey, Mr Wangchuk thought, 'They were not failures. They were just not there yet.'

* * *

Usually, the only marker of intelligence in India is our academic grades. Society often tells us that getting good grades is the only path to success. And anyone who has achieved success in spite of not getting good grades has done so through their natural talents, something fixed at birth.

Many of the college students I interviewed for this book felt that successful people have innate skills that ordinary people cannot develop. They often said with a smirk, 'If I were that talented, I would have done that too.'

We sometimes think that our natural abilities are fixed and define what we will achieve in our lives. But the opposite appears to be true.

In twelfth grade, I chose to leave my athletic ambitions for a career in business and academia. I was looking for inspiring self-help books to get some direction in my life. But I could not find good literature on what made Generation Zs successful in a developing country like India. Most of the available books were written by Western authors, narrating stories and studies of eras, people and places that had nothing to do with me.

The few Indian books I could find on this topic were so fluffy with positive thinking, random motivational quotes and philosophical literature that I was left feeling disappointed.

As any self-respecting overconfident teenager would, I dreamt of writing a book that would be better than any that existed.

But the challenge was, I had never been good at languages. I was scared of English; I remember scoring 8 out of 20 in my ninth standard tests. I spoke with a stammer. My pronunciation and spelling made me the laughing stock of my class. As a result, I generally felt insecure in settings that required English. I thought I would never overcome my fear of the language and the sense of inferiority that came with it.

However, just to give it a try, I enrolled myself in a two-year diploma course in creative writing in parallel with my bachelor's degree. To prepare myself as an author, I also read over 200 books, research papers and journal articles. Furthermore, I interviewed forty young overachievers in sports, academia, music, politics and entrepreneurship as part of the research process. And I surveyed over 300 students to understand the trends in their aspirations and the barriers they faced.

It took me nearly four years to complete this book. The English language was the most significant initial obstacle I had to overcome. Did it come easy to me? No. But it was undoubtedly rewarding.

If I were stuck in a fixed mindset and accepted my shortcoming in the English language, this book would never have happened.

Let me tell you an even more inspiring story of a young musician who discovered his passion, taught himself music and honed a mindset to learn new things that made him one of India's most celebrated young artists, and a Forbes 30 under 30 awardee in 2022.

* * *

Achyuth Jaigopal is a musician from Kerela. He is the co-founder and lead guitarist of the popular indie band When Chai Met Toast and plays the banjo, ukulele, acoustic guitar, electric guitar and nylon string guitar. His band now has 5 lakh monthly listeners on Spotify, and 3 lakh subscribers on YouTube. He was previously a member of the Raghu Dixit Project, a famous folk and Indie band. He has played at multiple international venues, including the Sydney Opera House and the Glastonbury Festival.

As a studio musician, he works with A.R. Rahman and many famous composers. He has performed in over 500 shows in different parts of the world.

Achyuth was born in Kochi, Kerela, in 1996. There were no musicians in his family. Both his parents are architects by profession. As a child, he was introduced to music through his dad's collection of songs by Bob Dylan, John Denver, Eric Clapton, ABBA, Bonnie M, Muhammad Rafi, Kishore Kumar and A.R. Rahman, among others.

Growing up, he was an ordinary student who played sports and chilled with friends.

One day, he found an old guitar lying around at home and started strumming randomly. When he was seven, his parents put him in a music class where he learnt Western classical guitar.

Although the seed of music was planted, Achyuth confesses, 'As a child, I was neither exceptionally talented nor the one who practised every day.'

Until the tenth standard, he studied in Kochi. In his eighth grade, at the age of fourteen, he had the mentor John Anthony, the founder of a few bands such as Karnatriix and Roots—A.R. Rahman's first band. John introduced him to different styles of music: blues, fingerstyle guitar and jazz.

Later, when he was sixteen, Achyuth went to Bali on vacation with his parents. They visited the Green School, built by the legendary architect John Hardy. Since his parents work in the field of sustainable architecture, they had to see it. Achyuth instantly fell in love with the school and applied there. It was an extraordinary opportunity for an eleventh grader. And that was where he started performing.

'I happened to be at an open mic in a small café called Coffee and Copper. My houseparent nudged me to perform my original written song. The café liked my guitar playing, and they called me back.' That is how his career as a musician was launched—in a coffee shop.

After high school, he got into the prestigious Berklee College of Music in New York. He sent in a video audition to be part of the Raghu Dixit Project. Then, one day, Raghu broke his hand. And Achyuth got a call out of the blue to fly to Bangalore. The band needed a guitarist. So, they allowed a seventeen-year-old to play at a show the next day.

'Within a month, I was on a flight to the UK for a tour. I could go to college, but I didn't want to let this opportunity go. So I stuck with the Raghu Dixit Project for close to two years. We played in Spain, England, two tours in the US, Australia, and many other countries such as Bhutan, Sri

Lanka, etc. So I must have played at least like 180 odd shows in that year and a half that I was with the band.'

While working with the senior musicians at the Raghu Dixit Project, Achyuth had to quickly grow into the lead guitarist role as his counterparts. He would seek feedback from his bandmates and spend countless hours in the studio practicing and perfecting his skills.

There have been many delightful moments in his career. But the most significant one was an incident in Kashmir. In a small school, about forty kilometres away from the nearest road, one of Achyuth's well-wishers used their song 'Firefly' to teach students English. The students liked the song so much that they made posters with the lyrics and stuck them on their classroom walls, and even sang the song for their school assemblies in the morning.

Achyuth's journey has been of following his heart, but he says, 'My core value is in being independent. Even if you take a different path, do not put the people who matter most to you in a difficult position. It's your own decision. So, you have to live up to it and work hard towards what you're doing.'

It is tempting to say that Achyuth was talented. But upon a closer look, his story has been of following his passion wholeheartedly, spending hours practising his instruments, being open to taking on new challenges, meeting new people and having a mindset to learn new things. If he had a fixed mindset, he would have been fixated on talent, sought constant validation and never tried to learn.

Instead, he used better strategies, taught himself more, practised harder and smarter, and worked around all the obstacles he faced to become the artist that he is today. Now, after listening to his story and his accomplishments, a distinction emerges between the two types of mindsets one could have. The distinction discussed in this chapter has been studied in depth by Dr Carol Dweck, and her masterpiece *Mindset* is highly recommended for anyone interested.

* * *

Growth versus a fixed mindset

How you think about yourself profoundly determines how you lead your life. If you believe that your abilities are fixed and unchangeable, you will go through life without improving at all.

If you have a fixed mindset, you will believe that your intelligence and skills are static. You will feel that there are some things you can, and some things you can never, do. As a result, you will go through life trying to show everyone that you are smart and avoid situations that will make you look dumb. Thus, you will never grow as a person.

Some of us are raised to constantly prove that we are intelligent. This can make one believe their level of intelligence has been carved in stone since birth. As a result, they feel a constant need to prove themselves to gain continuous approval from others.

I see quite a few of my friends stuck in the fixed mindset. Many of them go to good engineering and medical colleges. Yet, they are consumed by this goal to prove that they are smart everywhere they go, whether in college, in their jobs, in relationships, or even at casual parties. All occasions are approached as binary: will I look clever or not?

If you have a growth mindset, you will believe that your intelligence and most other abilities can be developed.[22] You think that your true potential is unknown yet unlimited, and you can achieve anything in life. Knowing that your intelligence can be developed will make you curious to learn and grow.

In the growth mindset, one believes that their talents right now are only a starting point. The essential qualities can be cultivated through effort, strategies and grit. Although everyone can have different intellectual abilities, they can grow these through deliberate practice.

A perspective from two mindsets

Look at the following situation, and note how you would react to it.

Imagine you are a student who has just moved to a metropolitan city for education. You come from a small town in India, you don't know anyone in the city, and you are all alone there. Your parents are in perpetual financial difficulty and struggle to make ends meet. Your dream is to get a PhD from a prestigious international university through a scholarship programme. You cannot afford to pay for tuition or coaching fees. And you face rejections and hardships in the application process. What would be your next steps?

Mindset 1

Firstly, I would have been heartbroken. Then, I would have told myself it is a highly competitive world out there. My chances of getting the scholarship were less than 1 per cent anyway.

Secondly, I would have compared my current achievements to those of students lesser accomplished than me and tried to feel good about the little distance I have come.

Thirdly, I would have thought, 'I was fooling myself even to dream of such a thing.'

Finally, I would have tried to rationalize the situation by saying, whatever happens is for the best. Then, thinking that I am just an average Indian student with lofty ambitions, I would have convinced myself to give up and find an easier target to achieve.

This is an example of a classic fixed mindset.

Mindset 2

Now let us look at the story of one of the youngest Union Public Service Commission (UPSC) exam toppers, a Delhi University gold medallist, and a pioneering researcher on Indian butterflies. An individual who overcame a situation worse than the one above to achieve one of the most ambitious goals in India: acceptance into the civil services.

In 1994, Himanshu was born in Shivpuri, a village near Bareilly in Uttar Pradesh. His father was a daily wage worker who did odd jobs in small shops in their village. He later started a roadside tea stall to make ends meet and climb out of poverty. Young Himanshu helped his father run the thela and interacted with everyone who stopped to drink tea.

There was no proper school in their village. So until the ninth standard, Himanshu would study at a small government school and scribble on a slate.

'Between the ninth and twelfth grades, I had to travel seventy kilometres every day to and from school on public transport.'

In the tenth and twelfth standards he scored 86 per cent and 84 per cent, respectively, which he says in all modesty was only 'reasonable and nothing great'.

'I had to walk most of my journey on my own. First, I could not afford to go to tuition or coaching classes, and later I got so used to self-study that I preferred it. It has a higher cost-benefit ratio and [promotes] the habit of diving into one field and studying as much as possible. This made me a deep generalist.'

After high school, he went to Hindu College in Delhi University to study for a bachelor's in science degree in botany. 'I have come this far on my own. I cannot stop. I have to go as far as I can.'

Himanshu's classmates came from privileged backgrounds, excellent schools, spoke in posh English and wore branded clothes. So, as you can imagine, it could get quite overwhelming for him in Delhi coming from a background such as his.

'At the beginning of college, I saw many people wearing fancy clothing, talking in fancy ways. So I knew if I had to make my value, I needed to outgrow and outsmart them.'

The feeling of inadequacy was natural. But he realized it was only a state of mind.

'I see a lot of people who are stuck in a web of poverty. I think poverty is a state of mind. If you believe that you are so poor that you cannot have or will never have resources in the future, then you are a poor person. But, on the other hand, if you can get one shred of hope in life, one ray of hope, an initial success, then you know what you want is achievable.'

After his undergraduate degree, he did a master's in environmental studies at Delhi University from 2014 to 2016. Here he worked very hard and won the university gold medal for topping the university program.

His pursuit in life has been a quest for knowledge. Education for him is to have a limitless arsenal of insights. He believes one can become a strong person knowledge-wise.

'I was so immersed in learning everything there was to learn that I couldn't develop a definite liking for one discipline.' This made him a deep generalist. After he finished his master's, he joined an MPhil course on environmental studies at Jiwaji University in 2017. There he again won a gold medal for holding the first position in his university.

His lifelong dream was to get a PhD from a prestigious international university.

'I got an excellent scholarship to go to a prestigious British university for a PhD programme. Unfortunately, I wasn't comfortable leaving my parents behind, and they didn't want to move to London either. It was a difficult choice to let go of my lifelong dream. When I rejected it, I decided to do something that would [match] the opportunity [I had] given up.'

He realized that working in a foreign country was not essential to earn a good salary. He felt it was more critical for him to work in India and help the people overcome hardships. He did not want to leave his parents and settle in a foreign nation as they had struggled a lot for him to achieve so much.

So, sitting for the UPSC exam was a natural choice for him. This is the highly competitive Indian civil service examination. Over 1.7 million people appear for it every year, and it has a qualification rate of only 0.15 per cent.

The habit of self-study that he had developed due to lack of money for tuition classes came in extremely handy.

'I realized that I write and think faster than other people. Since I was doing my MPhil simultaneously, I had to cover a lot of ground in a short time to beat my competition.'

In 2018, based solely on self-study and without the help of any coaching classes, Himanshu passed the exam with flying colours. He got allocated to the Indian Railway Traffic Services (IRTS). He also came in with an all-India rank of 8 in the Graduate Aptitude Test in Engineering (GATE).

Himanshu was not content with his score and was of the mindset that with better preparation and strategy, he could get a higher rank. In 2019, he made another attempt at the UPSC exams and topped them again. He was allocated to the prestigious Indian Police Services (IPS).

Still, for the third time, Himanshu felt he could improve his performance with a bit of creativity and tweaking a few of his approaches. He retook the exam in 2020, and finally became an Indian Administrative Services (IAS) officer.

Himanshu advises, 'Stop believing in the voice in you that says you are not good enough, it can't be done, or it requires way more than what you have. If you trust yourself, you can reach wherever you want in life.'

Today, Himanshu often guides students. 'It doesn't matter where you come from. It doesn't matter if your parents are poor or rich. It doesn't matter if you are highly educated or not. If you have the trust in yourself and if you can dream, you can reach it.'

He wears the simplest clothes one can imagine. Yet, he carries himself with confidence and the humility that comes from seeing the depths of poverty and coming out victorious.

'I do not see my struggling experiences as regressive in nature. On the contrary, they made me who I am today. It gives me a competitive edge. I have lived in poverty and been on the other side of inequality. I know what it is like to be on the ground.'

I noticed his ability to think of big ideas and explain them in simple language with a few words. It takes a depth of thought and a reservoir of experience to do so. Himanshu, at twenty-seven years of age, does this very well. He speaks with a Victorian vocabulary. He shifts between many stories and concludes with insights.

Therefore, his story shows that you are not a product of your circumstances. And you can choose to become who you want to be.

I spoke with Himanshu three times in the past three years—once after each of his successful UPSC attempts. It was mesmerizing to watch him evolve as a person and achieve every milestone he set out to achieve. Coming from a small town, having limited resources and being self-taught as against joining any coaching classes, Himanshu broke all barriers. He truly signifies a mindset of a champion—someone who keeps growing.

I was curious to learn more about this mindset and understand what makes people like Himanshu different from others.

A growth mindset

A growth mindset is basically about believing that your abilities can be developed.

It is not simply about being open-minded and flexible in accepting your mistakes. It is about being dedicated to growing your talents. It is not just about efforts but also about trying new strategies (and discarding the ones that are not working).

The table below developed after an in-depth reading on growth mindset literature, and interviewing industry experts, will help you identify the differences between growth and fixed mindsets.

The two mindsets

	Fixed mindset	Growth mindset
Success	It's about the outcome.	It's about the process, regardless of the outcome.
Preferences	Effortless success and constant validation.	Success is simply an outcome. Following curiosity and hard work are important virtues.
Truth	You think you know the absolute truth about yourself and the limits of your abilities.	You have some understanding of your strengths and weaknesses; you know you can develop your skills and life at large.
Failure	You see it as an obstacle on the way to development and change.	You regard it as the starting point of making a difference. You try to think what efforts will enable you to overcome the failure.
Confidence	Your confidence is more fragile. Setbacks pull you down.	Your confidence thrives irrespective of your failures (or even on the back of defeats). Further, you do not always need confidence. You will plunge into something even if you are not confident or not good at it.

	Fixed mindset	Growth mindset
Self-esteem	You want to be with people who make you feel you are without fault and therefore feel better about yourself.	You want to be surrounded by people who challenge you to become better.
Imperfections	Are shameful.	Are areas of growth.
Labels	Positive labels such as being intelligent, talented, etc., and negative labels such as being a loser, dumb, etc., mess with your mind. For example, if you get a positive label you are afraid of losing it. And if you are given a negative label, you are scared that it might be true.	Labels don't affect your performance.
Environment	In an external environment, when you are stereotyped for coming from a particular demographic such as your town, mother tongue, gender, etc., you have a shrinking sense of belonging.	You see things objectively and confront them with confidence.
In sports	Performance in sports depends on one's natural talents.	Performance depends on hard work and perseverance, and you continue to grow.

	Fixed mindset	Growth mindset
World view	The world is systematically categorized. People are the way they are, either inferior or superior. Therefore, you feel a need to regularly affirm that you are unique.	Everyone is a work in progress, and so are you.
Failure	Setbacks label you.	Setbacks are motivating and informative.
Relationships	It is either meant to be or not meant to be.	All relationships are capable of growth and change.
	If there is tension, and a relationship needs to be worked on, then there is something wrong with it and it wasn't meant to be.	There is always tension, but we can make it work.
	Couples must share the same views.	Couples have differences, and that's okay.
	Couples live happily ever after.	Couples work happily ever after.
Friendships	You stick with less accomplished friends so you feel better about yourself.	Irrespective of your accomplishments, you push each other to grow and be better.

	Fixed mindset	**Growth mindset**
Shyness	Shyness can take control of you.	You take control of shyness.
As parents	Your child has permanent traits, and you judge them for their skills.	Your child is a developing person, and you are committed to their development.
Heartbreaks	Your number one goal is revenge.	You move on by forgiving and forgetting. As they say in French, *tout comprendre c'est tout pardoner*, meaning, to understand all is to forgive all.
As students	You think that academic excellence depends largely on natural talents and abilities.	You simply follow your curiosity, expand your knowledge, and try to investigate the world in new ways.
In Indian mythology[3]	When Lord Shiva asked his sons to circle the world thrice, Kartikeya didn't think of the situation from a different lens. Instead, he took his father's words literally and rushed to prove his innate capabilities of power.	Ganesha showed a growth mindset when Lord Shiva asked him to circle the world three times. He didn't worry about what people thought of his slow vehicle and he brought forth his creative thinking to win.[3]

'Everyone is a mixture of fixed and growth mindset'
— Carol Dweck, *The Atlantic*

* * *

Many people have elements of both mindsets. Sometimes you may find yourself in the growth mindset and at other times in a fixed mindset. If you find yourself in a fixed mindset, you should investigate what triggers this. In addition, you need to be aware of the problems that make you feel your abilities are fixed and that put you in a place of judgment instead of development. Then you can work consciously to improve yourself.

Building a growth mindset

You can build a growth mindset by following these self-directed exercises as adapted from the interview with Stefanie Faye, an award-winning neuroscience specialist and educator. This exercise entails four steps: goal setting, learning about neuroplasticity, celebrating mistakes, and exposing yourself to micro experiences, while highlighting micro progress. This will lower your fear of failure and increase your willingness to go out of your comfort zone and grow as a person.

1. Have an other-ish goal. In his landmark book *Give and Take*, Adam Grant uses the term otherish as a person who is a giver, you will also see this in our Giving Back chapter.

In terms of goals, these are the opposite of selfish goals, and a bit different than the selfless goals, other-ish goals are the ones where you have your own interests in mind, while having a high concern for others too. As defined in the chapter on grit, you must have a higher-order goal. This goal should be motivated by your personal benefits and by a desire to help the world around you.

For example, at the time of writing this book, my personal long-term goal is to become an expert in the field of sustainable finance and help India achieve its net-zero carbon emission targets by 2070. This goal is at the intersection of my interests and qualifications in finance, and my desire to do something for my country.

2. Talk about neuroplasticity. Learn it, understand it and reflect on how it plays a role in your life.

Over the past century, it has been proven that our brain is highly dynamic and goes through profound changes over our lifetime. So by any means, our brain is not fixed.

According to Moheb Constandi, the author of the book *Neuroplasticity*, 'The adult brain is not only capable of changing, but it does so continuously throughout life, in response to everything we do and every experience we have.'

Neuroplasticity is the study on how our brain's capacity grows and changes over time with repetitive practice. Our ability to get better at any skill and our brain to restructure is observed not only at a young age, but in people across all ages.

Understanding that your brain can grow, become stronger, and you can acquire skills at any age will boost your confidence and help you improve learning. With the understanding of the science of Neuroplasticity, you will deviate from the stories around what you can, and you can't do. And this will enable you to take action towards developing skills and becoming a better learner.

An essential starting point can be Carol Dweck's book *Mindset*, and various books and podcasts on neuroplasticity and growth mindset.

Take notes, share them with your friends and family, and reflect on them.

3. Celebrate mistakes.

If you are trying something new, you are bound to make mistakes. And this only reflects that you are making an effort to improve. Mistakes help you. In fact, your brain rewires and grows neurobiologically with every mistake you make.

Reflect on the following questions: What are a few of the recent mistakes you made? How did you react to them? What did you learn about yourself through those mistakes? Something you wouldn't have known otherwise if it weren't for the obstacle or the challenge?

List out your favourite mistakes or rejections and three things you learnt from them.

Whenever you feel that you have failed at something, or have been rejected, or the results have been less than expected, you must reflect. You should point out two or three things that you would do differently. And celebrate the mistake by sharing your learnings with your family or treating yourself to your favourite cuisine.

4.   Expose yourself to micro experiences and highlight micro progress.

To improve at your given skill or reach your other-ish goal, you must take every small opportunity to practise your skill and highlight every small improvement you make.

Micro experiences are small opportunities you can expose yourself to for achieving your goals. For example, if my goal is to become expert in sustainable finance, then I could seek to read new research articles, share my learnings in class, on social media, or write a blog.

Highlighting micro progress means that you must reflect and celebrate on the small improvements that you make. In this process, you must not compare yourself with others who are already better than you at that skill, but just appreciate and continue making the tiny progress that you make everyday. To illustrate, if you want to get better at public speaking, you should take every opportunity to speak in your classroom or place of work, and notice small improvements you make, instead of comparing how far you are from someone who is great at it.

In your journey of growth, remember to have a practical outlook too. Growth mindset has now become popular term. But must be aware that you and your efforts as an individual are only half the picture in becoming successful. The system and your environment also plays a big factor in your success and failure.

Knowing this, you must still strive to work hard and with a growth mindset because then, and only then, do you stand a chance of being successful.

* * *

I used to often wonder, even with efforts, how far can one really go? How can we identify our true potential? Can we perfectly evaluate our strengths and weaknesses and what great things we go on to do with that level of self-knowledge?

I was hoping to discover some mathematical formula to learn what levels of achievements we can achieve in our lifetimes.

But it turns out everyone's potential is unknown and unknowable. Studies suggest that we are not as good at assessing our potential as we might think.

We tend to think that we are worse than the average at, say, juggling, living past the age of 100, and our ability to cope with the loss of loved ones. But, on the other hand, we overestimate our abilities to believe that we are far luckier, more virtuous, better drivers or better investors than the people around us.[4]

In short, we think we are worse than others in difficult areas where success is rare. In contrast, we believe we are better than others in the more straightforward areas where we usually feel capable.

Basically, we do not always objectively assess our true strengths and weaknesses. As a result, our self-judgments are often misplaced. And this can have a direct impact on our life outcomes. For example, if we have incorrect beliefs and discount ourselves from achieving something significant, we might let our potential down.

However, it appears that a few extraordinary people were exceptionally great at assessing themselves. In his book *Extraordinary Minds*, Howard Gardner studied four world-changers—Mozart, Sigmund Freud, Virginia Woolf and Mahatma Gandhi. He mentioned that these extraordinary individuals had a unique talent to measure their own strengths and weaknesses.[5]

This skill of self-evaluation and the drive to become better are the cornerstones of the growth mindset and appear among growth-minded people.

An individual with a tendency towards self-development, under the right circumstances, is able to actualize their potential and become everything they are capable of becoming.[6]

Therefore, it is crucial to adopt a growth mindset to realize your possibilities.

Let us look at the story of one of my favourite young athletes who has adopted a growth mindset and is living up to his potential on the international stage.

* * *

Shubham Jaglan is a sixteen-year-old golf prodigy from India. In 2015, he became the junior world champion at the age of eleven.

Shubham had participated in the IMG Junior World Championship for the previous three years and had even come close to winning it. All his golfing idols including Tiger

Woods and Phil Mickelson had won this event as juniors. So it was his dream to win it.

'It was in July 2015 in San Diego, California. I was in the ten to eleven age group, and I was two shots behind this guy named Jeffrey Guan from New Zealand, with only two holes to go. So, for the first time, I had around fifty or sixty people following me.'

The stakes were high, and the pressure was rising. Shubham's competitors had teams of aids and coaches following them around, while he was with his father, who was carrying his old club set.

Shubham's competitors, trained from the age of three to play golf in their high-tech facilities, were taller, more muscular, and could hit further. It was intimidating, but the eleven-year-old Shubham had a better mindset.

His coach told him, 'You have made it to the final group because you deserved it. You played great. You have the capability. So, don't think you're inferior to anybody in any way. You're just about as good, if not better, than any of the people you're going to be playing with. You deserve to top the leaders' board.'

On the last hole, he had to make a thirty-foot putt—a thirty-foot shot straight into the hole to win. A small error could cost him the world championship.

'Very difficult. I still remember it like it was yesterday. Left to right, hundreds of people standing, holding their breath. I remember just walking up and down the green, and I knew what I had to do. I made the shot. The ball took forever to go in the hole, all in slow motion. But then, when it did, it was all a celebration. I guess that was probably the happiest moment ever,' says the now seventeen-year-old.

Shubham, a junior world champion at the age of eleven, stood tall. He was following in the footsteps of his idols such as Tiger Woods and Phil Mickelson—making his own legacy.

Shubham was born in Israna village, near Panipat, Haryana, in a milkman's family. His family have been wrestlers for generations. However, Shubham's grandfather wanted him to try something different. Luckily, a non-resident Indian, Mr Kapoor Singh, from New Jersey, US, started a golf academy in Israna. So, at six years of age, Shubham was sent to try a game that no one in the village had heard of before.

'It was completely out of the blue. Nobody in my family or my village knew about golf. We had never heard of it before the NRI set up the academy and all my friends started going there.'

Shubham fell in love with the game right away. He was a calm and content kid, not very aggressive. He was good at his studies. The pace of the game was comforting. He found the greenery of the golf course alluring.

'I just loved how slow it was. And I was pretty good at it initially as compared to the other kids in the group, so that was kind of the motivating factor initially for me.'

Unfortunately, the academy shut down within only two months. 'Initially, we did not have to pay much, but later on, all of us realized how expensive golf was.'

Before the owner of the academy left, he told Shubham's dad how talented he was. He urged him to let Shubham continue playing golf. He gave him some equipment, and a few contacts to get in touch with so he could keep playing.

Instead of giving up on the sport given its price tag, Shubham's parents supported him to pursue the game.

'Playing golf in a village in Haryana, where there were not many facilities to access; it was very hard. My parents were putting in a lot of hard work.'

For the next year, Shubham practised in the fields. He learnt from YouTube and Facebook videos. He won over ten sub-junior events in a row, which got him media attention. Eventually, he met Amit Luthra, the founder of the Golf Foundation. They supported him in moving to Delhi for better training facilities.

'That was a turning point in my career. Because if I had stayed in my village, I wouldn't have had access to proper facilities to take my game to the next level.'

It was tough for his family to make a life-changing decision based solely on the potential they saw. Although there wasn't any concrete proof that Shubham would become a good golfer, it was a risk worth taking for his parents. And their efforts inspired Shubham to perform better.

Once Shubham got into the academy in Delhi, he worked relentlessly hard on and off the course to become a better athlete. Unfortunately, he did not have a solid muscular build or any seemingly natural physical advantages, nor was he remarkably better than his fellow players at technique. Interestingly, to make him hone his personality, his coach, Ms Nonita Lall Qureshi, put down a lot of conditions, including speaking in English. Otherwise, his lessons would be cancelled.

'The condition was that if I didn't speak to her in English, my coach didn't give me a lesson. And so, I had to learn English just to learn golf.'

The road wasn't easy. The privileged families in the sport tried to pull him down.

'I was continuously supported by the club and the foundation. This naturally created some feelings of envy among other members and parents of the children I was playing against and beating badly.'

After Shubham secured a few championship victories, there were a lot of complaints against him at the club, and he also felt lonely in training as he didn't have a lot of other kids his age to practice or play with. Mr Amit Luthra, the foundation's head, sat Shubham and his father down in his office one day. He was honest with them. 'You're going to come across people who don't really like you. Nine would love to kill you when you win these tournaments out of the ten people who have come to congratulate you. So don't really let that get to your head.'

Shubham had to learn to be polite with everyone while silently working on his game.

Tragedy struck just before the 2018 IMG Junior World Championships. Shubham got an injury that could have stopped his career.

'At age thirteen, I had gone for the World Championships in the US. Just one week before the event, I had terrible back pain. And we realized I had a stress fracture in my lower back.'

He couldn't pick up a golf club for eight months. So he was entirely out of the game and out of the rankings.

But in those months, he felt that he could be the best and beat everyone in the circuit.

'Even though I wasn't able to play, I tried my best to do whatever I could to still improve myself. I focused on my studies and physiotherapy during this downtime. Slowly, I was able to work out harder and recover faster. I never felt that I would never play again. I always believed that this was just another hurdle I needed to cross. And I did.'

After recovering from his injury, Shubham went on to win multiple international tournaments, and he is now the youngest member of the Indian men's national team.

Presently, he is playing golf at the University of South Florida on a scholarship. He aspires to turn professional in the next couple of years, participate in the PGA tours and start beating the world's best golfers in the next four years.

In this journey, habits have made all the difference.

'Working out, meditating, studying and practising are things I need to get done every day. Then, every night, I'll sit down and plan out what I'll be doing tomorrow. It's called time blocking. I read thirty or forty pages every day of any book that I'm reading at the moment. Those are two keystone habits.'

Introspectively, he says that the winds will never blow your way. It is your responsibility to adjust your stroke so that the wind carries the ball where it should land. But if it does not, don't blame the wind.

He says, 'I think in the pursuit of mastering something is when you become happy. So just pick up anything you are interested in and work really hard at it, learning as much as you can about getting better. And I think that is the best part about anything, any field you choose when you work non-stop to get better at it, that's just the best feeling in the world.'

Incredible feats are achieved by people like Shubham, who have the self-belief to learn and grow, have faith in their dreams, go through the grind and trust themselves.

7

Networking

'It's not what you know; it's who you know that matters more now than ever'

—Anonymous

Pablo Picasso and Vincent van Gogh have a lot in common. Both are considered modern gods in the field of arts. Both had distinct and easily identifiable styles. Both were ahead of their times. Although it has been decades since their deaths, their art is sold for tens of millions of dollars.

There is one big difference, though. Van Gogh died penniless, while Picasso left behind an estate worth $750 million (Rs 5,667 crore).

It might have something to do with the fact that Vincent van Gogh was a loner. On the other hand, the charming Pablo Picasso was an active member of many social spheres.[1]

Imagine Vincent Van Gogh, who lived in a small town in the south of France, as one singular 'node' with a few connections. On the other hand, Pablo Picasso lived in his various houses in Spain. He travelled all over the world and was part of multiple social 'hubs' with his vast network cutting across social, geographical and industrial boundaries.

As Professor Berns, in his book *Iconoclast*, observes, '[. . .] van Gogh's brother was his primary connection to the art world, and this connection was not plugged into the money that could have turned van Gogh into a living success.' In contrast, Picasso had strong connections with other artists, politicians and high society people. So he was always only one person away from knowing someone of importance.[2] And that is the reason for the difference in the commercial success achieved by the legends in their lifetimes.

You must ensure that you end up more like a Picasso than a van Gogh.*

> *Your network is your net worth.*
>
> —*Tim Sanders, New York Times*
> *bestselling author, and former Yahoo! executive*

Networking is about attempting to build, maintain and use informal relationships with people who can help you in your career by giving you access to resources and helping you reach your maximum potential.[3]

Studies have identified that individuals who engage in networking behaviours have better and more satisfying careers.[4]

---

* There are of course other factors that contributed to Vincent van Gogh having died poor such as his mental disorder (which might have made him a loner in the first place). But sill, it is important to note that the size and quality of your network correlates to your net worth.

In anything you aspire to achieve, you will need a mentor, investor, partner, promoter, or just an inspiring friend at some point in your life. The ability to access this person of your need is determined by your networking.

We live in a volatile world, as the onset of the COVID-19 pandemic has made clear. In this world, we must secure ourselves with opportunities that might not be readily available to us at present but will arrive only through networking and engaging in meaningful relationships with others.

In India, your power lies in who you know. This means surrounding yourself with a small but strategic and robust network—a network that works with you and for you.

> *Skill is fine, and genius is splendid, but the right contacts are more valuable than either.*
>
> —*Sir Arthur Conan Doyle, British writer*
> *and the creator of Sherlock Holmes*

* * *

In early 2019, I was nineteen years old, living abroad for the first time to study in Singapore. I did not know anyone there. As an ambitious young business student, I wanted to secure the best internship possible for my freshman summer. So I applied online to a dozen companies such as HP, UBS, Facebook, Google, Intel and several others. But unfortunately, I was rejected by all of them.

My college dean, Professor Golo, was pleased by the record-shattering thirty rejections I had collected in such a short time. This probably made me the most rejected freshman in the history of the college. Perhaps out of pity, Professor

Golo scribbled down three organizations' names on a Post-it note. 'Just a couple of companies that are creating value and impact in Singapore,' he said. 'You might want to check them out.'

One of them was Ashoka: Innovators for the Public, which is the world's fifth most impactful social good organization.[5] My interest in the non-profit world aligned with Ashoka. I had nothing to lose. So off I went to give it my best shot.

The following day, eager to secure a paid internship in Singapore, I decided to drop in at the offices of Ashoka and try to meet someone. I took a bus to Singapore's Central Business District. It was early in the morning, and I could see well-dressed professionals rushing in and out of the metro. A cup of coffee in one hand and laptop bag in the other, speaking with their bosses through their headsets, they really made me feel out of place.

I had a copy of my CV, reference letter and document that showed my work eligibility in Singapore. I boldly walked into the office. On a sofa right next to the door sat a lady checking her emails.

I knocked on the door to get her attention, and said, 'Hi, my name is Manthan, I am a freshman at college, and I would like to intern here. May I speak with Ms Sumitra Pasupathi, please?'

I knew about Sumitra because my professor had given me a brief about her: Cambridge University alumnus, twenty years of experience across continents and industries, founder of her own non-profit, and the country director of Ashoka.

A little surprised, she said, 'Yes, that's me. How can I help you?'

The lady I spoke to turned out to be the director herself. Everyone was a little surprised to see a young brown kid randomly walking in and demanding an internship from the director.

For the next ten minutes, she patiently heard me out as I told her my story, about my passion for social entrepreneurship, and of my desire to work for her at Ashoka.

She connected me to the human resources department right away. After three rounds of interviews, they offered me a paid internship. This turned out to be the best internship of my life. I helped manage Bosche's ChangemakerXchange (CXC) 2019 programme, which was a highly selective 5-day summit for changemakers, coordinating with teams in three countries and evaluating 2000 applicants for the CXC programme. I helped write a grant for Google.org. I got the opportunity to attend multiple corporate events in the city and meet the founders of many great companies from across Asia.

Now a close mentor to me, Sumitra confessed that she was impressed by my boldness in walking through the door and demanding an internship. And that attempt to make a connection helped me immensely in my career.

In this process, I learnt that you do not have to go to a fancy college, come from an established and connected family, or be rich to get opportunities and access to a world-class network.

More importantly, networking is not blandly reaching out to people. It is more about having the audacity to let people know you can add value to them. It is about authentic relationship-building.

Networking is about taking the few extra steps that anybody can take, but so few do.

The Ashoka internship opened me to a brilliant global network of changemakers. Many of whom offered to help and support during this book writing process. One of the former Ashoka consultants introduced me to a young changemaker who overcame many odds to put his foot in the door, expose himself to opportunities and build a great personal network along the way.

* * *

In 2020, I spoke with someone on the phone who was making waves way beyond his age. At nineteen, Akash Singh employed convicts at Kasna jail (G.B Nagar District Jail) to create art pieces and idols out of temple waste. He is the founder and CEO of Energinee Innovations, a Noida-based social impact start-up.

At Energinee, they collect temple waste and train jail inmates to make eco-friendly products out of it.

Akash Singh comes from a small town in western Uttar Pradesh called Khanpur, which is near Jewar, Greater Noida. Akash has always been an innovator and an entrepreneur.

About his family background, he jokes, 'Traditionally, Jats are either soldiers or farmers. So people laugh when I say I am an unlikely Jat trying to use my brains.'

Akash was educated in the town of Jewar, and he comes from a family of farmers.

'Until ninth standard, I had no clue what to do in life nor were my grades supportive of doing anything worthwhile,' he laughs.

When he was in the ninth standard, he designed a wind-harnessing machine that could be installed on buses and trains to generate electricity. In 2014, he was elated to learn that he was among the top twenty students selected for the Central

Board of Secondary Education (CBSE) national-level science exhibition. This inspired him to continue down the innovation path, and the uniqueness of innovation got him featured on various newspaper and TV channels.

'For the first time in my life, I realized I can be praised too!' he chuckles.

This inspired him to move to a bigger city, so he enrolled in a civil engineering course in Gurugram, Haryana. When he moved to the city as a sixteen-year-old, he had no friends or networks.

Nonetheless, he continued working on his wind-harnessing project. In 2016, at the India International Trade Fair, he met a scientist who advised him to go to the Prime Minister's Office (PMO) to talk about his project, and request its large-scale implementation in India. He relentlessly wrote letters, sent project details to the PMO and uploaded his ideas on the relevant website portals every week for four months. Finally, the PMO sent him a letter of appreciation and connected him to the Ministry of Railways. While their letter helped him immensely, his project proposal was pushed around from one office to another for a whole year.

Akash was frustrated by the time it took to get anything done in the ministries. So, for peace of mind and out of habit, he would go to the temple every week. There, he noticed how flowers, fruits, milk and incense sticks were being discarded everywhere around the temple. It was a mess. The pollution caused by this waste in the nearby lake had killed all its tortoises. So he chose to do something about it.

Over the next three months, he used his civil engineering know-how to make a binding material from a mixture of incense and coconut ash, which was much stronger than cement. He had the idea to turn this ash into other products and sell those in the market.

He reached out to dozens of people in the hope of securing financial grants and guidance. In a city where he knew no one, it took many attempts to build and use his contacts to create opportunities for himself. It involved a lot of hard work and struggle. He sometimes did not have the money to buy dinner, or had to sleep in street-side hamlets, under the open sky.

The same day I visited Ashoka's office in Singapore for an internship, I had also gatecrashed the International Table Tennis Federation, Amazon Web Services and Shopify offices in Singapore. I wanted to hand in my CV personally to their recruiters. I hoped this would increase my chances. However, in most places, a receptionist would ask me to wait, then after about thirty minutes, give me a business card of someone from HR. In a few instances, I wasn't even allowed inside the office; they asked me to go home and apply through the company website. None of these cold calls worked.

It was the same with Akash; he had to continue being bold in his outreach in the face of rejection.

Luckily, things clicked for Akash and he got tremendous support from the Atal Incubation Centre to develop his idea. There he quickly defined his problem statement, created a solution, made a business validation proposal and worked towards the scalability of the business.

One evening, the centre director called him to her office and said, 'Akash, you have to go to jail.' Of course, he was a little shocked to hear this.

They wanted to run a pilot project where they would train twenty-four inmates over fifteen days to make art pieces out of temple waste, and see if the idea takes off. If not, they would have had to scrap the plan.

With twenty-four inmates already registered for the fifteen-day pilot project, he started working with them to make idols from temple waste. Within two weeks, eighteen of them got bail and were out of his pilot programme. Akash and his team thought all the time, money and resources they had invested in training the inmates over the past two weeks had gone to vain as most of his inmates left the programme. Surprisingly, when he thought his efforts had failed, on the sixteenth day, he got applications from 250 inmates. Interestingly, the inmates thought the temple waste was magical and would help them get bail sooner. This was how Akash's temple-jail rehabilitation programme got started.

By the time he was twenty-one, Akash was managing a team of twenty-six people. He made sure every person felt like a family member and that their ideas were heard and implemented. This eventually brought him a lot of success.

Failure is feedback. And feedback is the breakfast of champions.
—A fortune cookie

Horizontal and vertical networking[6]

I have noticed that to be successful at networking, one does not have to connect with anyone and everyone. Instead, one must understand the concept of vertical and horizontal networking, and they must make deliberate attempts to communicate with a few but essential people.

A horizontal network basically means your friends are all from the same bracket as you. So, for example, imagine

Vincent van Gogh hanging out with a few artists in the south of France.

If you are an engineering student, your circle of friends would be a set of engineers or, at most, a few of your childhood friends pursuing different fields. Most of your friends might be from the same background in terms of age, experience, geography and family as you. This means you have a horizontal network.

Horizontal networks are excellent for social outings and having fun. But they rarely help with getting ahead in life or open doors to unforeseen opportunities.

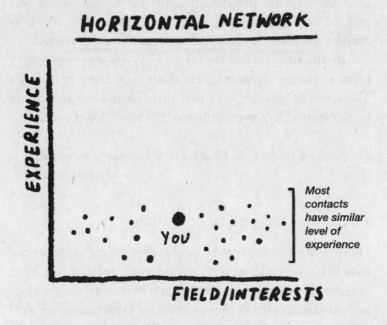

HORIZONTAL NETWORK

EXPERIENCE

YOU

Most contacts have similar level of experience

FIELD/INTERESTS

Now imagine Pablo Picasso hanging out with fellow painters, sculptors and playwrights in Paris and Barcelona, and politicians, academics, businessmen and industrialists in

VERTICAL NETWORK

Most contacts have more experience than you

Moscow and New York. In vertical networks, the connections are made at different stages in one's career and experience. They should preferably be higher than you.

* * *

In August 2015, Sheryl Sandberg, COO of Facebook, wrote about a nineteen-year-old software developer who had created an app that helped families detect early-stage developmental disorders in their children. Shortly after that post, this teenager raised over $1,07,000 (Rs 75 lakh) at a $1 million (Rs. 7.4 crore) valuation for his app. As soon as he got the cheque, he dropped out of college and became one of the leading tech experts in India.

The name of this founder is Harsh Songra. He is the founder of My Child App, head of technology at Qyuki Digital Media and a Forbes 30 Under 30 entrepreneur.

He was born with a neurological disorder called dyspraxia, which affects coordination and movement. But he was not diagnosed with it until he was nine years old.

Harsh's life is the improbable story of a tech-developer with no formal degree in engineering. His school teachers labelled him a dim student, who then displayed exceptional resourcefulness to impact tens of thousands of lives through his work at a very young age.

'I attribute all my success to my mentors and supporters. I am blessed to call Mr Luis Miranda, co-founder of HDFC bank, Devraj Sanyal, CEO and MD of Universal Music Group, among many industry experts as my mentors. I met them only because of networking.'

Today, if Harsh has a problem, he is confident that some influential person will give him solutions and help him get the work done.

'If I have an issue with the bank, government officials, or just start-up barriers, I will reach out to people who will easily solve it. These are not the people my dad introduced me to or I met through a family extension. These are the people who I made friends with.'

At fifteen years of age, instead of sending Facebook friend requests to girls from his school, he sent them to investors and CEOs. He made a Microsoft Excel sheet of all the people he wanted to connect with. He had a daily target of emailing fifty people. Although for every 100 people he reached out to only one person would reply, he got an opportunity to speak with industry legends.

'That was the best investment of my time I made,' he says.

One of the responses he got was from Guy Kawasaki, original chief evangelist at Apple in the 1990s, author of thirteen bestselling books, chief evangelist at Canva, and former special advisor to the CEO at Google for Motorola.

'A lot of industrialists, businessmen and CEOs replied to my email. I was surprised, how could this guy reply to me? This inspired me to send more emails.'

His emails were short. They were nothing special in terms of vocabulary and sentence structure. They were the standard emails a nineteen-year-old would write. But his perseverance was inspiring.

'I did the groundwork of finding and sending connection requests to people such as the CEOs, directors and founders of banks, venture capital firms, etc., when I was sixteen-seventeen. And this is why my life is floating instead of struggling right now.'

Harsh was born and raised in Bhopal, Madya Pradesh. He attended his first conference, organized by Nokia for Android App developers on its upcoming Nokia X platform, in Indore when he was in high school. There he met fellow attendees and shared his app ideas. Luckily, he was introduced to Nishant Kavi, head evangelist for Nokia, who encouraged his concept and boosted his morale.

As a result, he decided to enter all the networking events and conferences he possibly could. At every event he went to, he would make sure to meet everyone, shake hands and say, 'Hi, I am Harsh Songra. I am sixteen years old, and I run three start-ups. Would you speak to me, please?'

When I asked him where he got his confidence to approach people, he answered, 'I am from Bhopal. They are

from some metro city. Neither do they know me, nor do I
know them. Therefore, it became straightforward for me to
strike up conversations with anyone I wanted.'

When he was nineteen, he did not have money for servers.
One day he saw an ad on Facebook for a programme called
FBStart that offered to give $25,000 worth of credits for
servers. This programme aimed to help mobile app developers
with demonstrated expertise, and potential to disrupt their
focus industry to build and grow their apps. Harsh applied for
the FBStart programme and luckily got in.

After being part of the Facebook start-up programme, he
wanted to raise money for his app idea that would help families
detect early-stage developmental disorders in their children.
So he went to several app developer and tech conferences,
introduced himself to everyone and pitched his idea.

Interestingly, when he asked for $25,000 (Rs 18 lakh) or
$50,000 (Rs 36 lakh), no one said yes. However, when he asked
for $1,00,000 (Rs 75 lakh), many people said yes looking at this
young man's vision to scale his app and solve a big problem.

At one of these events, he was introduced to the founder
of 500 Startups, Dave McClure, who signed him a cheque for
$25,000 too.

He managed to raise over $1,07,000 (Rs 75 lakh) for 10
per cent equity of his start-up when he was just nineteen.
Once he had this amount in his bank, he dropped out of
college. After all, he wanted to run his own thing and did not
want a job because he wanted nothing to do with paper and
pen. Unless it was for signing cheques.

'The reason I was able to raise so much money was that
I was not afraid to go out and connect with people. If I went
to a conference where a thousand people attended, my goal

used to be that every one of the thousand people should know Harsh Songra attended the event.'

Initially, Harsh used to reach out to people to simply make friends and share good conversation.

'I just wanted to know people and talk to them. I would say, "You are an interesting person. I think I could add some value to your life, and you could definitely add a lot to my life. So can we have a chat?"'

In the journey of creating a world-class network, Harsh says we are all scared and nervous about what people will think if we ask them to connect. But it turns out most people are friendly. Moreover, most people will try to see the best in you and encourage your boldness.

Getting the first thirty connections is the most important. After that, you will enjoy the process of connecting.

'In networking, if you know the properties that define you, it is perfect for getting someone's attention,' he says.

Harsh's network includes people from the banking, film, journalism, non-profit, education, government, venture capital, music, tech and many more industries spread worldwide.

* * *

Three golden questions: How can I help you?
What ideas do you have for me?
Who else do you know that I should talk to?
—*Judy Robinett, Author of*
How to Be a Power Connector

No matter how successful, everyone needs help in some way. For instance, the president of a bank may need a good table tennis coach for his son, or a venture capital fund manager may be on your friend's podcast or may come to speak with students at your college. Seeking to add value first is a prominent feature of all power connector relationships. It's 'the law of reciprocity': when you give your time, effort and connections to help someone else, they naturally want to reciprocate.

'Think about how you can support the work of others and spread their messages,' says *Forbes* blogger Kathy Caprino. 'When you have the approach to serve others, instead of thanking me, myself and I, support is returned to you a hundredfold.'[7]

Initiating and making a connection in the first place is essential. But maintaining contact is another ball game. If you want to create a long-term connection, you need to connect with a person's core beliefs. You need to connect with something that makes the person tick and continue adding value to them in the long term.

After speaking with Jared Kleinert, USA Today's 'Most Connected Millennial', and reading various resources on networking, it appears that there is an art to adding value over to others in the long term.[8] Consider the following points for multiplying your network and building authentic relationships:

1. Add value appropriately.

You need to ensure that the value you provide is suited to the recipients. What goals are they pursuing? Which of the four critical resources, namely, opportunities, information, money and connections, are the most important for them to reach their goals?

2.   Solve their problems.

Everyone has problems of some kind, and it's often difficult to see a potential solution or access the resources you need. However, if you can identify the problem and provide a solution—by sharing relevant information, a critical introduction, a piece of strategy, a referral, a mentor, or other support—you will deepen the relationship quickly. Even though many people don't need you to solve their problems, they appreciate the gesture.

3.   Practice five-minute favours.

In his book *Give and Take: A Revolutionary Approach to Success*, Adam Grant describes how Silicon Valley networker Adam Rifkin does what he calls 'five-minute favours', which are any favour that takes less than five minutes. These small favours often make the most significant difference.

Things such as sending an email, or a message with an article ('I saw this article and thought it might be useful to you'); calling to say, 'I just met this person, and I think it would be worthwhile for the two of you to connect', lets people know you have them in mind. Dropping an encouraging five-star review of their book or podcast; or sharing their posts with your network with a personalized insight showcases that you care about their work. A simple encouragement can also go a long way.

4.   Always do what you say you will.

In today's world, talk is cheap. Everyone makes fake promises and over-commits. To stand out and to create trust, if you say you will do something, do it, and do it by the time you say you will. If you say you will make an introduction or that you'll let them in on an opportunity, or even just that you'll follow up by a particular time, keep your word.

5.   Add value multiple times before you make any request.

Warren Buffet once said, 'Trust takes years to build, seconds to break, and forever to repair.' Adding value, keeping your word, thinking about the needs of others and doing the little things are all ways you build trust in relationships. But if you make a request before you have a healthy trust established, all the value you've added can be discounted in a second. By adding value multiple times before you ask anything for yourself, you are setting yourself as a 'giver' in the recipients' eyes. When they think of you, they'll think of a valued resource, someone who is helpful, caring, a problem solver, attentive to their needs and willing to go the extra mile.

The value given with an expectation that you will get something in return is a transaction, not a relationship.

'The ability to get things done with collaborative networks is the next evolution in human productivity.'
—*Michael Leavitt and Rich McKeown,*
Finding Allies, Building Alliances

I started the Planet Impact podcast during my internship at Ashoka in Singapore when I was nineteen. It is a show about social entrepreneurship and change-making. I would reach out to dozens of accomplished Forbes 30 Under 30 awardees and Ashoka Fellows via email and ask if there was anything I could do for them, and if they had time, could they come to share their story with our listeners. It led me to great things.

One of the first few episodes was with Ms Kiran Bir Sethi, founder of Design for Change and Riverside School.

After the podcast recording, I asked her, 'Is there any way I can help you in your current projects?'

She asked in return, 'Where are you headed next for your studies?'

'Madrid,' I said.

'Great, we are organizing an event in Vatican City shortly; you can help our Madrid office in the preparations!' she said happily.

And just like that, I got myself an internship in Spain to go along with my exchange semester programme from September to December 2020.

I worked as an intern for Design for Change. Incidentally, they organized the world's most prominent design thinking summit—the I CAN Children's Global Summit.

I flew to Rome, Italy, to participate in the summit. Four thousand kids from sixty countries came there to present their ideas and stories. We met Pope Francis in a private setting. I also met many people from different industries who have helped me with my other projects.

None of this would have happened if it weren't for my first internship in Singapore. I was bold and naïve to knock on the door and ask for an internship. With nothing to lose, I went out and asked for what I felt was right.

Opportunity does not come to you. Instead, you must create it for yourself by putting your foot in the door. And creating a resilient network helps you in doing so.

You can only outwork and outsmart others for a while. If you really want to go far, you must out-collaborate others. Your network will always give you more opportunities than your individual talent and potential alone.

Building a solid network doesn't happen overnight. In 2011, Adam Rifkin became Fortune's Best Networker. He had more LinkedIn connections to 640 of the world's most influential people on *Fortune* magazine's list than anyone else in the world.[9]

'My network developed little by little," he tells the author Adam Grant in his book *Give and Take,* 'a minimal everyday kindness through small gestures, and acts of benevolence over a course of years with a desire to make lives better for the people I am connected to helped me reach here today.'

8

Leadership

'Leadership is accepting responsibility for enabling others
to achieve a shared purpose under conditions of uncertainty'
—Marshall Ganz, senior lecturer in
leadership, Harvard University

On a cold August morning in 2018, a fifteen-year-old Swedish girl decided to skip school. She chose to sit calmly outside the Swedish parliament with a wooden board that read 'School Strike for Climate'. Throughout the school hours of 8.30 a.m. to 3 p.m., she sat alone, protesting for the future of our planet.

The next day one person joined her in the protest. Then a few more joined. Then came hundreds. Then came thousands.

When she was eleven years old, she saw a video about the impact of climate change and extreme weather in her elementary school. This left her heartbroken. While her friends forgot about the graphic visuals of climate change disasters, she could not get over them.

Her name is Greta Thunberg. Today, as an eighteen-year-old, she speaks at the most prominent global forums such as the United Nations General Assembly and demands that global leaders take immediate action to combat climate change.

Greta suffers from Asperger's syndrome, which affects her ability to interact and communicate with others. Yet, she is considered their leader by thousands around the world. Greta was nominated for the Nobel Prize; she is the youngest recipient of TIME Person of the Year and has inspired many aspiring leaders worldwide.

Authentic leadership is meritocratic, and I wanted to learn what it takes to be a great leader.

I was born and raised in the small town of Ahmednagar in Maharashtra, India. When I was about six years old, I was fascinated by the game of table tennis. I quickly learnt the basics, and within a year, became the town's under-ten and under-twelve champion. At the age of ten, I requested my father to move me to Pune, Ahmednagar's nearest metropolitan city, so I could pursue my passion with the proper facilities. Away from my friends and extended family, I was home-schooled for the next three years as I focused on reaching my goal to play for my country.

I trained rigorously for seven hours a day, six days a week, for nearly six years. Despite lacking my counterparts' professional guidance and infrastructure, I pushed past the challenges to become the under-seventeen School Games Federation of India national champion twice when I was fifteen.

I went on to win two bronze medals for India at the Pacific School Games held in Adelaide, Australia, in 2015.

A lack of sporting infrastructure, financial resources and the opportunity cost were barriers to reaching my potential as an international athlete. However, this experience instilled in me a strong drive to make things better for the aspirational youth in my country. I wanted to explore innovative ways to help society. I chose to discontinue table tennis competitively to find a better way to do something for my country.

After my sporting journey, I explored various career avenues and searched for inspiration on becoming a successful young adult. At seventeen, I went on a month-long solo backpacking trip across India. I volunteered at various NGOs in my hometown. After discovering the benefits of social work and volunteering in changing one's perspective, I decided to start a non-profit with a group of friends that connected students to NGOs in our city.

As a teenage founder of the non-profit, I used to think that efficient leadership meant being a strict authoritarian and micromanaging people, as commonly observed in sports. Our non-profit grew to facilitate over 300 volunteers and partner with fifty non-profits around our city. We raised handsome amounts of money for different causes and ran weekly city cleaning drives. However, after a fallout with my fellow team members, I was removed from my own non-profit. As a result, I learnt how wrong I was. Being strict might get work done in the short run, but it was certainly not sustainable, effective or healthy in the long term.

* * *

In May 2019, I got an internship at the global NGO Ashoka: Innovators for the Public in Singapore. I was assigned to evaluate thousands of young leaders changing the world. This experience taught me about the making of young leaders.

I was tasked to assess over two thousand applications for the Ashoka ChangemakerXChange Thailand and Singapore 2019 programme, a five-day all-expenses paid experience for the world's top young social innovators and corporate intrapraneurs. This programme aims to develop a global community of young changemakers who can connect and develop cross-border collaborations. This highly selective programme accepts only a handful of eighteen- to thirty-five-year-old leaders from the social entrepreneurship space globally. Nearly 70 per cent of all applications came from India and neighbouring countries, and it was eye-opening to see the trends in what made these young leaders successful.

While interviewing over fifty shortlisted candidates, I noted that most leaders were not necessarily highly privileged. For example, they often came from rural or suburban areas in their countries. Moreover, they did not always go to elite schools or have an affluent network of supporters. They didn't have extraordinary technical skills.

Instead, they had early childhood experiences that inspired them to start their initiatives. The most successful young leaders told a great story. They were the people who built their initiatives from scratch with limited resources and enabled their peers to lead. Their work left a lasting impact on tens of thousands of people in their home country. I observed the following three key trends that set the selected candidates apart from the rest. And this also aligns with a fascinating study of social movements by the Harvard University professor Marshall Ganz titled *Leading Change: Leadership, Organization, and Social Movements*:[1]

Taking the Initiative

Telling a Story

Leading Strategically

Taking the initiative

'If you want to do something of significance, put yourself in a position to fail.'

—*Anonymous*

Leadership starts when you are inspired to take the first step. True leaders identify challenges, imagine a better way ahead, and act. If you are reading this book, it indicates that you have the drive to create change. In all the interviews and surveys I conducted for this book, I noticed tremendous potential in each of us. But being a self-starter sets leaders apart from their followers.

Taking the initiative means finding a challenge and taking a stance in solving it. In addition, it requires one to be confident and overcome one's fears, as discussed in the next chapter.

Mastering initiatives includes knowing that you can improve most situations, complaining less and not waiting for all things to be correct.

All of my small initiatives, such as writing this book, the *Planet Impact* podcast, another sustainable finance non-profit, or the business clubs at my college, among other projects, did not cost me much money or resources to start. Nevertheless, people encouraged and supported me to work on these initiatives despite some early resistance. Eventually, we built a strong community together.

Let me tell you a story of two teenage sisters who made the island of Bali ban single-use plastic bags, styrofoam and straws through their initiative Bye Bye Plastic Bags.

* * *

In 2013, if you walked around the island of Bali, you would find its golden beaches polluted with plastic waste. So two sisters, Melati and Isabel Wijsen, who were only twelve and ten years old, decided to change that.

They started Bye Bye Plastic Bags, a campaign to ban single-use plastic in their home island of Bali. At that time, Bali was generating enough plastic every day to cover a fourteen-storey building. Of this, 95 per cent was thrown away after a single use.

Bye Bye Plastic Bags was a movement to mobilize young people in Bali to create awareness and force the authorities to act.

'I think back about it seven years ago, at the age of twelve. I just [. . .] knew I could not be a bystander. Plastic pollution was everywhere, I mean, it was on the beaches, the rivers, the rice fields. So it was no rocket science to say, "What can we do?" So, you know, it was as simple as that, [we had] no business plan, no strategy, [we] just went straight into it had no idea what we were entering.'

Taking the initiative did not mean Melati and Isabel had a well figured out plan. They did not even have a clear goal to ban single-use plastic. They simply started by doing beach clean-ups, awareness drives and connecting with a lot of different people.

Initially, they started collecting signatures and running a petition to gain public buy-in for their cause. This quickly grew to 6000 signatures in twenty-four hours and over 1,00,000 signatures by the end of their campaign.

Despite the growing support from the locals and tourists alike, the government officials didn't heed the girls for over eighteen months. Then, inspired by one of their trips to India to speak at INK talks, one of India's foremost platforms for the exchange of cutting-edge ideas and inspiring stories, they decided to go on a hunger strike as a way to catch the attention of those in power.

Finally, in December 2018, the governor of Bali, Wayan Koster, announced a ban on single-use plastic, straws and styrofoam items such as cups and food containers.[2]

One thing I learnt from Melati's example was that she turned a complex systemic problem into a simple idea that everyone could follow. Her idea was Bye Bye Plastic Bags. The name of the movement tells you everything you need to know. She did specific things to achieve her goal: campaigns, clean-up drives, petitions, education, advocacy and even a hunger strike.

I spoke with Melati in early 2020 on my podcast. The lockdown in India had just started, and I had arrived to my hometown in Ahmednagar from my semester in Dubai.

When I spoke with her, she was only nineteen. Yet, she was already highly accomplished: a speaker at the United Nations and TED conferences, a TIME most influential teen and one of the youngest Forbes 30 Under 30.

In the interview, Melati spoke passionately about her new initiative: Youthopia. It is a non-profit that empowers youth by providing them with the tools to become changemakers.

Very quickly, she gave us a recipe to change the world. 'Firstly,' she said, 'understand how and where your role is. Then, where can you bring in a unique idea? Because if you can think differently and outside the box, that will get you places; it turns heads, and it gets you meetings with politicians and decision-makers.

'The second thing is, you cannot do it alone. You need to build a like-minded team around you.'

Leadership is a team sport. Once you take the initiative, you need to tell a great story and build strong relations with the people around you.

Telling your story

People are the actual fabric of any endeavour, and how tightly they are woven makes all the difference.

Influencing people starts with a powerful story. Look at any great leaders, social movements, big institutions, and even religion. You will find a strong narrative in the form of their mission and vision statements at their core.

Stories are compelling. They help you translate your values and your potential solutions into action.

One of my favourite social changemakers, and an internationally recognized advocate of the rights of the indigenous people was a shining embodiment of this leadership trait.

* * *

Archana Soreng is a twenty-five-year-old climate activist from India, and the only Indian to be named by UN Secretary-General Antonio Guterres to his youth advisory group on climate change. She recently participated in the UN Climate Change Conference COP 26 held at Scotland, UK, as an indigenous youth, She belongs to the Khadia Tribe and hails from the Sundergarh District of Odisha.

Archana works on documentation, preservation and promotion of the traditional knowledge and practices of indigenous communities. She pursued her master's in regulatory governance from Tata Institute of Social Sciences (TISS) Mumbai and there she was the president of the TISS Students Union.

She says, 'I believe that small steps can make a big difference and I experienced it in my own life.'

Growing up, Archana's mother motivated her to participate in all the competitions there were, such as singing, dancing, elocution, and so forth. This imbibed a spirit in her that participation was more important than winning or losing. And that increased her self-confidence.

She says, 'I can address many public gatherings especially young people and policymakers at the national and global level, it is because of my childhood foundations.'

A school essay competition she participated in, sparked her curiosity about her roots and the Khadia tribe. 'Nature is a source of life and identity' she wrote. She was inspired to learn the stories of her ancestors, who have been protecting the forests and nature for centuries. Through this process, she understood the depth of her tribe's relationship with the environment.

Archana's grandfather was a pioneer of forest protection in her village. He strongly believed that it is crucial to have a sustainable relationship with nature. Both her parents were active in the tribal movement and implementing Panchayati raj (a council of five members—a system of self-governance in rural India).

Her parents told her, 'If you want to lead a change that truly makes a difference in the society, then you must enter in policy making.' These words stayed with her and guided her throughout her journey. To create a change by advocating for the rights of indigenous people, she aligned all her decisions through childhood to enter governance and policymaking. She pursued humanities from Carmel School, Rourkela, and went to Patna Women's College run by the Apostolic Carmel sisters to pursue a bachelor's degree in political science.

During her undergraduate degree, she was also elected as the National Convener of Tribal Commission, AICUF (All India Catholic University Federation). In her role, she organized and participated in summer camps where they trained students on the Forest Rights Act, Panchayat Extension to Scheduled Areas (PESA) Act, and the indigenous ways of forest and land conservation. And that is where everything changed for her.

In 2015, she went to Chhattisgarh for a national camp and stayed with the communities for around twenty-four hours. She witnessed that the communities there lived a very environment-friendly life, and ate from plates that were made from leaves. These plates were not thrown out but fed to cattle. There was no concept of waste. The people there were hospitable and generous. But despite that, the community faced serious problems of displacement, mining, human trafficking, illiteracy, atrocities against women because of land grabbing, etc. She also realized that these practices and the situation were similar to her region as well. And that was when her parents' teachings came ringing back. She had to rise to a position of influence at the policy-level decision-making to create constructive change on the ground. Thereafter, she chose to pursue a masters degree in regulatory governance from Tata Institute of Social Sciences, Mumbai.

'We must go back to our elders and learn from them. The untimely death of my father in 2017, made me realize that the elder generation will not be with us for long. It is important for us to learn from their experience in protecting nature, forests, rivers and entire biodiversity.'

She spent hundreds of hours on the ground in the tribal communities trying to document and preserve traditional knowledge and promote it at the state and national level. She was inspired to bring indigenous practices under global limelight, and she went on to participate in various United Nations events such as the Global Youth Caucus at UNCCD COP 14 New Delhi and 66th Session of CESCR on Land and ICESCR at Geneva Head Quarters of UN Office, Switzerland. She has also addressed among some of the key world leaders ranging from HRH Prince Charles, Prince of Wales, the prime minister of UK Mr Boris Johnson.

Later in July 2020, she was selected as one of the seven members and the only Indian to be a part of the UN Secretary General's Youth advisory group on Climate Change

She vividly remembers the first meeting with the UN Secretary-General where she engaged with the global leaders in an honest open dialogue.

In the first meeting, the deputy general told her, 'Never forget your roots, and keep working for your people.'

She reflected deeply on the struggles of her ancestors and was inspired to continue advocating for rights of indigenous communities. She shares the three guiding principles on leadership that has helped her in her professional journey and continues to do so is, 'Embrace your identity, be proud of your roots, and speak up.'

After interacting with young leaders from across the regions, she realized that adequate representation is very important in policymaking spaces and often there were no indigenous representatives apart from her. While she was grateful for the opportunity, she wanted to increase indigenous representation at the top level.

In championing her rights at the global stage, she says, 'In a leadership position, it's important how you articulate your perspectives in a firm yet a polite way to the administration.'

Archana's leadership journey started from being monitor in the class, and taking small responsibilities in the school and hostel, then from being a pupil leader in high school to becoming the president of the students union of TISS during her post-graduate studies.

Archana's leadership journey truly involved taking many small steps, that are now making a big difference to her community. From her experiences, she advices aspiring young leaders, by saying, 'It is important to contextualize the issues to grassroots and speak up. Once you work on the ground, you can tell your story with conviction. And that will inspire important stakeholders to help and support you. Once you stand for a cause, share your story, people will start aligning with you, and you will build meaningful relationships.'

Once you have a story to tell, you must start reaching out to people with similar thought processes, connect with stakeholders who can make good interventions, and show them what is the need of the hour.

As you navigate your own story, writing a few hundred words to reflect on your journey so far through the following exercise will be helpful. Make sure you reflect deeply on the situation or a challenge you faced, the choices you made, the tasks you performed, the actions you took and the outcomes of your activities.

Present a narrative or a story from your professional, academic or personal life that has one distinct example of a time when:

- You used your intellect to identify an opportunity or a problem and crafted a solution.
- You used your communication and interpersonal skills to inspire a team effort to implement a solution.
- You pushed through obstacles and made a positive change in your community.

Talk about the example in detail, highlight how you grew as a person, focus on how you saw yourself, your surroundings and the future you wanted to create.

---

* * *

Leading strategically

In November 2019, I was fortunate to volunteer at the Design for Change I CAN Children's Global Summit, held in Vatican City, Rome, and attended by 4000 children from seventy countries. There we met His Holiness Pope Francis in a private setting.

Within the same week, my friends and I joined over 5,00,000 others to protest on the streets of Madrid ahead of the United Nations Climate Change Conference COP25 in support of Greta Thunberg's Fridays for Future and Climate Strike.[3]

In early 2020, I participated in Al Gore's Climate Reality Leadership Corp programme with thousands of individuals with micro-movements to combat climate change. Former Vice President Gore's efforts to counteract climate change won him the Nobel Peace Prize in 2007.

When I looked closely at these three movements that I participated in, I realized that they were characterized by strategies devised to gain maximum impact.

Strategies are essential because we all have limited resources. Therefore, one needs to ensure that all resources are mobilized most efficiently to achieve the preferred outcomes.

As a leader, you must clearly define the desired outcomes, make things happen on time, keep people accountable and evaluate your results constantly. These things must be thought about and learnt through experience.

I was fortunate to interview one of the highly influential young leaders, who started an international movement, that went on to become the world's largest offline social network.

This initiative he started at age nineteen, eventually grew into a movement comprizing 28,000 young organizers across thirty-five countries, 220 cities in India and 7,500 schools globally within ten years.

Rishabh Shah, the founder of India's International Movement to Unite Nations (IIMUN), created quite a storm by putting the idea of India on a world map. Rishabh's IIMUN replicates the workings of the Indian parliament and multilateral organizations for school students to engage in debates on international relations and global politics.

Born in 1991, Rishabh was brought up in South Bombay. He had a slightly more privileged childhood, and he grew up with a lot of western influence.

In seventh grade, Rishabh was caught dozing off in one of the history classes on the second world war, and the subsequent creation of the United Nations. To turn him around, the teacher asked Rishabh to represent the school in one of the upcoming Model United Nations (MUN) competitions. MUNs are an academic simulation of the United Nations where students act as delegates of various nations and try to solve real-world problems.

Rishabh recalls, 'I started doing Model United Nation conferences very early on in 2002 when I was eleven.'

He had a humble beginning in the world of debating. As a timid seventh grader, he knew little about the Model United Nation's procedures. As the youngest person in a conference of 300 students, he was chosen to represent Sudan. With all the interruptions and counter-arguments by his fellow students, he felt intimidated and left the room crying. He declared to the teachers that this would be the first and the last time he would do public speaking.

Eventually, the teachers encouraged him to speak on a topic of his preference, and he got a round of applause for it. This boosted his morale.

In the next few years, the MUN conferences opened him to people from diverse backgrounds and perspectives. This exposure was an eye-opener for him.

Rishabh went on to participate and even judge hundreds of MUN conferences regionally and internationally including Harvard World MUN, The Hague International MUN, and the ones in Australia, France, among many others. He was enamoured by the Western system of education. Everything there was done exuberantly.

But he recalls, 'In these MUNs, I noticed that Harvard was there for the United States, Hague was there for Europe, but we had none in India. Here we had to study and follow the procedures that were westernized, as against Indianized.'

Upon his return to India, his grandfather too pointed out that as a future leader of their family business of their iron and steel company, he was expected to talk to people who are more rooted in Indian culture and not necessarily the western ones that he had engaged with at MUNs. So he needed to learn more about his roots.

He says, 'In the Indian schooling system, we are not taught about our culture elaborately. With the advent of the International Baccalaureate (IB) programme, our students lose touch with our roots'.

He wanted to change that. As a nineteen-year-old, he set an objective to, 'unite the world by spreading the idea of India among the next generation of world leaders', this will propagate the Indian principles of peace, non-violence, tolerance, comradery and unity in diversity globally. So as a first-year college student, he started the India's International Movement to Unite Nations (IIMUN).

'I just wanted young school and college students to drive this movement, and not any senior professionals, who might have personal agendas to impose. I am happy about our key achievement that our initiative was started and is now run by the young people who want to change the world.'

In 2011, the concept of the Model United Nations was relatively unknown and restricted to only a few schools in the Indian subcontinent. After doing orientation workshops in 200 schools across dozens of Indian cities, the first IIMUN conference in Mumbai was attended by more than 1000 students. Many senior politicians, heads of multinational organizations and Bollywood celebrities came to support their movement. Rishabh felt truly elated and relieved. It was rewarding to see smart young students debate about India and the world and become glocal citizens—the ones who are globally aware and locally proactive.

Doing one conference in their own city was easy but growing to conduct 220 national and thirty-five international conferences annually in less than eight years was significantly challenging.

In scaling to schools in different cities and countries, he had to make students understand what IIMUN stood for. Through pro-bono workshops, Rishabh's team would make students aware, and sensitize them about global issues.

They also had to maintain quality, consistency and thought. He overcame that by recruiting driven students from across India and setting up a core council for quality control.

Young students were motivated, and there was no stopping for the IIMUN.

Rishabh says, 'The common thread that united all of us was that young people believed in spreading the idea of India. At that juncture, a lot of people were moving towards the west, highly influenced by the English culture in their outlook, but many of them realized that there's so much in their own country. I was lucky enough to find that kind of people in my initial phase, who believed in the idea of India. I truly believed that we needed to teach young people to look at the world from the Indian perspective, and understand India better.'

In the rapid expansion of the movement, Rishabh learnt that enabling young people with power in turn helped him to achieve greater results than having a central authority to run everything. He established local teams in each city, which became essential in sustainably growing the IIMUN across India.

Rishabh happily reflects, 'The beauty of the initiative is visible, each participant took charge in spreading their idea of India, not Tagore's, Nehru's or Modi's, or even my idea of India. All of these young people today belong to different political parties, businesses, cinema houses, etc. and they have in their own way propagated an idea of India in their work. As long as they are trying to advocate our Indian values of peace, non-violence, camaraderie and brotherhood, then I think our team has done a good job uniting the world in the best way possible.

IIMUN now has a self-sustaining structure that is run by students. IIMUN's board of advisors now includes Dr Ajay Priamal, Mr A. R. Rahman, Dr Shashi Tharoor, Ambassador Prakash Shah, Dr Suresh Prabhu, Dr Nadir Godrej, Mr Rakesh Jhunjhunwala and Dr P.T. Usha among many other eminent Indian industrialists, politicians, statesmen and various other Indian leaders.

In this journey of becoming a youth leader and honing the next generation of leaders, Rishabh wasn't too motivated by fame. He started an initiative when he saw a gap and kept on building it because of its impact. His colleagues appreciate Rishabh's down to earth nature, and passion to make a difference.

It was rewarding to speak with Melati, Archana and Rishabh, and read a lot of literature on leadership. While to me leadership appeared to be in taking an initiative, telling a story and leading strategically, I was equally curious to know what leadership was *not* about. And I found that leadership wasn't really about the more popular things among us youth: grades and followers.

* * *

Leadership is not about grades

As a college student studying business, finance and entrepreneurship, I felt that the traditional curriculum doesn't teach us anything about leadership. The academic information provided in colleges is excellent. It helps build a structure in thinking that is effective. But colleges in general, especially in India, teach us compliance, not leadership.

A former Yale professor, William Deresiewicz, wrote a book called *Excellent Sheep* that talks about how the elite schools in the US are making compliant people filled with facts but no social and emotional development.

The regular exams test how well we recall abstract information and concepts. But these academic skills don't help us build something of value.

The certificates that our colleges give us when we graduate are essential credentials. The word *credential* comes from the Latin word *credere,* meaning 'to trust or believe'. That is the institute's stamp certifying that we as a candidate for employment are suitable. But are we qualified to lead change?

In taking the initiative, telling a story and leading a group of people, your grades and GPA do not matter. No one will orient their decision to join your team, invest in you and support you based on your GPA. Likewise, your GPA is not a substitute for you to go out and network, inspire people and lead. Your drive is what makes you do that.

Leadership is not about showmanship

When I was seven years old, I remember taking a computer class to learn Microsoft Paint and other essential computer tools. I also took coaching classes for various other subjects: abacus, drawing, mathematics, table tennis, skating, dance and swimming, among others. It was not about excelling at anything; it was about experiencing multiple avenues and seeing what I liked.

But when I started fifth standard and moved to Pune to seriously pursue table tennis, the opposite became true. It wasn't about experiencing and learning new things and not falling behind; it was about getting ahead. Everyone was in a race to show they were more intelligent or better than the rest. The teachers, parents and families of my friends in primary and secondary school were excited about how their children could out-perform the rest of us.

In the race to stand out, everyone was going to programming classes, solving the Rubik's Cube, playing the guitar, participating in Model United Nations or other competitions, volunteering at non-profits, and finding different ways to look better. Doing activities lost meaning. They became tools of signalling. It was all about impressing someone.

Then came Instagram. Our generation was raised to understand that the image we portray matters more than our actual work, and we embraced this social media, like fish to water.

So, what does all of this have to do with initiative and leadership?

We have turned initiative and leadership into a confirmation show. Leadership has become somewhat of a competition in winning the most titles, increasing followership on Instagram and being famous.

But unfortunately, this leads young people to think about influence, followership and social media engagement instead of launching a well thought out initiative, telling an authentic story, building healthy relationships with team members, and creating a dynamic culture.

What makes a good leader?

In all the interviews I did for this book, it appeared that true leaders are exceptionally humble, and they have a deep desire to make a difference.

True leaders have a lot of modesty. They do not talk about themselves. They don't have a personal ambition to be famous persons. Instead, they are simple people who want to create extraordinary things. They rely on inspiring with their authentic story and values. When giving credit, they are generous, and they attribute their success to other people and even luck.

And they have a ferocious determination. Leaders have an unstoppable will to take on things. They have the drive to do anything that needs to get done. They are focused on long-term results, irrespective of how difficult it might be to achieve them. When taking responsibility for poor results, they never blame other people or external factors; they look inwards.

Once you understand what leadership is and is not about, you must know that you as a young person are well placed to be a leader today. We young people are deeply aware of issues around us and are at the age where we have time but no family responsibilities. We are at the age where we can look at authority from a critical lens, are optimistic about the future and have the energy to create change.

We live in challenging times. Multiple crises keep happening. We have the COVID-19 pandemic, climate change, racism, massive inequality, failing democracies, religious conflicts, political and economic polarization and so on. The news and social media create addicts and fill viewers with anxiety and fear.

People with skills, robust belief systems and motivation see these events as opportunities. Likewise, initiators and leaders thrive in these environments.

* * *

As a twenty-one-year-old who grew up in India and met inspiring leaders worldwide, I can tell you that leading in India is more socially and emotionally challenging than in the developed economies. As a result, leadership can be lonely and isolating.

Your journey to become an unstoppable leader will be difficult. The critics will get on your nerves, you will face many challenges, and quitting will seem to be an easy and natural choice. However, believing in your values and story is necessary. If you stand firmly by your values and your authentic leadership story, you will be fine.

To live by a set of values is not only about acknowledging what your beliefs are, but it is about practising them. It means that all your behaviours, actions and thoughts are aligned with those beliefs.

I was always fascinated to learn early life incidents that shaped the people who we now know as great leaders. Let me share a final story of someone who went on to become a global leader in one of India's beloved industries. Throughout his life, he has been known to be one of the humblest leaders in the world, who stuck by his values, and honed a great team to create one of the most lasting impacts on the country.

In 1974, a young Indian was detained in Bulgaria for seventy-two hours without food or water. His only offence was that he asked someone about the struggles of living in a socialist country. During his time in detainment, this young engineer had time to reflect on his leftist commitments. This experience taught him that entrepreneurialism and job creation was the only way for growth and poverty alleviation.

This young engineer's name was Narayana Murthy. He is the 'father' of the Indian IT sector and one of the most outstanding entrepreneurs of all time.

Mr Murthy was born in a small town in Karnataka, in a very modest middle-class family. He got his bachelor's in electrical engineering from the University of Mysore and then a master's degree from the Indian Institute of Technology at Kanpur. Later, he worked at IIM-Ahmedabad as a chief systems programmer and at Patni Computer Systems in Pune before starting Infosys.[4]

Mr Murthy and a group of six friends started Infosys in 1981. Their initial investment was Rs 10,000, which Mr Murthy borrowed from his wife.

In the 1980s, it was challenging to do business in India. The government back then had shackling anti-business rules and regulations. Although paying powerful people off could have helped him overcome these barriers, Mr Murthy chose to do business with honesty and good values.

In 1990, Infosys received a buyout offer for a whopping Rs 2 crore. Mr Murthy offered to buy out his co-founders instead of selling the company. But all the co-founders decided to stay on.

Mr Murthy has repeatedly demonstrated the importance of having strong values such as integrity and conviction as a leader. In a journey to revolutionize an industry, a country and an era, Mr Murthy showcased the power of initiative, building a solid relationship with his team, having values in his leadership story that helped him lead strategically.

Greta, Melati, Archana, Rishabh and Mr Murthy have been true embodiments of great leaders in their own rights. I hope you too can take inspiration to start your initiative, narrate a great story and lead change.

9

Confidence

'You either walk inside your story and own it or you stand
outside your story and hustle for your worthiness'
—Brené Brown, the author of *Daring Greatly*
and five other *New York Times* best sellers

It's hard to overestimate the symbolic and systemic importance
of Dr B.R. Ambedkar.[1] He was born in 1891 in Mhow, a
small town in Madhya Pradesh, in abject poverty. He was the
youngest of his fourteen siblings. His family belonged to the
'Mahar' caste, which was considered untouchable, and suffered
socio-economic discrimination throughout their lives. No one
would have thought that a student who was only allowed to
sit on a piece of gunny cloth at school would become the chief
architect of the great Indian constitution. It is difficult for many
of us today to understand the pains of being untouchable.

His family originally came from Dapoli taluka of Ratnagiri
district, Maharashtra. They lived at the edge of a village that

was predominantly Hindu. A Mahar's job was to go through the town daily to clean its most unpleasant filth, run sundry errands, and collect food at the doors of the houses of upper-caste families. Although the village was home, they could not touch nor be touched by anyone living there. This was only the tip of the discrimination Dr Ambedkar faced early in his life. Yet, Dr Ambedkar lived with confidence, fighting fearlessly anything that came in his way.

Dr Ambedkar was a brilliant student, and education became his respite. He was the first untouchable to enter a university—he graduated from Elphinstone College in 1912 with a degree in economics and political science. Then he won a scholarship from the Maharaja of Baroda to pursue his master's and PhD at Columbia University in New York City in 1916. In 1917, he moved to London to join the post-graduate department of the London School of Economics. But he was obliged to return to India to serve the state of Baroda in 1918. Later, in 1921, he moved to London to complete his education and received a master's degree from the London School of Economics, a DSc in economics, and was also admitted to the British bar as a barrister. He became the first Indian to complete a doctorate overseas.

In 1918, after spending five years in Europe and America, the memory that he was an untouchable was wiped out. But when he returned to India, he once again became conscious of the discrimination faced by those of his caste. He was deeply agitated as he did not have a place to go once he arrived in Baroda. None of the Hindu hotels, Vishis, would accept him. In Baroda, his friends, who had studied with him in America, hesitated to allow him to live with them. Guesthouses run by people of other religions such as Parsis were hesitant to accommodate him, only allowing him to stay in a small room filled with rubbish under a fake Parsi name. His time in the Accountant General's Office of the Maharaja of Baroda was equally tricky as he was ridiculed and denounced.

To fight against this overwhelming systemic oppression and secure the rights of the depressed classes in India, he had to become nothing but 'unstoppable'. He and his family faced an unending stream of threats and harassment from the upper castes in professional and personal settings.

In 1931, his demand for a separate electorate for the depressed classes at the Second Round Table Conference held in London to discuss the constitutional reform in India, was opposed by Mahatma Gandhi. But in 1932, under the Poona Pact, he secured reservations for the depressed classes in the regional legislative assemblies and the central council of states.

In 1956, two months before his passing, Dr Ambedkar converted to Buddhism with 3,65,000 of his followers in Nagpur. His cremation ceremony was attended by hundreds of thousands of his supporters. He was awarded the Bharat Ratna, India's highest civilian honour, posthumously, in 1990.

We all know Dr B.R. Ambedkar as the Chief Architect of our Indian constitution. But, upon a closer look at his story, what do we learn from it? How can someone go through so many hardships and change a systemically oppressive regime that had held sway for hundreds of years?

So how did Dr B.R. Ambedkar do it? How does an individual carry the responsibility of fighting for the rights of arguably the world's most suppressed class in the face of social isolation, physical harm and the hopes of thousands? After reading his biography and dozens of essays, one of the answers emerged in his unmatched value system and grounded confidence.

* * *

It was a warm and clear September morning when I first spoke to Dr Rajeev Gowda, a respected former Member of Parliament in the Rajya Sabha from South Bangalore. He narrated the following part of Theodore Roosevelt's 1910 speech given at the University of Paris. Former US President Roosevelt had come to give his 'Citizenship in a Republic' speech that emphasized that the success of a republic rested not on the brilliance of its citizens but on disciplined work and character, the quality of its people. [2]

Man in the arena

It is not the critic who counts; not the man who points out how the strong man stumbles or where the doer of deeds could have done them better. The credit belongs to the man who is actually in the arena, whose face is marred by dust and sweat and blood; who strives valiantly; who errs, who comes short again and again, because there is no effort without error and shortcoming; but who does actually strive to do the deeds; who knows great enthusiasms, the great devotions; who spends himself in a worthy cause; who at best knows, in the end, the triumph of high achievement, and who at the worst, if he fails, at least fails while daring greatly, so that his place shall never be with those cold and timid souls who neither know victory nor defeat.

—*Theodore Roosevelt*[3]

This speech, along with Dr Gowda's insights, and lessons from Brené Brown's excellent book *Daring Greatly*, taught me three things.

First, it reaffirmed my belief that the brave and confident will emerge victorious despite all the failures and rejections. I have never met a successful person who has done something worth doing without failing, disappointing someone else, or having heartbreaks.

Second, one needs to cherish vulnerability during the phases of failure and uncertainty. For many successful people, it is never about winning or losing. It's not about the outcomes. It is about showing up even though they cannot control the results. They show up to do their duty and stick with the process. This can be observed in Chapter 2, verse 47 of the Bhagwat Geeta:

karmany-evādhikāras te mā phaleshu kadāchana
mā karma-phala-hetur bhūr mā te sango 'stvakarmani

Which translates to

'You have a right to perform your duties, but you are not entitled to the fruits of your actions. Therefore, never consider yourself to be the cause of the results of your activities, nor be attached to inaction.'[4]

Finally, if someone is not in the arena of getting their butt kicked from time to time, or if they have not done anything of significant value through hardship, then their opinions or feedback should not interest you.

Thousands of people never do anything in their lives. They just sit and put all their energies into passing judgement and comments on someone trying to build something. If someone gives you this hollow criticism when they are not putting themselves on the line, then what they have to say should not interest you.

What does it take to be confident in times of turmoil?

Naturally, as a twenty-one-year-old, my life experience is limited. Thus, I studied dozens of impactful people, young and old, surveyed and interviewed hundreds of students my age, and read numerous books and research papers. In this study, one trend emerged clearly—you cannot succeed without putting yourself in the arena and marching with grounded confidence. A notion that Abhay Rangan's story demonstrates.

* * *

Abhay is the twenty-five-year-old founder of Goodmylk, India's biggest plant-based company, which has raised over $1.8 million (Rs 13.5 crores) in funding. Abhay was included in the Forbes 30 Under 30 list twice, in 2019 and 2020. When we spoke with him in August 2020, he was getting married in Seattle, USA.

Abhay was always an above-average student and a strong animal rights activist.

'The food system today is broken; people are not eating as sustainably as we would have hoped', he said when he started his campaigns to promote veganism and animal rights as a young teenager.

At fifteen, he started an animal rights initiative known as Society of Animal Rights (SARV). Over the next three years, it grew to 600 volunteers and covered more than ten cities. At its peak, it was one of the most active animal rights grassroots networks in the country.

During one of his campaigns, someone said to him, 'Abhay, I want to become a vegan, but all the vegan options are so expensive.'

A litre of cow milk costs Rs 50, while the vegan alternatives start at Rs 300 a litre. That lack of affordable vegan options stuck with him.

Abhay's parents had been vegans for a long time. He wanted to start a company that brought affordable vegan options to the market. He and his parents had a conversation and created the for-profit side of his SARV movement. They wanted to give people who wished to consume plant-based dairy food affordable options.

Soon after, Abhay made a decision. 'I dropped out of engineering in my second year. I had meagre attendance. Meanwhile, Goodmylk was getting more steam, and we wanted to raise funds at that point.'

Goodmylk showed a lot of potential, but there were no financial results. When Abhay broke the news of failing in college, his parents were saddened. His father was an IITian, and his mother was an engineer too.

Many perils and frustrations lay ahead, such as breaking into the investor community, which was a challenge. As a one-man-army, Abhay felt his lack of awareness held him back from taking risks. Another frustration that Abhay had to overcome after dropping out of college was of scaling their manufacturing capacities. His mother was still manufacturing Goodmylk products at home, and Abhay used to deliver these products on his bike. They scaled up so much that it was hard for his mother to keep up with the orders alone.

He recalls a situation that deeply affected him. His mother said to him, 'Abhay, I feel overwhelmed, it is really hard to continue manufacturing at our home kitchen.'

To this, Abhay didn't have an answer. They both were in tears in that moment.

'I think that was very, very powerful for me. I'd never cried in years. It was the first time I broke down. But after that, I told my mom, give me three months. I will make sure that you never have to manufacture again, and that is what I did. So, I'm delighted that it turned out that way. It was the lowest point for me, to see my mother go through so much.'

When Abhay made it to the Forbes 30 Under 30 list for the first time in 2019, his parents were overjoyed. 'My mom was just skipping around the house. It was a sense of relief for my parents. Because this is probably the replacement for the degree that they've always wanted from me.'

Four years later, in 2022, Goodmylk became one of India's largest and fastest-growing plant-based companies, with $1.8 million (Rs 13.5 crores) in funding and a team of more than fifty talented people.

Abhay notes that the real world doesn't care too much for potential and the titles these awards offer as much as they care for actual results. 'I was always wondering what would happen if the company ever hit a few crores in revenue. And today we are there.'

When asked, the only suggestion Abhay has for his sixteen-year-old self is to take more risks.

'The ages between twenty and thirty are great times to take risks because we do not have as many responsibilities. Suppose I knew at sixteen, as now I do, that risk is proportional to reward; I would have taken more calculated risks. I would have taken as much risk as possible without being over risked.'

Abhay says, 'Taking risks unlocks rewards. You should take more risks, have conviction in what you do, and learn to deal with the emotional ups and downs that are inevitable in your journey.'

Once you have decided what you want to do and evaluated the risk and reward ratio, you will need to go forth despite the paralysing fear of failure and public ridicule. Having a deep sense of confidence in your abilities helps you overcome these fears and emerge victorious.

* * *

Creating something new is often a lonely journey. However, words like loneliness, empathy and those describing other human emotions aren't often mentioned in the traditional leadership literature. Overcoming challenges and phases of uncertainty require a sense of grounded confidence.

Grounded confidence is the process of having well-rooted faith in yourself while learning, relearning, losing, winning and going through life, even in the face of fear. This is not a reckless kind of confidence that is arrogant and shallow. The 'fake it till you make it' type of confidence may work in the short term, but it can take you into a suffocating place and keep you small.

Instead, grounded confidence is a more inwardly looking self-aware kind of confidence built on practise, constant learning and patience. This type of confidence lifts you and the people around you up and encourages effort. Here a part of Brene Brown framework from her fascinating book *Daring Greatly* comes in handy.[5]

You will face tough decisions, challenging opponents and emotionally charged situations in the journey towards greatness. But, in this journey, grounded confidence will act as a rudder to your boat, preventing you from getting carried away.

GROUNDED CONFIDENCE

=

RUMBLE SKILLS + CURIOSITY + PATIENCE + PRACTICE

Rumble skills: The skill to engage in difficult conversations. Rumble is American slang for 'let's have a real conversation, even though it may be tough'. This conversation can be with yourself or the people around you to approach difficult things.

Brene Brown narrates the importance of rumbling in her book *Dare to Lead*: '[. . .] having the skill to hold the tense situation with calm and confidence will allow you to be empathetic, meet the challenges, and stay curious.'[6]

Despite failing in his engineering course, waiting for financial validation of his idea, and having to overcome manufacturing limitations, Abhay displayed rumbling skills in his conversations with his mother and himself.

Curiosity: It is often uncomfortable to admit that we don't know something. It is uncommon to be curious about something, go down a path to find something new even though the outcome might be uncertain. Unfortunately, our ego makes us feel like we are all-knowing sometimes. But this feeds our insecurity and restricts our personal growth.

To be curious means to be okay with uncertainty. It means to accept that one doesn't know all the correct answers, but one must continue questioning and learning.

The original thinking and lived experience that emerges from following your curiosity is a tremendous source of confidence. Your interests and enthusiasm will take you to unusual places, and it will be worth it.

One must overcome the sense of incuriosity, as Stephen Fry rightly said: 'The only reason people do not know much is that they do not care much. They are incurious. Incuriosity is the oddest and most foolish failing there is.'

One thing our society values greatly is order. It often seeks to suppress curiosity, as we may have experienced in our schools and colleges. In medieval European society, anyone who was curious or enquired too much about the working of the Catholic church was defamed. But through the ages of the renaissance, reformation and enlightenment, societies began to encourage the curious. As a result, there was an explosion of ideas and scientific advancements.

Patience: As mentioned by Rich Karlgaard, in the book *Late Bloomers*, our world is obsessed with early achievement.[7] I admit that many of the prodigious under-twenty-five-year-olds I interviewed for this book are examples of this obsessed world. But they and the many industry experts I spoke to admit that success is not about quick fixes and early achievements, but a long-term satisfaction and purposeful life.

Patience is the key when achieving your goals. Your work can take a while to manifest, and all you need to be is patient. The quick-fix way of life that we see in the age of social media encourages us to give up on our goals when they don't manifest as rapidly as we'd hoped and move on to the next thing. This can never be fulfilling. Often, your goals are not escaping you; you either have not put in the effort you need or expect things to happen instantaneously. Practise a little patience.

Practise: Easy learning does not build vital skills. Often, teachers find an easy way to teach kids and quickly assess if they have grasped a concept. However, these are not necessarily effective methods. Success needs deliberate efforts. There should be a desirable level of difficulty.

As we saw in Hard Work Over Talent chapter, it takes ten thousand hours of deliberate practise to succeed at something. Your confidence in your abilities will only come from the hours that you have invested in your skills. Likewise, to have grounded confidence in the slippery spots in your journey will come from practise. You will have to make deliberate efforts to have difficult conversations with yourself and the people around you, have vulnerability, courage, curiosity and patience.

* * *

One of the people that I have deeply admired and followed for the longest time is a social media influencer. She dared to take a path less taken, engaged in impactful conversations with thousands of strangers, stayed curious, and patiently built her brand with deliberate efforts.

Karishma Mehta is the founder of Humans of Bombay, a page with over two million followers on Instagram. She shares the stories of success, failures, hopes, dreams and desires of ordinary people.

It took her over eight years of working twelve hours a day, fifty-two weeks a year, before becoming a success.

Karishma was born in Mumbai, went to Bombay Scottish School and an international high school in Bengaluru. She went on to get her undergraduate degree from the University of Nottingham, UK.

When she graduated with a degree in business and economics, most of her friends started high-paying jobs straight out of college. A few of her friends got into top consulting and asset management firms in the UK.

At twenty-one, she was not too sure about what she wanted to do with her life. She came back home, to Mumbai, for a sabbatical. She had always wanted to start some kind of story-telling platform. While in college, she discovered, Humans of New York, a popular Facebook page started in November 2010 by photographer Brandon Stanton that shares the stories of New York City inhabitants. Intrigued she googled 'Humans of Mumbai' but didn't find anything, So she thought to herself, 'Why not start something similar to this as a Facebook page?'

She quickly made a primary logo for Humans of Bombay on Microsoft Word by selecting a random font she liked.

At first, her parents did not understand what she was doing. They were a bit worried. However, her friends, who followed the Humans of New York page, had some idea of what she was up to. They supported her in the initial days while providing a healthy dose of criticism.

'I always had a fetish for people and their stories, and this was a perfect starting point for that,' she says. Thus began the story of Humans of Bombay on 28 January 2014.[8]

The first person she approached said 'no' to her request to cover her story. It was a young girl in a frilly pink dress. She wanted to take a picture of her, but her parents refused, point-blank.[9]

In college, she had never taken a course in photography. So, she learnt to handle a camera by watching YouTube videos. Initially, she went out to shoot for five hours a day.

Then, she shared one story a day on her Facebook page after writing the story and editing the photos. In addition to this, she would take on freelance writing work. She never earned a penny from the Humans of Bombay initiative, until much later, with the book she launched.

'I am a business and economics major, and what I am doing right now is not at all connected to what I studied. And I think that's okay. It is about what you really want to do, what you feel will get you to a particular place in life, and just going for it.'

To stop someone randomly on the streets and ask, 'Can I take a photograph of you? Can you tell me about your life story?' was definitely a weird thing to do at first.

Engaging a stranger in a five or six-minute conversation is difficult. Rejections are constant and not easy to digest. But she adds, 'You need to understand the point after which insistence becomes intrusion into someone's privacy.' So, she usually waits in the background and observes people. [10]

Even today, eight years after starting this page, with over two million followers on Instagram, she feels a bit nervous before initiating a conversation with a stranger.

She started as a solopreneur with one camera, working from home, and has become an organization with a team of fifteen, working out of a great office location in Mumbai and with millions of followers.

In her journey, Karishma had confidence and faith to listen to her gut. Instead of ignoring her passion and pursuing a safe route of banking as her friends, Karishma crafted her own path. In building a community of more than 20 lakh people and covering more than 4000 stories so far, she maintained her curiosity to share the stories of ordinary people and being patient with the process.

When Karishma started her photo-blogging journey and asked strangers to share their stories, she faced hours of rejections. Nine of the first ten people she first approached declined to share their stories. But she says, 'I kept going and kept facing rejections, but I ultimately got enough stories to start a Facebook page.'[11]

As you dare to do something new, you face rejections, but they are an important part of the process, and they should be celebrated.

* * *

Dealing with rejections, and the art of hustling

'Failure is the condiment that gives success its flavour.'
—*Truman Capote, an American novelist, and playwright*

What did it feel like when you had a crush on someone, but they didn't like you back? What was it like when you applied for a college, job or a scholarship, but you got rejected? Do you remember the pain when you wanted something really badly but didn't get it?

Rejections are the only constants in our journey, and we need to learn how to take them in stride. If you are getting rejections, that means you are living your life to the fullest.

The only cure to the painful feeling of being rejected is conditioning. The faster you experience as many rejections as possible, the better it will be for your growth. The following exercise will help.

You need to define your short-term goal. For example, it could be getting an internship, a job, a scholarship, mentorship, guests for your podcast or anything else.

Then make a list of people or places you need to reach out to achieve your goal, and keep track of all the places and people you have already reached out to.

Reward yourself with something nice such as chocolate, ice cream, your favourite meal, or anything that you can look forward to after every seven rejections.

Each rejection will get you closer to either your goal or your next treat. A win-win situation.

Goal:		
1	8	15
2	9	16
3	10	17
4	11	18
5	12	19
6	13	20
7	14	21
Treat	Treat	Treat

Let's look at the story of an acclaimed artist who overcame a series of rejections from the best art schools in India and went on to truly make a mark on the industry.

* * *

Debangshu Moulik is a multidisciplinary artist based out of Pune, India. His works have been featured by the official Instagram, *Vice* magazine, Snapchat and Google, among many other influential websites.

At twenty years of age, his art has made him financially independent. He was born in a middle-class Bengali family in Pune. He got rejected by most top design schools that he applied to. Today, more than 50,000 people follow him for his artwork through his Instagram page.

When one meets Debangshu, he seems like an average twenty-or-so-year-old. He wears glasses with thick black frames. When he walks, he carries himself with a dreamy float.

He has always had artistic elements in his blood. His father used to be a photographer.

'From the age of twenty-two to thirty-five, my dad worked as a photographer in Calcutta. And then he went into corporate life. He was a material manager or something in Tata Motors.'

His mother is a psychologist. When he was a kid, his mother would read him many books and help him draw simple characters.

The drawing room of his house is filled with random art pieces, books in Bengali, Hindi and English, sculptures, and a coloured piece of a TV antenna-dish. It's one of the new canvases for Debangshu's creations.

Debangshu works all the time. He works hard. If he is not working, he is dreaming of working. However, his success came unconventionally.

Since childhood, we are told that we must pass the tenth and twelfth standard exams with perfect scores if we want to make it in life. Then, we must get into a good college. And we are told that is the only way to become successful. Debangshu was told the same. The fear of failing was paralysing.

'All the students who wanted to go to art schools, their parents had made them join these art classes that lasted seven to eight hours a day. That idea didn't resonate with me. I told my parents there is this online course by Pixar Artists. Might as well invest in this one so I will learn about art. I do not want to learn how to crack an exam. But I want to learn the art—how do I express myself better. That is how I basically learnt in the eleventh and twelfth.'

Debangshu used to learn in the classes on Skillshare, Coursera and YouTube, all the online learning platforms, and applied for a lot of freelance work. However, he got a ton of rejections on the way.

'There has been this constant rejection because sometimes the client doesn't like your design etc. At one point, I counted them, and [I had gotten] about 250 [rejections]. And this was only in the eleventh standard.'

After completing twelfth standard, Debangshu got rejections from all the colleges that he wanted to get into. Everyone told him that he would not make it as an artist if he didn't get into those colleges. He felt highly rejected.

Debangshu did not end up getting into any college except Srishti School of Design in Bengaluru. 'But their fees were so high it didn't make sense [. . .] it was like [Rs] 4 lakh per year, which I couldn't afford to pay from my own pocket, so I thought it would be best if I kept learning on my own,' he says.

So he stayed put in Pune. He enrolled in a local art school called Abhinava, which strangely didn't require an entrance test. He simply walked into the office, and they said, 'Yes, you can simply start now.'

But still, the failure of not getting into any college was absolute. Nonetheless, he spent all his time making content. Learning about design, animation, video-making, editing, Photoshop etc.

'When I do not work, I just feel depressed. It's this weird thing, like I can't take holidays.'

Earlier, the failure and rejection would stop his workflow for a couple of days. He would question whether he should be making art. But now, it has become a part of life. During the COVID-19 pandemic, he has built a routine to wake up early in the morning, do twelve Surya namaskars, then make a to-do list, and note down five things that he is grateful for, followed by light drawing exercise and then start working until 6 p.m. after which he will work on his personal projects. These things in his everyday life helped him overcome his feelings of anxiety, and fear of failure.

One of the projects he worked on was a zine, which is a rougher form of a magazine. It can be made at a local Xerox shop. It's a direct way to express yourself through print media. It doesn't have a high cost. It can be as simple as a PDF.

'I posted a zine called "Old Shirt", one of my first pieces. I put three months' worth of it for free on the internet because I just wanted people to see it. Within two days, the *Vice* creative segment did this small piece on me, and it meant the world to me,' he recounts. 'Two months later, I got featured on the Instagram official page.' And from there on, he has worked regularly with Vice media, Google, Instagram, Snapchat etc.

If a kid who was rejected as many times as Debangshu was now has 50,000 people looking at his work on Instagram, then that means anyone can be a success. The art of hustling and overcoming rejections should be at the core of all of us.

Overcoming modern fears

Our ambitions make us start our journey towards our success. But our fears become the real roadblocks in our journey.

As a table tennis player, I used to be terrorized by the fear of failure. So much so that I consulted a sports psychologist, who eventually helped me win state and national tournaments. My fear of failure was so prominent that I would freeze and choke at critical times. I lost at least a dozen crucial games out of the sheer fear of not being good enough. I used to be scared of public ridicule and losing to lower-ranked players. The memories of losing the team's quarterfinals in the 2016 National Championships and losing my games in the semi-finals at the Pacific School Games in Adelaide, Australia, in 2015 haunt me even today.

One of my more prominent memories is from 2013. An under-fifteen state-ranking tournament was being held in Nasik. I had recently won my debut Maharashtra state-ranking tournament, and I was state number one for the first time. It was unreal for me. In the round of sixteen, I had to play a cadet's player (under-twelve-year-old) who was much younger than me and had a lower ranking. But I was so fixated on how embarrassing it would be if I lost this match that I actually lost. That too in straight sets, 0-3.

It was not fun, but it taught me a valuable lesson. The fear of failing is worse than failure itself. So the loss in that game wasn't as embarrassing as I thought it would be.

The fear that stops us from doing the things that move us towards reaching our goals is known as 'Atychiphobia'.

There are three types of fears identified by Gregory Berns in his book *Iconoclast: A Neuroscientist Reveals How to Think Differently*.[12]

The first is ambiguity, or the fear of the unknown. For example, if you want to go to college in the US, then your fears could be along the lines of, 'What does an application to a college in the US look like?' Or, 'How do I make my application stand out?' Such a fear basically emerges from not having enough information about something you face.

Second is the fear of failure. Although it is accounted for as 'risk', we all know it as the fear of losing money, getting bad grades, failing at a responsibility or in a relationship.

And finally is the fear of public ridicule or looking stupid. For many, there is nothing harsher than embarrassing yourself in front of your friends and family.

Grounded confidence helps us overcome these fears. And these fears are not trivial. Interestingly, over one-third of the population is afraid of public speaking.[13] When you are scared, your body is under stress. Of course, different things might trigger stress in people. But our bodies react in the same way: the heart beats faster, our blood pressure rises, we start to sweat, our fingers tremble and our voice cracks.

This is captured by Eminem in his song 'Lose Yourself' when he raps,

> His palms are sweaty, knees weak, arms are heavy,
> There's vomit on his sweater already, mom's spaghetti,
> He's nervous, but on the surface, he looks calm and ready to
>   drop bombs,
> But he keeps on forgetting what he wrote down, the whole
>   crowd goes so loud,
> He opens his mouth, but the words won't come out,
> He's choking how, everybody's joking now,
> The clock's run out, time's up, over, bloah!

Our stress system becomes highly stimulated and overrides our brain. Our body goes into the fight or flight mode. This reaction is so powerful that it derails many driven people. The ability to tame these stress reactions and strive is one of the biggest obstacles you will face to becoming unstoppable. Fear can be paralysing and stops the average person dead in their tracks.

But if you have a grounded sense of confidence in your abilities, then you can endure in the long durations of stress and fear and emerge successful.

Nobody knows stress and fear as much as a solo entrepreneur trying to build a business from scratch all alone.

> *One of the most significant discoveries a man makes, one of his great surprises, is to find he can do what he was afraid he couldn't do.*
>
> —*Henry Ford, founder of Ford Motor Company*

I was eighteen when I first read Ronnie Screwvala's autobiography *Dream with Your Eyes Open: An Entrepreneurial Journey* at a library in Mumbai. I was initially attracted by his excellent book title. I was later rewarded by the story of Mr Screwvala, the Parsi boy who went on to become one of the most successful serial entrepreneurs in the country.

From his modest beginnings in Mumbai to becoming one of TIME magazine's 100 most influential people globally, and named among twenty-five of the most powerful people in Asia by *Fortune* magazine, Mr Screwvala has done it all. He is the founder of UTV (now Walt Disney India), Unilazer Ventures, Swades Foundation, the unicorn start-up UpGrad, and the author of two of my favourite books, *Dream with Your Eyes Open* and *Skill it, Kill It.*

His life has been one roller coaster ride, and he is my personal idol. At eighteen, he organized one of the first rock and roll concerts in Mumbai and ended up with a Rs 50,000 hole in his pocket. In the 1970s, that was a big sum.

He went from high school at Cathedral straight into the second year of a Bachelor of Commerce (BCom) degree at Sydenham College. There, out of self-confessed arrogance and over-confidence, he failed a year.

He had an innate curiosity about the world around him, and he was open to all experiences with zero plan. When he was in the UK for a short trip in his early twenties, he saw two toothbrush manufacturing machines headed for the scrap heap. He inspected the machines and guessed they could easily be used for another ten years.

'I was standing in a British brush factory, staring at two bulky, grey, state-of-the-art toothbrush machines without a rupee in my pocket, no clue about the oral hygiene industry, and no strategy to import those hulking boxes back home.' That was how he started his company, Laser.

On the many setbacks that lay ahead, Mr Screwvala reflects, 'Failure is unavoidable. One of the most enduring lessons everyone in business learns is that not all great ideas succeed. Account for risks. Embrace failure. Note that failure is only a comma, not a full stop. You do not fail in life when one thing goes wrong. No matter how grim today feels, there will always be a tomorrow.'[14]

While most of us wonder how we will be successful as we don't come from the right background or cities, or don't have the right education and connections, he says, 'It really does not matter what socio-economic background you come from. It is irrelevant if you come from a big city or a small town if you have family connections or not. If you have the thirst to succeed, the intrinsic confidence in your abilities, the guts to take sensible risks and a go-getting attitude, you will prevail.'

When people ask him, what is the right time to start something, he says, 'The right time or age to start is when you feel confident, driven and ready to jump. Most impediments to entrepreneurship are put in place by people who do not have the imagination to dream. So go into every fight certain you're going to win.'

Mr Screwvala writes in his book *Dream With Your Eyes Open*, that in India, we've become part of an echo chamber critical of people who work hard to realize their dreams. From their safe perches along life's sidelines, competitors, naysayers and dream-killers criticize and pull people down instead of joining life's beautiful, wondrous, often shambolic dance. Most of these critics have never created or built anything, nor will they ever understand the challenges and the great satisfaction of steering a ship to its destination. Even so, they act as though they are the experts in the room. They are hypocritical to the extreme. But unstoppable leaders need to endure this. This is the real world.

As Mr Scewvala says, 'Let criticism and public failure strengthen you, and not diminish you. In the end, you are only answerable to yourself. The art of recalibration requires confidence and courage of conviction.'

10

Giving Back

'The more I help out, the more successful I become. But I measure success in what it has done for the people around me. That is the real accolade'[1]

—Adam Grant, author of *Give and Take: A Revolutionary Approach to Success*

When you meet Mrs Anu Aga[2] at her Thermax India corporate office in Pune, you will be taken aback by her calmness and positivity. She has had a difficult life. She has dealt with irreparable losses and emotional turmoil. Yet, she has displayed strength, generosity and altruism in her journey.

Mrs Aga is a trained social worker, was a committed wife and a mother. But when the time came, she took the reins of an ailing company to become its CEO and orchestrate one of the biggest turnarounds ever witnessed in corporate India. In addition, she was a respected parliamentarian in the upper house for six years.

In her early life, she was a bright student. She earned a bachelor's degree in economics and politics from St Xavier's College, Mumbai. Through the Social Service League of the college, she attended two camps per year—rural and urban—where she spent her time and energy to help the underprivileged. After graduation, a career in social work seemed like the most obvious choice. She got her master's degree from Tata Institute of Social Sciences (TISS) in medical and psychiatric social work.

While at TISS, she met her future husband, Rohinton Aga. They soon got married in 1965. Their first child, Meher, was born in 1966. Their son, Kurush, was born in 1972.

In 1982, unfortunately, her husband, Rohinton, had a massive heart attack. While going through a bypass surgery, he suffered a stroke that left him paralysed. While supporting her husband's recovery, Mrs Aga also started working in the HR department of Thermax in 1985. From 1991–96, she was appointed as the director of human resources.

When her daughter gave birth to her first child, Mrs Aga spent six months in the UK. Upon her return, Rohinton was supposed to pick her up. But he suffered his second heart attack and sadly passed away.

Within two days of her husband's death, the board of Thermax appointed Anu Aga as the executive chairperson of the company. Thermax shares had plunged from Rs 400 to Rs 36 and she assumed the responsibility to recuperate the company.

Over the next two years, she had to take complex decisions in order to turn the company around. From the head of human resources to the executive chairman of the company, she took over the reins magnificently. Under her leadership, Thermax was an excellent turnaround success.

Barely a year after her husband's death, she lost her mother-in-law. And a fortnight later, in the cruellest blow of all, her twenty-five-year-old son, Kurush, passed away in a car accident.

Despite all the pain and suffering, Thermax remained her point of focus. When she stepped down as chairman in 2004, Thermax saw the highest order in its history—intake of Rs 867 crore, which was an 86 per cent increase from the previous year, and completed the turnaround phase successfully.

After stepping down as a chairman, Mrs Aga dedicated her time to social work and primarily through the non-profit organization Akanksha that educates less privileged children from slum areas and provides them with vocational opportunities. She directed Akanksha's journey in Pune and Mumbai in its early stages. Later she helped Shaheen Mistri, the founder of Akanksha, a social activist and an educator, launch Teach for India, a part of a global movement that recruits graduates and professionals and trains them to teach students from low-income families in municipal schools.

The decision to devote herself to philanthropy was also prompted by Mrs Aga's belief that true happiness lies in serving humanity and helping the needy. Mrs Aga has passed on her spiritual awareness and social sensitivity to her daughter and Thermax. As a result, the corporation became one of the earliest Indian companies to set aside 1 per cent—and now 2 per cent—of its profits for social projects.

For Mrs Aga, corporate social responsibility is not a buzzword; she is committed to it not just by writing cheques but by being deeply involved with the two NGOs, Teach for

India and Akanksha. For example, in one of the schools, she and the schoolchildren cleaned the dirty toilets. There was a gasp of disbelief from the staff and students when they saw the former chairperson of Thermax Group demonstrating how much water to use when cleaning.

It's usually easier to simply write a cheque to help someone than to sit beside them and help them one at a time. Mrs Aga chose the more challenging route.

Mrs Anu Aga was awarded the Padma Shri in 2010 for her service in the field of social work.

* * *

The land of givers

India has been blessed with larger-than-life givers such as Mother Teresa and Mahatma Gandhi. They sacrificed their lives to bring about massive changes in society. We have also had doyens such as Jamsetji Tata, who emerged as the world's most prominent philanthropist in the last 100 years, donating $102 billion (Rs 7.6 lakh crore) to people.[3] More recently, Azim Premji became India's most generous person, donating Rs 7904 crore in 2020 alone.[4] Anu Aga single-handedly shaped the lives of thousands of school children in the primary education system. In addition, we have thousands of unsung heroes such as social workers, non-profit leaders, philanthropists and dutiful citizens.

It is tempting to say that these people achieved great heights in their personal lives, enabling them to become generous. But the opposite appears to be true. The habit of giving made them who they are today.

The act of giving doesn't require you to be wealthy and successful before being generous. In contrast, giving can become a tool for you to reach your potential and achieve sustainable success. To be a giver doesn't require extraordinary acts of sacrifice. Instead, it requires you to do small things with other people's interests at heart.

As described by Adam Grant in his book *Give and Take: A Revolutionary Approach to Success*, there are three types of people: givers, takers and matchers. Anchored on the two extremes of the spectrum are the givers and takers.[5]

The takers are the ones who try to get as much as possible from other people and contribute as little as possible in return. They think that is the shortest and most direct path to achieving their personal goals.

On the other hand, there are a few strange people called 'givers'. These are the people who want to contribute and add value. But, of course, they aren't saints. They don't necessarily volunteer every weekend with NGOs, adopt stray pets, donate tons of money, or run family foundations. But they are open to giving advice, sharing knowledge, making connections, providing mentorship to juniors, and helping their peers in their projects *without* any strings attached.

There are a few people who are pure givers or pure takers. Most people lie in the range between these two points. They can be defined as matchers. These are the people who try to maintain an even balance of giving and taking. If I scratch your back, you will scratch mine, is their philosophy.

Adam Grant conducted research to find out where do all three of these types of people end up on the success scale at a workplace. It was found that a certain kind of giver is over-represented at the bottom of the success scale. They are the selfless givers. A selfless giver will often put other's priorities first and risk burning out or even being exploited by the takers.

Interestingly, guess who is at the top of the success metrics?

Adam Grant found out that it's not the takers or the matchers. It was the givers again who succeeded more than the takers and matchers. Their advantages in domain knowledge such as networking, collaboration, influencing and evaluating helped them rise to the top.

A lot of this is because of the trust, goodwill and reputation that they have built.

*　*　*

Life is not about winning a competition; it's about contribution

I used to think life was a zero-sum game, if one person has to win then someone else has to lose.

I grew up playing table tennis with the dream of becoming an international athlete. Naturally, in an individual sport, for someone to win, someone had to lose. Table tennis was not a simple hobby as it might have been for many. It meant business to me.

I considered myself a hard worker. I spent six to eight hours, six days a week, for almost seven years in practice, on the track field, at the gym, or in my room analysing videos, meditating, journaling or reading about the game. This instilled in me a mindset where 'I' was at the centre of everything. I used to think my training, tournaments and routine should be everyone's top priority.

I would push my family, friends and well-wishers to adjust to my schedule. I felt entitled to maximize personal gains as much as I could to improve my performance and not think too much about others. This made me think like a *taker*.

I felt winning the competition would lead to ultimate happiness for my friends, family and me. But when I won two gold medals at the School Games Federation of India National Championships in 2014-15 and two bronze medals at the Pacific School Games in Adelaide, Australia, in 2015, I felt empty.

After beating the competition from the district to the global level, I should have felt victorious. Instead, very few people showed up to celebrate with me, and I felt hollow.

Eventually, at seventeen, when I left table tennis, I solo backpacked through India for a month. Spending time on our Indian streets in different towns gave me perspective on both my privilege and insignificance.

Then, I found my happiness in volunteering at local NGOs and teaching table tennis for free to children at primary schools in Pune. Throughout the next few years in college, I volunteered at global non-profits and NGOs. I found volunteering and community service to be far more fulfilling than the traditional finance and business roles.

In my freshman year at college, one of my favourite professors, Professor Golo, taught the sustainability and corporate social responsibility class. I would visit his office just to chat, and in one of these conversations I asked him, 'Professor, you are an Oxford and Cambridge graduate, why are you teaching us? Why didn't you choose to work at a multinational company and try to be a billionaire?'

To this, he responded, 'Manthan, for me being a billionaire is to impact a billion lives, not make a billion dollars. And from this cabin, I am doing just that.'

That answer stuck with me, and everywhere I went after I saw *impact*. All the successful people I have met since then have had the innate trait of kindness and generosity, and the one thing they want to do is make an impact.

This was even more apparent when I interviewed the fifty young changemakers during my internship at Ashoka in Singapore for Bosche's ChangemakerXchange[6] and the dozens of trailblazers subsequently for my Planet Impact podcast. Their ambitions and their stories of overcoming challenges always started with the purpose of giving something to society and making a difference.

Consequentially, I re-evaluated myself and consciously tried to move from being a taker to being a giver. I tried to imbibe an approach of how I could help the other person, without any strings attached. I ended my conversations by asking how I could help. And it opened me to multiple new opportunities, such as writing this book, running a podcast, starting many initiatives, and even meeting HH Pope Francis in a private sitting in 2019.

Furthermore, in this process of trying to add value to the lives of the people around me, I made numerous wonderful friendships and shared meaningful conversations with hundreds of people. And these have now become the memories I celebrate and cherish over any material achievements.

The value of giving and being a part of the community has made my life far more fulfilling.

Instead of trading value, I now strive to add value for other people without any expectations or agenda of gaining something in return.

It turns out life is more of a team sport than an individual game. Life is more about contribution than competition.

And from my short experience, I can assure you that becoming a giver is a skill that can be learnt.

* * *

Giving brings happiness

Before starting this book, my college group and I undertook a four-month-long college research project. We wanted to identify what the aspirations and drivers of success were of Generation Z. So we surveyed over 300 students across colleges in India, Singapore and Dubai from diverse cultural, geographical and economic backgrounds.

When asked, 'What do you want from life?', more than half said, 'I want to be happy.'

But where does happiness come from? Does wealth bring you contentment?

Many billionaires have viewed 'giving' as a source of energy and happiness. For example, Sir Richard Branson, the founder of the Virgin empire, pledged to give away $3 billion (Rs 22,600 crores) in ten years to reduce global warming. That is about $820,000 or Rs 6 crore per day, every day, for ten years.[7]

Interestingly, Richard Branson was a giver even before he was rich. He started his first charity, Student Valley Centre, when he was still a broke seventeen-year-old.[8] He made a list of problems students faced and targeted the more serious ones, such as unwanted pregnancies and abortion. Then he reached out to dozens of doctors and convinced them to treat the students free of cost. He spent multiple nights consoling students who were contemplating suicide. This gave him energy for his own work.

Research shows that giving can boost happiness, motivate people, give them meaning, and even help them earn more money.[9] Most of us might think that spending money on ourselves will make us happy. But studies have shown that the opposite is true. When people spent money on themselves, there was no change in their happiness level. But when they chose to spend money on others, they felt significantly happier.[10]

It's not just about giving money, but giving time can also increase your happiness and satisfaction. This is because giving adds meaning to our lives, it distracts us from our personal problems, and helps us feel valued by others.[11] Also, Neuroscience shows that giving activates reward and meaning centres in the brain, which send us purpose and pleasure signals when we act for the benefit of others.[12]

In addition, the most effective givers are the ones who have an otherish approach (when you're willing to give more than you receive, but still keep your own interests in sight and use them as a guide for choosing when, where, how, and to whom you give), as we saw in the Growth Mindset chapter. This approach wherein you give more than you receive, and you do so by keeping your ambitions and interest in sight and the ability to choose who you help elevates your mood.[13]

Giving in turn leads to life-happiness, and happiness can motivate people to work harder, smarter and longer. Wouldn't you agree that you would put extra effort into a demanding project and set challenging goals for yourself when you were happy about it?

Giving leads to sustained success

The givers, matchers and takers are equally ambitious in life.[14] It's just the way they go about finding success that is different. All three types of people certainly achieve success in their life at some point, and to some degree. But it is something different and distinctively beautiful when the givers succeed.

Givers' success spreads and cascades. And the people around the givers are happy and rooting for their success. On the other hand, when takers win, it is usually at someone's expense. Research proves that when takers win, people envy them, and they look for an opportunity to knock them down.[15]

In contrast, when people like Mrs Anu Aga win, people are rooting for them and supporting them instead of looking to pull them down at the next opportunity.

The givers' success trickles down to the people around them and enhances their success too. Givers genuinely create value and not just claim to create value. It is a fun journey when everyone wants you to succeed.

I am very happy to share a story of two givers who are solving a big problem in Nepal. As college graduates, they started a passion project with a genuine care for others and keeping their interests in mind. Little did they know that it would impact tens of thousands of people in their country and boost their personal and professional lives.

* * *

Jesselina Rana and Shubhangi Rana became Forbes 30-under-30 social entrepreneurs for starting Pad2Go in

2018. Pad2Go is young-women-led social enterprize based in Nepal that focuses on menstrual health.

Jesselina and Shubhangi were both born and raised in Kathmandu, Nepal. Jesselina completed her BA LLB from National Law University, New Delhi, and Shubhangi completed her B. Tech in Civil Engineering from National Institute of Technology, Warangal, Telangana.

In 2018, after completing their undergraduate studies in India, they returned to Nepal, and started looking for jobs. In the meantime, instead of sitting idle, they wanted to do something for the society. In Nepal, they felt that the women's rights sector still had many challenges to overcome, and the taboo surrounding menstruation was an issue that deeply touched both of their interests. The stigma around menstruation had impacted them both despite being from an urban background.

Shubhangi remembers, 'We were not allowed to enter the kitchen and the prayer room. These small things really affected our self-esteem growing up. Even in schools today the boys tease the girls about their menstruation. This affects the female literacy rate in Nepal too.'

It is estimated that around 89 per cent menstruating individuals face some form of restriction in Nepal.[16] These restrictions range from being excluded from participating in daily activities to being kept outside in cowsheds in the more extreme cases. Further, in the matter of hygiene, a WaterAid study in Nepal found that 83 per cent of the girls used cloth while only 17 per cent used pads.[17]

It was a big problem that they wanted to address creatively.

Jesselina says, 'A lot of NGOs work around menstrual health management, however none had approached it through an innovative social enterprize route. And we wanted it to be different.'

Jesselina had seen vending machines in her university in India. Those didn't exist in Nepal, not even for cold drinks and snacks at movie theatres. So she and Shubhangi had an innovative idea of using vending machines to dispense pads and sanitary products. It was a creative way to break down and eradicate visual and psychological taboos.

In 2018, they became the pioneers in introducing Nepal's first sanitary napkin vending machines. By 2021, they had already installed over 286 machines across all seven provinces in Nepal. In total these machines now support 60,000+ menstruating individuals. Further, Pad2Go's educational programmes helped 65,000+ young boys and girls all over Nepal learn about menstrual hygiene. In only one year since their start, they reached a break-even point, much quicker than other startups in Nepal.

In doing so, they built a lot of goodwill and reputation in their society and left a lasting impact.

The girls in Sindhupalchok, a rural hilly region in northern Nepal, had never seen either a vending machine or a disposable sanitary pad. Once Pad2Go vending machines were installed, this school observed an increase in girls attendance as compared to other schools that did not have these machines.

In the flood-prone region of Terai families often had to take recourse in the school grounds, and women could not soak their cloth pads in sun. Pad2Go vending machines and the disposable sanitary pads helped women overcome challenges in accessing menstrual products in those pressing times.

In the national capital of Kathmandu, Pad2Go vending machines in five main cinema theaters left an impact beyond their expectations. Shubhangi and Jesselina were pleasantly surprised to learn how valuable their machines were not only for the movie goers but also the cinema staff members who worked six-hour shifts and didn't have time to go out and buy sanitary pads.

Pad2Go had many unintended positive benefits in rural and urban areas alike. Over the three years of their initiative, Shubhangi and Jesselina gained valuable skills in entrepreneurship, building a network, and collaborating with multinational organisations. Now, they are using their influence to get the government to remove the 13 per cent luxury tax that is imposed on menstrual products in Nepal.

As two recent graduates, starting a social enterprize was not an easy choice. They had invested five years learning law and four years in civil engineering, respectively. They were passionate about their careers and wanted to be financially secure as well. So, Pad2Go was started as a passion project.

Their story taught me that one can have multiple passions and they can achieve significant goals with an otherish approach in their giving. Shubhangi and Jesselina had a genuine care for others. And they went about giving back on their own terms while maintaining their personal interests and ambitions.

Shubhangi and Jesselina built trust with people in their community over the years, and that has been rewarding for them.

Pad2Go gave them an essential energy boost to succeed in their own careers.

Jesselina says, 'Pad2Go started as a passion project. Very slowly we realized the value it added to both our lives—it balanced out our creative side and made us persevere. From a passion project it turned into one of the greatest learning moments of our lives.'

Shubhangi and Jesselina's success trickled down in their community. Pad2Go now has four paid interns in their team. They also trained 30 young people for about three months on campaigning and changemaking. These young people are being mentored to be the next leaders and starting their own non-profits someday.

Jesselina is now pursuing a Master of Law (LLM) from Harvard Law School, and Shubhangi is now an Engineering Officer at CDM Smith in Nepal working on diverse infrastructural projects. They aspire to continue creating lasting social change in their community, both on the ground and at the policy level.

* * *

Not being a pushover

As a giver, you stand the risk of being a pushover. People might try to take advantage of you. I have had my fair share of experiences in this too.

After high school, I took a gap year to get real-life work experience before deciding on a college. I worked for a sports and wellness brand as a salesperson for gym trainers' certification courses. This company was the fastest growing gym chain in India. At my interview, they asked me my expectations with regard to a salary. I naively said, 'Nothing, I just want to learn.' They took that very much to heart and hired me on the spot on a stipend of Rs 5000 per month that didn't even cover the petrol costs of travelling

25 kms a day. My job was to sell the courses to as many people as possible.

On my first day, my boss handed me a cell phone and an Excel sheet with a few hundred numbers of people in Pune on it and said, 'Get at least 100 people to enrol for the next batch.'

I had just turned eighteen that month. I had no knowledge or relevant experience in selling. I gathered up the courage to start making the calls. The first sixteen calls I made, they either disconnected as I was in the middle of introducing myself or waited a moment longer to make it clear to never call them again.

The next few calls were better, but the prospective clients were visibly uncomfortable about the course. So, I started inventing discounts offers, instalment options, referral schemes and any incentives programmes I could think of on the spot as I went. I was handing out courses like it was Diwali, at prices lower than the competitors.

Still, after nearly a couple hundred rejections, I signed up only three clients in a whole month. To put this in perspective, my counterparts in other departments were signing at least three members or Rs 50,000 in revenue *every* day. I was practically giving out money and discounts and being overly helpful. But I was still losing revenue. I was pathetic at my job.

This was not the first time I had gone out of my way to give and failed.

The second story goes back to when I was fifteen years old.

In the table tennis circuit, I was a tall, skinny guy with specs who always carried the most oversized kit bags possible.

I was in the eleventh standard in junior college and playing in the state circuit for the fifth time.

To be on the state team, I needed to win at least five of the seven matches against the top-ranked players in our state of Maharashtra. I started strong and won four matches one after the other, defeating a couple of much higher-ranked players.

One of my friends had lost three matches right in the beginning, and it was apparent he would not make the state team if he did not win against a leading player. So, I conceded my match against him so he would stand a chance. This is clearly against the principles of sports, but hey, friendships first, right?

He returned the favour by winning the remainder of his matches in straight sets. There was a tie for a spot on the team. After the selectors checked the score sheets of all players, I missed the place on the team by *one* game. Guess who took that spot? Yes, the friend I had helped.

In this too I had helped out someone else at my personal cost.

Coming back to my job as a salesperson, I realized that only giving out discounts didn't work because people didn't see the value in deeply discounted services. They thought the quality of the product was poor. And I was not convincing enough. Then I tried to be a bit more assertive and empathetic; I asked them about their problems and ambitions; I told a better story about my sports background; I showed them how they would have a great career in the fitness industry and fulfil a bigger purpose of making India healthier. Then, I started making more sales.

In the next two months, I single-handedly sold out two batches and made in-hand revenues of Rs 10 lakh. At eighteen, I was promoted to sales manager. For a while, I had two MBA students who were a few years older than me as interns. I got my first business card. I travelled to other gyms to lecture and motivate their trainers and worked with other club managers on the sales front.

This experience made me realize that there is a thin line between selfless giving and otherish giving.

GIVERS, TAKERS AND MATCHERS AT WORK.

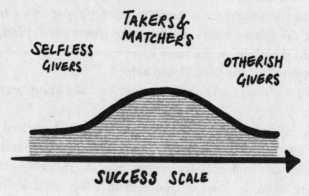

Givers, takers and matchers at work[18]

Selfless givers drop everything they are doing to help others and fall behind in their own work. On the other hand, otherish givers are intelligent and strategic about their giving. They have learnt to successfully navigate a world with matchers and takers so others don't take advantage of them.

How to give

After my table tennis career, and in my gap year, I felt the happiest when volunteering at a Teach for India school, cleaning roads, working at non-profits, helping at the local orphanage, or teaching young schoolchildren.

In this volunteer work, I saw a few senior level working professionals show up for community service every weekend. When I asked them how were they so consistent, and how did they take out time from their schedule? They said they allocated a few hours every weekend morning just for the volunteer work because it made them feel rewarded.

I was curious to know how many hours one dedicated to volunteering for the greatest effects. It appears that,one hundred is a magical number of hours to volunteer. A hundred hours a year breaks down to two hours a week per year. And this leads to more happiness and a longer life.[19] Research of Australian adults showed that people who volunteered between 100 and 180 hours were more satisfied with their lives than those who volunteered for less than 100 hours or more than 180 hours.[20] This number seems to be magical because it will energize you instead of draining and exhausting you.

During these hours of volunteering, don't be a purely selfless giver. Have an otherish approach. Focus your giving in the area you are passionate about.

Pick one or two ways of helping that you enjoy and excel at, rather than being a jack of all trades. This will also allow you to gain a reputation as someone with particular expertise that you want to share instead of a nice person who is freely available.

In your journey of giving, always keep an eye out for takers. Make sure to quickly scan for sincerity. If they seem like someone who would maximize taking, then politely let them pass. Often there will be people who try to take advantage of you. You need to start doing sincerity screening to weed them out. Get a sense of who is genuine and who is not.

* * *

Rise of the service economy

In the short term, you will not receive the benefits of giving. It is not an instant gratification game that our generation is hooked to. But in the long term, the givers build goodwill and trust and eventually have a reputation, strong relationships, and merit in the community, which enhances their success.

Today we work in teams more than ever. Whether submitting college projects or being a parliamentarian, we are always part of some team or the other. The performance of these teams depends on the givers to share information, provide help, mentor and volunteer for the tasks that no one else is willing to do.

Even if you do not work in teams, it's probable that your job is related to the service industry. Previous generations worked largely in agriculture or the manufacturing industry, and they didn't have to collaborate with other people as much as one has to at present. But the contribution of the service sector to India's GDP increased from 29 per cent in 1950 to 57 per cent in 2011.[21] This sector employs nearly a quarter of all working Indians, that is, almost 450 million people.[22]

As the Indian economy gradually moves towards the service sector, an increasing number of people's careers will depend on their established relationships and reputations that might arrive from being a giver. Especially in a society like India, where business is done on goodwill and word of mouth, I bet you will want to be in a relationship with a giver. And people will want to be in a relationship with you if you are one.

* * *

Personally, the successful people I admire the most are givers. Many of them shaped my academic and professional life. And I feel that I am responsible for paying forward what I have learnt from them.

The most magnetic thing about them is that they got to the top without cutting others down. Rather, they found ways to increase the size of the pie for everyone instead of taking the most significant slice for themselves. With this, I would like to end this book with the story of my mentor, from whom I learnt the intricacies of giving.

Sumitra Pasupathy is the managing director of global partnerships at Ashoka: Innovators for the Public. Previously, she was the country director of Ashoka for Singapore and Malaysia when I worked for her as an intern. She is the co-founder and on the board of directors of Playeum Ltd., a Singapore-based, independent, and award-winning non-profit organisation that inspires creativity in twenty-first-century children.

She grew up in Kuala Lumpur, Malaysia, in a typical middle-class family. Her parents were civil servants.

She was a good student, and she applied to University of Cambridge and got a scholarship to pursue her higher education there.

Sumitra graduated from the University of Cambridge in 1995 with a degree in Chemical Engineering. She also became the first female president of the Engineering Society at Cambridge.

Then she worked in the UK and Brussels, and went on to get an MBA from INSEAD in 2001. She lead a very successful corporate career for the years to come.

In 2008, when she came back to Singapore, her oldest son was two years old and she saw that the Singaporean schools were a bit too academically focused and lacked room for children to explore, play and be creative. So she and her partner, Jennifer Loh, started Playeum Children's Centre for Creativity, a safe space for families and children to express themselves and play differently[23]. It now has two executive directors, and it has taken on a life of its own.

In 2015, as Playeum was doing well, Sumitra was invited to join Ashoka as the country director for Singapore and Malaysia. Ashoka was founded 40 years ago on the idea that the most potent force for good globally is a social entrepreneur: a person driven by an innovative idea that can help correct an entrenched problem.

As a director now, Sumitra was not only generous to give me, a random student who walked in the door requesting an internship, an actual offer. But also while working for her in the Ashoka office at Singapore, I noticed something that I hadn't in my previous work and internship environments. Sumitra and her team had made the Ashoka environment very kind and empathetic. Sumitra in particular would see each of the employees as an individual beyond just their work titles and was compassionate without expecting anything in return. Despite being the country director, she generously took hours

of her time to flesh out a few of my projects, as well as help me
navigate my career steps ahead.

This too was felt by Ara Kusuma, a friend, a fellow
Ashoka employee, and the founder of a leading Indonesian
social venture, Aha! Project, who says, 'In the early days of
the Aha! Project in 2020, Sumitra generously supported me,
came on as the board of advisors and connected me to many
influential people, including a coach for personal growth and
leadership development. This greatly helped in the expansion
of Aha! Project in Indonesia.'

Going out of the way to help her mentees is one of the
traits I admire her for. During my conversations with Sumitra
in the office, I learnt that the skill she embodies in both her
organizations—Playeum and Ashoka—of creative problem
solving, and doing good by keeping other's interest at heart
will be essential skills for anyone to become successful today.

Sumitra says, 'Today, the world is changing incredibly
fast. We are seeing a great change and drastic increases in
inequalities now in our society than we ever did before.
And this change is only growing faster and faster. In the
environment of rapid change, the changemakers—people
who are constantly problem-solving and contributing—will
be successful.'

In this change, Sumitra an the Ashoka team are trying
to create an 'everyone a changemaker' world. They do so by
inspiring people to find their power and agency, build essential
skills and create a better world for all.

We live in a world with a massive population of young
people, with over 230 million in India. So I asked Sumitra, 'In
this rapidly changing world, what skills for us young people
will be important to grow and thrive?'

She replied, 'The people with the new leadership skills, grit, creativity and empathy along with a desire to contribute will help them thrive in this environment. People will these skills will get ahead because head's of institutions, whether it's for profit, not for profit, or government will want them to work in their organisations.'

And I think that truly summed it all for me. In the course of writing this book, I observed that all successful young people in this book had the main trait as mentioned in their respective chapters, but one thing that was common among them all was that they were givers.

In this rapidly evolving world, one cannot survive alone. One truly needs a community to succeed. Being a giver enables you to build goodwill and trust with your community. At a personal level too, doing things for others adds meaning to your life, and makes you happy. And as a giver your success cascades. People root for your success.

As we saw previously, there are many ways of giving, from sharing knowledge and supporting your peers to starting a non-profit, from doing simple things with others' interests at heart to bringing big social change. At all levels, if you strive to give more than you receive, and keep others as well as your own interests in sight then you will be unstoppable.

Acknowledgements

I started thinking about this book when I was eighteen. It took me nearly four years, or about 20 percent of my lifetime, to complete this book. In these years of work, countless people blessed me with their unconditional support for which I am very grateful.

I would like to thank my ever-loving parents and my brother, Tanmay, for their generous emotional and financial support throughout the years of this project. They gave me space and freedom to write without asking any questions. Their unconditional love and the countless cups of my mother's masala chai made this book possible.

I would like to extend my deepest gratitude to Radhika Marwah, my commissioning editor, for taking a chance on me and so kindly guiding me on all aspects of the book and beyond. I am very thankful to Gunjan Ahlawat for creating such a beautiful cover design. Saloni Mittal, Shreya Dhawan, and Radhika Agarwal worked immensely hard on the book manuscript and helped me significantly upgrade the quality of my work for which I am incredibly indebted. Many thanks to the entire team at Penguin Random House for giving more attention to this book than the first-time authors can usually demand and making the whole publishing process feel much smoother than anticipated.

As a first-time author, I am incredibly lucky to have landed Penguin. I am deeply indebted to Varsha Adusumilli for introducing me to the world of publishing and being a pillar of support in each phase of writing this book. I owe a big thanks to Trisha Bora, who generously championed my book idea, connected me to the people at Penguin, and made this book possible in the first place. Special thanks to Manu S Pillai and Mohamed Zeeshan for your advice and guidance throughout the project.

I cannot begin to express my thanks to Eric Koester, founder of the Creator Institute, for teaching me the fundamentals of book writing. I owe a debt of gratitude to the ever-gracious Natalie Lucas, my developmental editor, for discussing early themes, book structures, stories, and chapters of the project, and sharply editing the early drafts that formed the became the foundation of this book.

I owe a bigger debt of gratitude to the experts and thought leaders who very generously took the time to speak with me. Without their depth of knowledge, this book would have been incomplete. Aparna Piramal Raje, Prakash Iyer, Kiran Bir Sethi, Ronnie Screwvala, Pavan Soni, Col. Pagay, Stefanie Faye, and Caroline Stokes, truly many thanks for your insights and guidance. Special thanks to Dr Bijal Oza not only for your mentorship but also for your generosity in designing a self-assessment exercise, especially for this book.

There were a few kind souls, no less than youth icons themselves, who spared a month of their lives to help me in the early book research and interviewee outreach process. I am very thankful to the Unstoppable fellows - Pratik Parihar, Noopur Patil, Nikita Yeole, and Rajat Jaiswal – for their priceless contributions.

I cannot begin to thank Prof. Golo who spent many evenings, including Christmas eve, speaking with me and pushing me to finish the book. Special thanks to my confidant Devika Malik for her profound belief in this project, and your constant encouragement.

This book would be incomplete without my friends Devdatta Fadnavis, RJ Tarun, Taabish Ali Khan, Raghav Bansal, Vamika Arora, Sundetbay Jumamuratov, Rayyan Khokhar, Jatin Julka, Jasim Patel, Neha Rana, Pooja Pipalia, Jerico Agdan, Jennifer Lambert, Caitlyn Lubas, and several others, each of whom has been a pillar of support. Many thanks to Ujjwal Bansal who spent hours brainstorming potential book title and subtitle ideas with me. Thanks also to Gabriel Fordan who made sure the book gets the website it deserves.

I wish to thank my mentors and former bosses who truly shaped the way I looked at the world and found my place in it: Dr Arunabha Ghosh, Shuva Raha, Kiran Bir Sethi, Sumitra Pasupathy Dr Sharayu Bhakare and Piya Mukherjee.

Most importantly, I am extremely grateful to all the trailblazers who opened their hearts to share and reflect on their life experiences: Anam Hashim, Dipa Karmarkar, Kunal Pandagale, Sandeep Chaudhary, Deepak Ramola, Pratishtha Deveshwar, Manav Thakkar, Achanta Sharath Kamal, Dutee Chand, Vedangi Kulkarni, Ritviz, Dr Rajeev Gowda, Anirudh

Sharma, Akshat Mittal, Sanket Deshpande, Dr Karan Jani, Prabhat Koli, Praful Billore, Krishna Allavaru, Reshma Qureshi, Jazz Sethi, Gurmehar Kaur, Achyuth Jaigopal, Himanshu Gupta, Shubham Jaglan, Akash Singh, Harsh Songra, Rishabh Shah, Melati Wijsen, Archana Soreng, Abhay Rangan, Debangshu Moulik, Shubhangi and Jesselina Rana. Thanks to each one of you for trusting me with your story and speaking with me so kindly through the interview and multiple follow-ups over the years of this project. I hope the chapters come close enough to justify the enormously inspiring lives that each one of you has led.

Many of these interviews would have never happened if it weren't for the extreme generosity of a few angel figures. People from unexpected corners of the world went way beyond to help me with the book. One of them being Kshitij Korde. I have never met anyone so selfless and ever ready to help, as he. Kshitij connected me to many stalwarts you read in the book such as Dr Rajeev Gowda, Mr Krishna Allavaru and Rishabh Shah. He spent several hours talking about the various aspects of the book, reading the chapters, and providing great insight with tremendous kindness. Special thanks to Nishaad Shah for introducing me to Kshitij and providing me with valuable inputs in the early stages of the book writing process.

I would like to acknowledge the very moving gesture of Kunal Pandagale who at the end of our two-hour-long interview donated a sizable figure to the Snehalaya orphanage out of the blue. I very much appreciate Henna Brar and the entire team of IncInk, the independent record label and artist collective that puts thought-provoking artwork, in helping me arrange the interview with Kunal and their advice throughout the project.

Many thanks to Achyuth Jaigopal and Shubham Jaglan for sharing their stories with such kindness and humility, and for introducing me to other guests in the book. Sincere thanks to Rahul Sinha and Ishita Mehta of *Under the Radar*, for helping me interview Ritviz.

Thanks to Chirag Shetty and the team of GoSports Foundation and Olympic Gold Quest for a great amount of assistance in setting up the interviews of Dipa Karmarkar, Sandeep Chaudhary, and Dutee Chand.

I appreciate the entire team of IIMUN - India's International Movement to Unite Nations – for their incredible work and their assistance in patiently helping me with the interview of Rishabh Shah and my multiple follow-up questions.

I also had the pleasure of working with Debangshu Moulik on the illustrations for this book, and I very much appreciate his assistance throughout the process.

I am truly blessed to have Vedangi Kulkarni, Archana Soreng, Pratishtha Deveshwar, Akash Singh and Jazz Sethi who not only shared their most inspiring stories but also provided sustained encouragement and support throughout this project.

I owe a huge thanks to Samira Khan and Akanksha Khurana for their guidance, and for connecting me to a few of the most inspiring young changemakers in the Indian subcontinent. A huge thanks to Ara Kusuma for her encouragement during a very challenging time, and for her advice and edits in a few of the most important stories of the book.

Gurmehar Kaur and Deepak Ramola are the authors I look up to. I gratefully acknowledge their support and valuable advice not only in the multiple interviews for the book I requested but also at each stage of the publishing process. I am very much grateful to Vivan Marwaha and Shivam Shankar Singh for sharing the tips and insights in the final stages of publishing.

I am eternally grateful to each person I met in this book journey.

Notes

Introduction

1   Helliwell, J. F., Huang, H., Wang, S., and Norton, M. (2020). *Social Environments for World Happiness.* World Happiness Report, 2020, p. 34.

2   Ibid.

3   Jha, Shweta. Panda, Elim & Singh, Adtiya. (2021). *India Skills Report, 2021*, p. 62. Wheebox. https://indiaeducationforum.org/pdf/ISR-2021.pdf.

   And Economic Times. (2021, February 23). *India Skills Report 2021: More than half of BTech graduates lack tech skills; women are more employable—ET Government.* ETGovernment.com. https://government.economictimes.indiatimes.com/news/education/india-skills-report-2021-more-than-half-of-b-tech-graduates-lack-tech-skills-women-are-more-employable/81169237.

4   Punia, K. (2020, May 12). *Future of unemployment and the informal sector of India.* ORF. https://www.orfonline.org/expert-speak/future-of-unemployment-and-the-informal-sector-of-india-63190/.

5   *Countries by Projected GDP per capita 2021—StatisticsTimes. com.* (n.d.). https://statisticstimes.com/economy/countries-by-projected-gdp-capita.php.

6   IMF. (2021, October). *World Economic Outlook Database.* International Monetary Fund. https://www.imf.org/en/Publications/WEO/weo-database/2021/October/weo-report.

7   Kestel, Dévora & van Ommeren, Mark. (2019). *Suicide in the world—Global Health Estimates.* World Health Organization.

8   Jha, Abhishek. (2021, October 29). *Suicides increase 10% to highest since 1967, accidental deaths down 11%: National data.* Hindustan Times. https://www.hindustantimes.com/india-news/suicides-increase-10-to-highest-since-1967-accidental-deaths-down-11-national-data-101635455348072.html.

9   Patel, V., Ramasundarahettige, C., Vijayakumar, L., Thakur, J. S., Gajalakshmi, V., Gururaj, G., Suraweera, W., & Jha, P. (2012). *Suicide mortality in India: A nationally representative survey.* The Lancet, 379(9834), p. 2343–2351. https://doi.org/10.1016/S0140-6736(12)60606-0.

10 Garai, S. (2020, January 29). *Student suicides rising, 28 lives lost every day.* The Hindu. https://www.thehindu.com/news/national/student-suicides-rising-28-lives-lost-every-day/article30685085.ece.

11 Chakravarty, M. (2018, October 23). *Richest 10% of Indians own over 3/4th of wealth in India.* Mint. https://www.livemint.com/Money/iH2aBEUDpG06hM78diSSEJ/Richest-10-of-Indians-own-over-34th-of-wealth-in-India.html.

    And Credit Suisse. (2018). *Global wealth report 2018.* Research Department, Credit Suiss Investment Banking. https://www.credit-suisse.com/about-us/en/reports-research/global-wealth-report.html.

12 Knight Frank Research, Shirley, A., Bailey, L., Kate Allen, Grainne Gilmore, Taimur Khan, & Tom Bill. (2016). *Knight Frank's Wealth Report 2016.* https://content.knightfrank.com/research/83/documents/en/wealth-report-2016-3579.pdf.

And PTI. (2015, March 9). *Indian ultra-rich population to double by 2024: Knight Frank.* Economic Times. https://economictimes.indiatimes.com/news/economy/indicators/indian-ultra-rich-population-to-double-by-2024-knight-frank/articleshow/46504347.cms.

13 Agarwal, N. (2020, February 27). *Oyo's Ritesh Agarwal is the world's second youngest self-made billionaire.* Mint. https://www.livemint.com/companies/people/oyo-s-ritesh-agarwal-is-the-world-s-second-youngest-self-made-billionaire-11582782072380.html.

Chapter 1: Grit and Perseverance

1 Duckworth, A. L. (2013, April). *Grit: The power of passion and perseverance.* https://www.ted.com/talks/angela_lee_duckworth_grit_the_power_of_passion_and_perseverance.

2 Banerjee, Aritra. (2019, October 5). *Why Do So Many NDA Cadets Leave Training? The Reality Will Shock You.* SSBCrack. https://www.ssbcrack.com/2019/10/why-do-so-many-nda-cadets-leave-training.html.

3 Outlook Web Bureau. (2018, January 5). *More Than 1,200 Cadets Quit NDA In Last 10 Years Due To Ragging, Torture, Excessive Punishment: Report.* Outlook. Https://Www.Outlookindia.Com/. https://www.outlookindia.com/website/story/more-than-1200-cadets-quit-nda-in-last-10-years-due-to-ragging-torture-excessive/306441.

4 Col. Pagay. (2021, April 28). *NDA Recruitment* (M. Shah, Interviewer) [Telephone].

And Outlook Web Bureau. (2018, January 5). *More than 1,200 Cadets Quit NDA in Last 10 Years Due to Ragging, Torture, Excessive Punishment: Report.* Outlook. Https://Www.Outlookindia.Com/. https://www.outlookindia.com/website/story/more-than-1200-cadets-quit-nda-in-last-10-years-due-to-ragging-torture-excessive/306441.

5 Duckworth, A. (2016). *Grit: The Power of Passion and Perseverance.* Simon and Schuster.

6   Pate, A. N., Payakachat, N., Harrell, T. K., Pate, K. A., Caldwell, D. J., & Franks, A. M. (2017). *Measurement of Grit and Correlation to Student Pharmacist Academic Performance.* American Journal of Pharmaceutical Education, 81(6), p. 105. https://doi.org/10.5688/ajpe816105.

7   Miller-Matero, L. R., Martinez, S., MacLean, L., Yaremchuk, K., & Ko, A. B. (2018). *Grit: A predictor of medical student performance.* Education for Health (Abingdon, England), 31(2), p. 109–113. https://doi.org/10.4103/efh.EfH_152_16.

8   Kwon, H. W. (2018). *The sociology of grit: Cross-cultural approaches to social stratification.* University of Iowa. https://iro.uiowa.edu/esploro/outputs/doctoral/The-sociology-of-grit-cross-cultural-approaches/9983776796902771.

9   Breene, K. (2016, November 7). *6 surprising facts about India's exploding middle class.* World Economic Forum. https://www.weforum.org/agenda/2016/11/6-surprising-facts-about-india-s-exploding-middle-class/.

10   *Saving Face in India.* (n.d.). (Retrieved 2021, December 23). https://www.cultureready.org/resource/saving-face-india.

11   Jayakrishnan. (2017, December 22). *This Lady Rider Is Pulling Out All Stops to Reach Her Goals.* Times of India. https://timesofindia.indiatimes.com/city/hyderabad/this-lady-rider-is-pulling-out-all-stops-to-reach-her-goals/articleshow/62196091.cms.

12   Schwantes, M. (2020, July 29). *Warren Buffett's 25/5 Rule Has Been Debunked. Here's What You Should Do Instead.* Inc.com. https://www.inc.com/marcel-schwantes/warren-buffett-25-5-rule-career-goals.html.

13   Adapted from Duckworth, A. & Gross, J. (2014). *Self-Control and Grit: Related but Separable Determinants of Success.* Current Directions in Psychological Science, 23, p. 319–325. https://doi.org/10.1177/0963721414541462.

14   Dasgupta, Priyanka. (2016, August 17). *Dipa Karmakar's parents thrilled with her Khel Ratna recommendation.* Times of India. https://timesofindia.indiatimes.com/sports/rio-2016-olympics/india-in-

olympics-2016/miscellaneous/Dipa-Karmakars-parents-thrilled-with-her-Khel-Ratna-recommendation/articleshow/53744879.cms.

15   Bhattacharya, Nilesh. (2016, August 22). *Rio 2016: Nursery that trained Dipa Karmakar has poor equipment.* Times of India. https://timesofindia.indiatimes.com/sports/rio-2016-olympics/india-in-olympics-2016/gymnastics/rio-2016-nursery-that-trained-dipa-karmakar-has-poor-equipment/articleshow/53804212.cms.

16   Maurer, R. (2014). *One Small Step Can Change Your Life: The Kaizen Way.* Workman Publishing.

17   Duckworth, A. (2016). *Grit: The Power of Passion and Perseverance.* Simon and Schuster.

18   Ibid.

Chapter 2: Courage

1   Francis, S. L., & Renewal, T. C. (2018). *The Courage Way: Leading and Living with Integrity.* ReadHowYouWant.com, Limited.

2   Rudolph, S. H. (1963). *The New Courage: An Essay on Gandhi's Psychology*.* World Politics, 16(1), p. 98–117. https://doi.org/10.2307/2009253.

3   Fleming, Sean. (2019, October 2). *Who was Mahatma Gandhi and what impact did he have on India?* World Economic Forum. https://www.weforum.org/agenda/2019/10/mahatma-gandhi-who-what-impact-india/.

4   Rachman, S. (1990). *Fear and Courage.* W.H. Freeman.

5   *The Nobel Peace Prize 2014: Malala Yousafzai Biographical.* (n.d.). NobelPrize.Org. (Retrieved 2021, December 25). https://www.nobelprize.org/prizes/peace/2014/yousafzai/biographical/.

6   *Malala Yousafzai addresses United Nations Youth Assembly—Office of the Secretary-General's Envoy on Youth.* (2013, September 10). https://www.un.org/youthenvoy/video/malala-yousafzai-addresses-united-nations-youth-assembly/.

7   Dungate, L., & Armstrong, J. (2011, February 14). *Lion's Whiskers: What is Social Courage? What Is Social Courage?* http://www. lionswhiskers.com/2011/02/what-is-social-courage.html.

8   Howard, M., & Fox, F. (2020). *Does gender have a significant relationship with social courage? Test of dual sequentially mediated pathways.* Personality and Individual Differences, 159, 109904. https://doi.org/10.1016/j.paid.2020.109904.

9   *Indian sprinter cleared after 'gender test' suspension.* (2015, July 28). Al Jazeera. https://www.aljazeera.com/sports/2015/7/28/indian-sprinter-cleared-after-gender-test-suspension.

10 Swami, Narayan. (2012, July 24). *Santhi Soundarajan: Asiad medallist labours at brick kiln | Off the field News.* Times of India. https://timesofindia.indiatimes.com/sports/off-the-field/asiad-medallist-labours-at-brick-kiln/articleshow/15112611.cms.

11 *What role does the Court of Arbitration for Sport CAS play?* (2021, November 23). International Olympic Committee. https:// olympics.com/ioc/faq/roles-and-responsibilities-of-the-ioc-and-its-partners/what-role-does-the-court-of-arbitration-for-sport-cas-play.

12 *Sprinter Dutee Chand cleared to compete after CAS ruling.* (2015, July 28). Reuters. https://www.reuters.com/article/athletics-world-gender-india-idINKCN0Q20DZ20150728.

13 Ives, M. (2019, May 20). *Sprinter Dutee Chand Becomes India's First Openly Gay Athlete.* New York Times. https://www.nytimes. com/2019/05/20/world/asia/india-dutee-chand-gay.html.

14 Altidor, W. (2017). *Creative Courage: Leveraging Imagination, Collaboration, and Innovation to Create Success Beyond Your Wildest Dreams.* John Wiley & Sons.

15 Francis, S. L., & Renewal, T. C. for C. and. (2018). *The Courage Way: Leading and Living with Integrity.* ReadHowYouWant.com, Limited.

16 Ware, B. (2012a). *The Top Five Regrets of the Dying: A Life Transformed by the Dearly Departing.* Hay House, Inc.

17 Ibid.

18 *Biography | Rajeev Gowda*. (n.d.). (Retrieved 2021, December 25). http://rajeevgowda.in/Biography.aspx.

19 Ibid.

Chapter 3: Creativity and Innovation

1 Han, J. (2006, February). *The radical promise of the multi-touch interface*. https://www.ted.com/talks/jeff_han_the_radical_promise_of_the_multi_touch_interface?language=sw.

2 Routh, Benu Joshi. (2016, February 11). *30 Under 30: Anirudh Sharma—Innovator-in-chief*. Forbes India. https://www.forbesindia.com/article/30-under-30/30-under-30-anirudh-sharma-innovatorinchief/42201/1.

3 Schwab, Klaus. (2016, January 14). *The Fourth Industrial Revolution: What it means and how to respond*. World Economic Forum. https://www.weforum.org/agenda/2016/01/the-fourth-industrial-revolution-what-it-means-and-how-to-respond/.

4 *IDEO Design Thinking*. (n.d.). (Retrieved 2021, December 21). IDEO | Design Thinking. https://designthinking.ideo.com/.

5 Gravity Recovery and Climate Experiment. (n.d.). (Retrieved 2022, February 15). *Grace—Earth Missions—NASA Jet Propulsion Laboratory*. NASA Jet Propulsion Laboratory (JPL). https://www.jpl.nasa.gov/missions/gravity-recovery-and-climate-experiment-grace.

6 Shah, M. (2021, March 26). *Kiran Bir Sethi: Design for Change and Riverside School* (No. 22). https://planetimpactpod.com/episodes/kiran-bir-sethi

7 Sethi, Kiran Bir. (n.d.). (Retrieved 2022, February 15). *Design for Change*. https://dfcworld.org/SITE.

8 Kiran Bir Sethi. (2020). Stories of Change. Design for Change | Stories of Change. https://stories.dfcworld.org/

9 Biswas, S. (2020, March 30). *Coronavirus: India's pandemic lockdown turns into a human tragedy*. BBC News. https://www.bbc.com/news/world-asia-india-52086274.

10   Simonton, D. K. (1999). *Origins of Genius: Darwinian Perspectives on Creativity*. Oxford University Press.

11   *Failing for Success: Thomas Edison.* (n.d.). (Retrieved 2022, March 20). https://www.intellectualventures.com/buzz/insights/failing-for-success-thomas-edison

12   *The Wright Story.* (n.d.). (Retrieved 2022, March 20). from https://www.wright-brothers.org/History_Wing/Wright_Story/Wright_Story_Intro/Wright_Story_Intro.htm

13   *From carbon to canvas.* (2016, August 8). The Hindu. https://www.thehindu.com/features/metroplus/From-carbon-to-canvas/article14558704.ece.

14   Kelley, T., & Kelley, D. (2013). *Creative Confidence: Unleashing the Creative Potential Within Us All*. Crown.

15   Ibid.

Chapter 4: Hard Work over Talent

1   Abrams, C. (2019, June 23). *Oyo Has Remade India's Hotel Business. Now It Is Going Global*. Wall Street Journal. https://www.wsj.com/articles/oyo-has-remade-indias-hotel-business-now-it-is-going-global-11561311205.

2   Gupta, A. (2020, February 17). *Annual Report Card FY 2019*. Official OYO Blog. https://www.oyorooms.com/officialoyoblog/2020/02/17/annual-report-card-fy-2019/index.php.

3   *Nonconformist.* (n.d.). (Retrieved 2021, December 6). https://dictionary.cambridge.org/dictionary/english/nonconformist.

4   Gladwell, M. (2008). *Outliers: The Story of Success*. Little, Brown.

5   Ericsson, K. A., Prietula, M. J., & Cokely, E. T. (2007, July 1). *The Making of an Expert*. Harvard Business Review. https://hbr.org/2007/07/the-making-of-an-expert.

6   Chambliss, D. F. (1989). *The Mundanity of Excellence: An Ethnographic Report on Stratification and Olympic*

Swimmers. Sociological Theory, 7(1). p. 70–86. https://doi.
org/10.2307/202063.

7   Ibid.

8   *Bio—Dr. Karan Jani | Astrophysicist.* (n.d.). (Retrieved 2021,
December 22)

Dr. Karan Jani. https://www.karanjani.com/bio.

9   *Breakthrough Prize—Special Breakthrough Prize in Fundamental
Physics Awarded for Detection of Gravitational Waves 100 Years After
Albert Einstein Predicted Their Existence.* (n.d.). (Retrieved 2021,
December 22). https://breakthroughprize.org/News/32.

10 Roe, A. (1953). *The Making of a Scientist.* Dodd, Mead.

11 Ericsson, K. A., Krampe, R. T., & Tesch-Romer, C. (1993). *The
Role of Deliberate Practice in the Acquisition of Expert Performance.*
Psychological Review, 100(3), p. 363–406.

12 *Prabhat Raju Koli—Openwaterpedia.* (n.d.). (Retrieved 2021,
December   22).   https://www.openwaterpedia.com/index.
php?title=Prabhat_Raju_Koli.

13 *Oceans Seven | LongSwims Database.* (n.d.). (Retrieved 2021,
December 22). https://longswims.com/oceans-seven/.

Chapter 5: Emotional Intelligence

1   Basu, Anindita. (2016, August 25). *Mahabharata.* World History
Encyclopedia. https://www.worldhistory.org/Mahabharata/.

2   Mark, J. J. (2020, June 15). *Bhagavad Gita.* World History
Encyclopedia. https://www.worldhistory.org/Bhagavad_Gita/.

3   Dr Meenakshi, K. & Gayathri, N. (2013). *Emotional Intelligence
in the Indian Context.* Global Journal of Human Social Science
Linguistics and Education, 13(8), p. 8.

    And Gayathri, N., & Meenakshi, K. (2019). *Emotional
Intelligence to Emotional Stability – a Repertoire of Knowledge from
the Bhagavad Gita.* International Journal of Recent Technology
and Engineering, 7(6), p. 3.

4   Goleman, D. (2006). *Emotional Intelligence.* Bantam Books.

5   Vaillant, G. E. (1995). *Adaptation to Life*. Harvard University Press.

6   Ibid.

7   Margaret Talbot. (2005, May 29). *Best in Class*. New Yorker. https://www.newyorker.com/magazine/2005/06/06/best-in-class.

8   Fisher, Anne & Goleman, Daniel. (1998, October 26). *Success Secret: A High Emotional IQ*. https://archive.fortune.com/magazines/fortune/fortune_archive/1998/10/26/249986/index.htm.

9   Schutte, N. S., Malouff, J. M., Simunek, M., McKenley, J., & Hollander, S. (2002). *Characteristic emotional intelligence and emotional well-being*. Cognition and Emotion, 16(6), p. 769–785. https://doi.org/10.1080/02699930143000482.

10   Tajeddini, R. (2014). *Emotional Intelligence and Self Esteem among Indian and Foreign Students—(A Comparative Study)*. International Journal of Humanities and Social Science Invention, 3(6), p. 10.

11   Rice-Oxley, M. (2019, June 3). *Mental illness: Is there really a global epidemic?* Guardian. https://www.theguardian.com/society/2019/jun/03/mental-illness-is-there-really-a-global-epidemic.

          And PTI. (2017, December 30). *India facing possible mental health epidemic, warns President*. Economic Times. https://economictimes.indiatimes.com/news/politics-and-nation/india-facing-possible-mental-health-epidemic-warns-president/articleshow/62308115.cms?from=mdr.

12   Borner, K., Gayes, L., & Hall, J. (2015). *Friendship During Childhood and Cultural Variations*. International Encyclopedia of the Social & Behavioral Sciences. https://doi.org/10.1016/B978-0-08-097086-8.23184-X.

13   Kevin Lui. (2016, September 9). *Acid-Attack Survivor Reshma Qureshi Hits the Catwalk*. Time. https://time.com/4485099/reshma-qureshi-new-york-fashion-week-acid-attack/.

14   Lauren Landry. (2019a, April 3). *Emotional Intelligence in Leadership: Why It's Important*. Business Insights: Blog. https://online.hbs.edu/blog/post/emotional-intelligence-in-leadership.

And Lauren Landry. (2019b, October 23). *How to Develop Emotional Intelligence Skills | HBS Online*. Business Insights: Blog. https://online.hbs.edu/blog/post/emotional-intelligence-skills.

15 Goleman, D. (2004, January 1). *What Makes a Leader?* Harvard Business Review. https://hbr.org/2004/01/what-makes-a-leader.

16 Ott, C. (2017). *What is Emotional Intelligence?* Ohio State University. https://ohio4h.org/sites/ohio4h/files/imce/Emotional%20Intelligence%20Background.pdf.

17 Mayer, J., & Stevens, A. (1994). *An Emerging Understanding of the Reflective (Meta-) Experience of Mood*. Journal of Research in Personality, 28, p. 351–373. https://doi.org/10.1006/jrpe.1994.1025.

18 Chamorro-Premuzic, T. (2013, May 29). *Can You Really Improve Your Emotional Intelligence?* Harvard Business Review. https://hbr.org/2013/05/can-you-really-improve-your-em.

19 Chadwick, G., & Raines, S. (2008). *Zen Coffee: A Guide to Mindful Meditation*. Mystical Mindscapes.

20 Kaur, G. (2018). *Small Acts of Freedom*. Penguin Random House India Private Limited.

21 Ibid.

22 Gayathri, N., & Meenakshi, K. (2019). *Emotional Intelligence to Emotional Stability—a Repertoire of Knowledge from the Bhagavad Gita*. 7(6), p. 3.

23 Ibid.

Chapter 6: Growth Mindset

1 PTI. (2017, September 9). *Private schools can't be the answer to the nation's needs: Sonam Wangchuk*. Economic Times. https://economictimes.indiatimes.com/news/politics-and-nation/private-schools-cant-be-the-answer-to-the-nations-needs-sonam-wangchuk/articleshow/60442826.cms?from=mdr.

2 Dweck, C. (2012). *Mindset: Changing the Way You think To Fulfil Your Potential*. Hachette UK.

3   *Ganesha Vs Kartikeya—The game of Mindset | LinkedIn.* (2020). https://www.linkedin.com/pulse/ganesha-vs-kartikeya-game-mindset-vatsal-anand/?articleId=6675093174677053440.

4   Moore, D. A., & Small, D. A. (2007). *Error and bias in comparative judgment: On being both better and worse than we think we are.* Journal of Personality and Social Psychology, p. 972–989.

5   Gardner, H. E. (2008). *Extraordinary Minds: Portraits of 4 Exceptional Individuals And An Examination Of Our Own Extraordinariness.* Basic Books.

6   Maslow, A. H., & Green, C. D. (1943). *A theory of human motivation.* Psychological Review, p. 370–396.

Chapter 7: Networking

1   Hayashi, A. M. (2008, October 1). *Why Picasso Outearned van Gogh.* MIT Sloan Management Review. https://sloanreview.mit.edu/article/why-picasso-outearned-van-gogh/.

2   Berns, G. (2010). *Iconoclast: A Neuroscientist Reveals how to Think Differently.* Harvard Business Press.

3   Wolff, H.-G., & Moser, K. (2009). *Effects of Networking on Career Success: A Longitudinal Study.* The Journal of Applied Psychology, 94, 196–206. https://doi.org/10.1037/a0013350.

4   Forret, M. L., & Dougherty, T. W. (2004). *Networking Behaviors and Career Outcomes: Differences for Men and Women?* Journal of Organizational Behavior, 25(3), p. 419–437.

5   *Ashoka Rated One of the Top Five Most Impactful Social Good Organizations | Ashoka | Everyone a Changemaker.* (2021, January 27). https://www.ashoka.org/en-gb/story/ashoka-rated-one-top-five-most-impactful-social-good-organizations.
        And *The World Top 200 NGOs list by NGO Advisor.* (2021). NGO Advisor. https://www.ngoadvisor.net/top-200-ngos-world.

6   Adapted from Zak Slayback. (2019). *How to Get Ahead: A Proven 6-Step System to Unleash Your Personal Brand and Build a World-*

Class Network So Opportunities Come To You. McGraw-Hill. https://learning.oreilly.com/library/view/how-to-get/9781260441857/ch5.xhtml.

7   Caprino, K. (2014, June 17). *The 5 Worst Blunders Most Networkers Make*. Forbes. https://www.forbes.com/sites/kathycaprino/2014/06/17/the-5-worst-blunders-most-networkers-make/.

8   Shah, M. (2020). *Jared Kleinert: Most Connected Millennial* (No. 9). https://open.spotify.com/episode/0cdfZ0LblbF3xYssdgW5sX

9   Jessica Shambora. (2011, February 9). *Fortune's best networker*. Fortune. https://fortune.com/2011/02/09/fortunes-best-networker/.

Chapter 8: Leadership

1   Ganz, M. (2008). *Leading Change: Leadership, Organization, and Social Movements*.

2   *Bali bans single-use plastics, targets 70 per cent reduction in 2019*. (2018, December 26). Straits Times. https://www.straitstimes.com/asia/se-asia/bali-bans-single-use-plastics-targets-70-per-cent-reduction-in-2019.

3   Barbiroglio, E. (2019, December 6). *COP25: Greta Thunberg Arrives In Madrid*. Forbes. https://www.forbes.com/sites/emanuelabarbiroglio/2019/12/06/cop25-greta-thunberg-arrives-in-madrid/.

4   Adapted from Belludi, N. (2006, August 20). *The Legacy of Infosys' Narayana Murthy*. Right Attitudes. https://www.RightAttitudes.com/2006/08/20/the-legacy-of-infosys-narayana-murthy/.

Chapter 9: Confidence

1   Moon, V. (Ed.). (1993). *Dr. Babasaheb Ambedkar: Writings and Speeches* (Vol. 12). Education Department, Mumbai: Government of Maharashtra. p. 661–691, https://mea.gov.in/Images/attach/amb/Volume_12.pdf.

And Patel, J., Taraporevala, S., Sadhu, A., Pavara, D., Mammootty, Kulkarni, S., Gokhale, M., Haldipur, A., & Phadake, Ya. D., India, Ministry of Social Justice and Empowerment, Bhagyshree Enterprises and Entertainments, Air-India, National Film Development Corporation of India, & Maharashtra (India), U. D. V. (Firm). (2008). *Dr. Babasaheb Ambedkar.* Ultra Distributors Pvt Ltd.

2   McKinney, M. (2010, April 23). *Theodore Roosevelt's The Man in the Arena Speech 100th Anniversary | Leading Blog: A Leadership Blog.* https://www.leadershipnow.com/leadingblog/.

3   Allen, J. G., & Edwards, G. C. (1990). *Man in the arena—Speeches and essays by Theodore Roosevelt. Presidential Studies Quarterly,* XX(4), p. 863.

4   Mukundananda, S. (n.d.). *Chapter 2, Verse 47 – Bhagavad Gita, The Song of God – Swami Mukundananda.* (Retrieved 2021, November 30). https://www.holy-bhagavad-gita.org/chapter/2/verse/47.
    And Swami Swarupananda. (1996). *Shrimad Bhagavad Geeta.* Advaita Ashrama.

5   Brown, B. (2018). *Dare to Lead: Brave Work. Tough Conversations. Whole Hearts.* New York: Random House. p. 136.

6   Ibid.

7   Karlgaard, R. (2019). *Late Bloomers: The Power of Patience in a World Obsessed with Early Achievement.* Currency. p. 210.

8   Sharma, S. (2014, May 25). *Karishma Mehta, the face behind Humans of Bombay.* YourStory. https://yourstory.com/2014/05/karishma-mehta-face-behind-humans-bombay/amp.

9   Joshi, P. (2016, May 5). *Meet Karishma Mehta, the woman behind Humans of Bombay.* Hindustan Times. https://www.hindustantimes.com/art-and-culture/meet-karishma-mehta-the-woman-behind-humans-of-bombay/story-Zwhwt3VJmysEGx62ZsuukJ.html.

10 Ibid.

11 Hanson, J. (2021, May 26). *Lessons From The 20-Something Who Is Healing The World One Post At A Time.* Forbes. https://

www.forbes.com/sites/janehanson/2021/05/26/lessons-from-the-20-something-who-is-healing-the-world-one-post-at-a-time/.

12   Berns, G. (2010). *Iconoclast: A Neuroscientist Reveals how to Think Differently.* Boston: Harvard Business Press. p. 96–100.

13   Stein, M. B., Walker, J. R., & Forde, D. R. (1996). *Public-Speaking Fears in a Community Sample: Prevalence, Impact on Functioning, and Diagnostic Classification.* Archives of General Psychiatry, 53(2), p. 169–174. https://doi.org/10.1001/archpsyc.1996.01830020087010.

14   Screwvala, R. (2015). *Dream with Your Eyes Open: An Entrepreneurial Journey.* Mumbai: Rupa Publications India Pvt. Limited. p. 92–94.

Chapter 10: Giving Back

1   Grant, A. (2013). *Give and Take: Why Helping Others Drives Our Success.* Penguin Publishing Group.

2   Adapted from Jain, G. (2018). *Arnavaz "Anu" Aga: (Penguin Petit).* Penguin Random House India Private Limited.
     And Jain, Gunjan. (2016, August 24). *Forbes India—Anu Aga: A Life Shaped by Tragedy, and the Courage to Face It.* Forbes India. https://www.forbesindia.com/article/recliner/anu-aga-a-lifes-shaped-by-tragedy-and-the-courage-to-face-it/44109/1.
     And Anu Aga. (2014, February 22). Death: Anu Aga at TEDxPune. https://www.youtube.com/watch?v=W_WwWc EmP_E.
     And Thermax Limited. (2004). *Thermax Limited Annual Report 2003-2004.* p. 2. https://www.thermaxglobal.com/wp-content/uploads/2020/02/2003-04.pdf.

3   Gaurav, Kunal. (2021, June 23). *Jamsetji Tata world's top philanthropist in 100 years, two Indians in top 50. Here's the list.* Hindustan Times. https://www.hindustantimes.com/world-news/

jamsetji-tata-world-s-top-philanthropist-in-100-years-two-indians-in-top-50-101624451361182.html.

4   Gill, Prabhjote. (2021, April 29). *Azim Premji donated ten times more than even Shiv Nadar And Mukesh Ambani in 2020.* Business Insider. https://www.businessinsider.in/thelife/personalities/news/azim-premji-shiv-nadar-and-mukesh-ambani-are-among-the-top-10-most-generous-entrepreneurs-in-india/slidelist/82310107.cms.

5   Adapted from Knowledge@Wharton. (2013, April 10). *Givers vs. Takers: The Surprising Truth about Who Gets Ahead.* Knowledge@Wharton. https://knowledge.wharton.upenn.edu/article/givers-vs-takers-the-surprising-truth-about-who-gets-ahead/.
    And Grant, A. (2013). *Give and Take: Why Helping Others Drives Our Success.* Penguin Publishing Group.

6   *ChangemakerXchange—Global community of young social innovators.* (n.d.). ChangemakerXchange. https://changemakerxchange.org/.

7   Milmo, D., & Adam, D. (2006, September 22). *Branson pledges $3bn transport profits to fight global warming.* Guardian. https://www.theguardian.com/environment/2006/sep/22/travelnews.frontpagenews.

8   Branson, Richard (2017, February 9). *How I started seven different businesses as a teenager.* Virgin.com. https://virgin.com/branson-family/richard-branson-blog/how-i-started-seven-different-businesses-teenager.

9   Marsh, Jason & Suttie, Jill. (2010, December 13). *5 Ways Giving Is Good for You.* Greater Good. https://greatergood.berkeley.edu/article/item/5_ways_giving_is_good_for_you.

10 Walsh, Colleen. (2008, April 17). Money spent on others can buy happiness. *Harvard Gazette.* https://news.harvard.edu/gazette/story/2008/04/money-spent-on-others-can-buy-happiness/.

11 Grant, A. (2013). *Give and Take: Why Helping Others Drives Our Success.* Penguin Publishing Group.

12 Crocker, J., Canevello, A., & Brown, A. A. (2017). *Social Motivation: Costs and Benefits of Selfishness and Otherishness.* Annual

Review of Psychology, 68(1), p. 299–325. https://doi.org/10.1146/annurev-psych-010416-044145.

13 Allen, S., & Suttie, J. (2015, December 21). *How Our Brains Make Us Generous*. Greater Good. https://greatergood.berkeley.edu/article/item/how_our_brains_make_us_generous.

14 Popova, M. (2013, April 10). Givers, Takers, and Matchers: The Surprising Psychology of Success. *The Marginalian*. https://www.brainpickings.org/2013/04/10/adam-grant-give-and-take/.

15 Kim, E., & Glomb, T. M. (2010). *Get smarty pants: Cognitive ability, personality, and victimization*. The Journal of Applied Psychology, 95(5), p. 889–901. https://doi.org/10.1037/a0019985.

16 Karki, K. B., Poudel, P. C., Rothchild, J., Pope, N., Bobin, N. C., Gurung, Y., Basnet, M., Poudel, M., & Sherpa, L. Y. (2017). *Menstrual Health and Hygiene Management in Nepal*. p. 1–96.

17 WaterAid (2009). *Is Menstrual Hygiene And Management An Issue For Adolescent School Girls? A Comparative Study of Four Schools in Different Settings of Nepal*. Kathmandu, Nepal: WaterAid.

18 Adapted from Grant, A. (2015, July 20). *The difference between workplace givers, takers and matchers*. The Globe and Mail. https://www.theglobeandmail.com/report-on-business/careers/leadership-lab/the-difference-between-workplace-givers-takers-and-matchers/article25594837/.

19 Luoh, M.-C., & Herzog, A. (2003). *Individual Consequences of Volunteer and Paid Work in Old Age: Health and Mortality*. Journal of Health and Social Behavior, 43, p. 490–509. https://doi.org/10.2307/3090239.

20 Windsor, T. D., Anstey, K. J., & Rodgers, B. (2008). *Volunteering and Psychological Well-Being Among Young-Old Adults: How Much Is Too Much?* The Gerontologist, 48(1), p. 59–70. https://doi.org/10.1093/geront/48.1.59.

21 Latha, M. & Shanmugam, Dr V. (2014). *Growth of Service Sector in India*. IOSR Journal of Humanities and Social Science, 19, p. 8–12. https://doi.org/10.9790/0837-19140812.

22   *India—Distribution of the workforce across economic sectors 2019.*
     (n.d.). Statista. https://www.statista.com/statistics/271320/
     distribution-of-the-workforce-across-economic-sectors-in-india/.
23   Chia, E. (2020, December 7). *Let your kids take the lead and other
     top tips on how to play with your kids.* Straits Times. https://www.
     straitstimes.com/singapore/parenting-education/let-your-kids-
     take-the-lead-and-other-top-tips-on-how-to-play-with